ESSENTIALS OF BUSINESS WRITING AND SPEAKING

A CANADIAN GUIDE

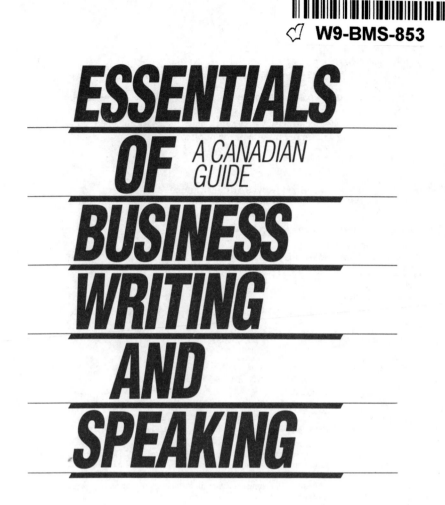

Beverley Reid
Communications Instructor, Capilano College, North Vancouver, British Columbia

L. Sue Baugh

Maridell Fryar

David Thomas

Copp Clark Pitman Ltd.
A Longman Company
Toronto

ISBN 0-7730-4917-7

EDITING: Jennie Bedford
DESIGN & PAGE MAKE-UP: Brant Cowie/ArtPlus Limited
PRINTING & BINDING: Webcom Limited

Canadian Cataloguing in Publication Data

Reid, Beverley (S. Beverley)
Essentials of business writing and speaking

1st Canadian ed.
Includes index.
ISBN 0-7730-4917-7

1. Commercial correspondence. 2. Business report writing. 3. English language — Business English. I. Title.

HF5721.R44 1989 **808.066651** **C88-095374-8**

For Peter, David, Robin, Thomas, and Matthew

Acknowledgments
I would like to acknowledge the following people for their assistance and support in the completion of this book:

- **my students** for their continued enthusiasm. (On many occasions over the past 20 years I have wondered who was teaching whom!). I particularly thank **Cam Heryet** and **Rick Neal** for allowing me to use materials which they wrote in my classes.
- **Pat Biggins, George Modenesi**, and **Suzanne Clouthier** for their help with the necessary research.
- **Brown & Collett** for permission to reprint their snap set memorandum form.
- **The Corporation of the Township of Richmond** for permission to reprint their application form.
- **3M Canada Inc.** for permission to reprint their Post-It telephone message form.
- **Marion Elliott** and **Jennie Bedford** at **Copp Clark Pitman** for their wisdom and patience in guiding the project.
- **Debbie Bentham** for her friendship and the endless hours of typing required by the manuscript.
- **My family** for continuing to ride the range with me.

BEVERLEY REID

The publisher also wishes to thank **Dr. Marjorie Holmes** of Algonquin College of Applied Arts and Technology, Nepean, Ontario, for her review of the manuscript as it was being prepared, and also the input that was received from **Kay Vanstone** of Seneca College of Applied Arts and Technology, Willowdale, Ontario, and **Margaret Dombeck** of Centennial College of Applied Arts and Technology, Scarborough, Ontario.

Copp Clark Pitman Ltd.
2775 Matheson Boulevard East
Mississauga, Ontario
L4W 4P7
Printed and bound in Canada

3 4 5 6 4917-7 95 94 93

CONTENTS

PREFACE

Computer systems have revolutionized the way we communicate in business. Data, text, voice, and graphics networks enable business personnel to exchange information and make decisions more rapidly than ever before. Today, one individual can generate, file, store, process, distribute, and retrieve volumes of information that would have previously taken scores of people to handle.

Sophisticated hardware and software, however, do not alter the fundamentals of communication. The message still originates in the mind of the sender and must be understood by the receiver. Human beings are responsible for the content, organization, wording, and format of information communicated. Skill in saying precisely and accurately what you mean is essential.

The ability to write and speak well transcends the electronic office. No matter how complicated the equipment or the means of transmission, you will still write letters, memos, and reports, make oral presentations, and answer telephones.

Along with advances in electronic technology has come a greater understanding of the dynamics of human communication. We are more aware of the importance of the non-verbal factors in the messages we send and receive. An unattractively prepared letter containing spelling and grammatical errors, for example, will be less favourably received than one with impeccable appearance and content. Similarly, a speaker who has little or no rapport with an audience will be much less effective than one who demonstrates positive non-verbal skills. A lack of eye contact in a job interview can make the difference between success or failure. The unpleasant telephone manner of an employee can cost a business money and goodwill.

Good communication is no accident. It is the result of careful listening, good writing and speaking skills, and an awareness of the non-verbal factors in the messages you send. The guidelines and examples in this book can help you become the effective business communicator you would like to be.

HOW TO USE THIS BOOK

This book is designed to help you find answers to your specific business writing and speaking problems quickly and efficiently.

Finding What You Need

To get the greatest benefit from this book, you should be familiar with six ways you can locate the guidelines, information, and examples you need.

1. Read through Chapter 1. "Three Steps to Effective Writing" summarizes a step-by-step approach to good writing you can use for any type of business communication. The approach breaks down the writing process into three stages: *prewriting* (planning and researching); *writing* (organizing, outlining, and writing first draft); and *revising* (rewriting and proofreading). These three steps will help you prepare, plan, and write your letters, memos, reports, and other types of communication.

2. Read through Chapter 13. "Public Speaking" describes a step-by-step approach to different types of oral presentations. In addition to dealing with styles and types of speeches, the chapter breaks down the public speaking process into three stages: *researching*; *organizing and preparing*; and *rehearsing and delivering*.

3. Use Specific Sections. Sections 1 through 3 cover specific types of business writing. Beginners will appreciate the detailed guidelines and examples in section chapters that show how to create effective business messages. Experienced writers can use the chapters' quick reviews, checklists, samples, and activities to strengthen writing skills they have already developed.

4. Use Specific Chapters. You can select the particular business communication you need — letter, memo, proposal — and turn to the chapter covering that topic. You may, for example, need guidelines for writing a press release. Chapter 12 contains brief tips for creating press releases as well as complete examples commonly used in business.

5. Use the Activities. You can practise and strengthen your business writing and speaking skills by selecting activities which are presented at the end of chapters.

6. Use the Index. This text includes a cross-referenced index to help you find related topics or subjects when you are not sure what to call them. You may, for example, want to know how many dots to put in a quotation to show you have omitted part of it. Under the heading "Quotations" you will find an entry "ellipses" and a page number. You will also find the same entry under "Period."

Special Features of This Book

Whether you are a beginning or experienced business writer and speaker, you will find several features of this book particularly valuable.

1. Reviewing Business Style. While there is no special language for business writing, certain points of style — tone, clarity, accuracy, brevity — are important to your message. Chapter 2, "Style in Business Writing"; Chapter 3, "Choosing the Right Word"; Chapter 9, "Organizing and Writing Business Reports"; and Chapter 12, "Proposals and Press Releases"; provide brief, vivid reviews of major points in business style. These guidelines can help you write messages that will influence your readers and get results.

2. Finding Business Information. In the Information Age, locating the data you need can cost considerable time and money. Chapter 11, "Finding Business Information," shows you how to locate data sources and use the computer to save time gathering information. Advances in electronic communications technology have brought vast quantities of data within the reach of both individuals and companies.

3. Reviewing Grammar and Style. The Appendix provides a practical and thorough review of grammar, style, and spelling questions that plague most business writers. Sections A through E cover parts of speech, sentence structure, punctuation, capitalization, abbreviations, numbers, and spelling guidelines. You can review an entire section or look up specific topics in the index to locate the exact information you need.

4. Reviewing Oral Communication in Business. Section 4 deals with several types of oral communication. It shows you how to structure an oral presentation, choose and prepare visual aids, improve telephone skills, and master dictation techniques.

5. Finding the Right Job. Section 5, "The Job Search," covers résumés, job applications, and various employment letters you will need to find the job you want. You will learn how to create an attention-getting résumé; fill out job applications; and write letters of application, appreciation, acceptance, refusal, recommendation, and resignation. A well-written letter is one of the best ways to introduce yourself to a prospective employer.

SECTION 1

BUSINESS WRITING TODAY

CHAPTER 1 THREE STEPS TO EFFECTIVE WRITING

Many competent, articulate business people experience a moment of panic when they must write a report, memo, or letter. Faced with putting their thoughts in writing, they become confused about what to say, how to say it, and how to manage the mechanics of grammar, spelling, and format.

If you are one of these people — and many of us are — relax. Like any business task, writing is manageable once you break it down into a series of smaller steps. Good writing is the result of good planning and clear thinking. The steps outlined in this book will help you identify your purpose in writing any type of business communication, clarify your thinking about what you want to say, and show you how to go about the actual process of getting your message to the reader.

This chapter presents an overview of the three basic steps to effective writing. You will see how to apply these steps in more detail in the chapters on business letters, memos, proposals and press releases, and special writing projects. Once you have a grasp of the principles of good writing, you will be able to use them for any written message, regardless of its length or complexity. The three steps to effective writing are:

Step One: **Prewriting** — planning and researching

Step Two: **Writing** — organizing, outlining, and writing the first draft

Step Three: **Revising** — reworking and editing the draft, proofreading, final keyboarding and printing

Step One: Prewriting

Before you begin any project, you must decide what you want to accomplish and how you wish to accomplish it. You begin with a *concept*: a question, a problem, a new situation. You gather *facts* to support the concept. What is the question? What type of problem is it? How much can you learn about the situation? Your *finished product* is a letter, a report, a memo.

In step one, prewriting, you are defining the concept and gathering the facts that will serve as material for step two, writing.

Planning

All your written communications in business should seek to answer these questions:

1. What is the *purpose* of this message? Why am I writing it?
2. Who is the *audience* ? Whom do I want to influence?
3. What do I want to say? What is the *scope* of my subject?

First, decide on a *purpose*. Do you want to sell a new product or replace an old one? Do you want to supply information or ask for a favour? In one or two sentences or a brief paragraph, state the purpose of your message. If necessary, talk the subject over with others until you have a clear idea of your objective.

Second, think about your *audience*. What should readers know or be able to do after reading your message? What is their level of understanding or expertise regarding the subject? Do you want to persuade them to do or to accept something? What are their interests and motivations — profit, comfort, health, convenience, savings?

Put yourself in the readers' place as much as you can and look at your subject from their perspective; for example, when reporting on company year-end performance, you would write different reports to the vice president of sales, the marketing manager, the president of the company, and the stockholders. Each reader would want to know different types of information and would have different levels of expertise. You need to tailor your message to the level and interests of the audience.

Answers to the first and second questions will help you answer the third: What do you want to say and what is the *scope* of your subject? You must distinguish between information the reader needs to know and information that is merely nice to know; for example, in your year-end performance report, you would include product sales figures but not a history of the product in Canadian culture — unless the reader specifically had requested it. You must limit your subject and focus on specific topics.

Researching

By answering the first three questions, you determine what information you will need for your writing. The amount of research required can vary greatly, depending on the subject and purpose. In general, you have five basic sources of information:

1. **Libraries** — public, specialized, and industry libraries
2. **Other people** — interviews with experts and others, questionnaires, surveys
3. **Industry and government** — industry associations and groups, government agencies and officials
4. **Your own company** — files, history, personnel
5. **Your own knowledge** — experience, training, education.

Your research may be as brief as jotting down sales figures from memory or as lengthy as several weeks or months of gathering data for a report on new site locations. Replying to customer inquiries or complaints can involve research lasting from a few minutes to several days or weeks. If your job requires research, learn how to use the various research tools available through libraries and other reference sources. Chapter 11, "Finding Business Information," provides a list of resources for locating data quickly.

When gathering information, remember the three cardinal rules of journalism: *accuracy, accuracy*, and *accuracy*. Make sure you copy or quote information correctly and have the data to support your statements. Nothing loses a reader's confidence in a writer's work more quickly than discovering errors in the material. Two or three careless mistakes can cast doubt on the credibility of the entire document. Check your facts and spelling.

Step Two: Writing

You have established your purpose, identified your audience, defined your topic, and gathered your data. Now you are ready for the second step — organizing, outlining, and writing the first draft.

Organizing

How you organize your material depends on your subject and your purpose for writing; for example, if you are giving instructions on machine assembly, you would choose a step-by-step approach to explain how to put the machine together. If you are making a special offer to a customer or breaking bad news to a client, you would put the most important information first and then fill in the details. Each type of letter or report has a specific purpose that will determine how you organize and arrange the material for the most effective presentation.

Outlining

Once you have chosen how to organize your material, the next step is outlining what you want to say and the order in which you want to say it. You will find sample outlines throughout this book. An outline breaks down a large topic into manageable bits and helps ensure that your writing flows logically from one part to another. The outline corresponds to a blueprint for a building. The more complete the blueprint, the easier it is to construct the building. Likewise, the more detailed the outline, the easier it will be to write the letter, report, or memo. Developing the outline enables you to see the process of your thinking at an early stage. You can spot gaps in data or logic quickly and fill them in before you get to the writing stage.

Outlining is also a good time to think about illustrations or graphics. Will your sales figures mean more to the reader if you show them in a bar chart or coloured pie chart? With the graphics capabilities of many computers, you can create illustrations for text easily. Check through your outline to determine where illustrations could make your presentation more effective.

Writing the First Draft

Once your outline is complete, you are ready to write your first draft. Many writers make a common mistake at this point. They try to get it right the first time. They may work on a paragraph for hours, fine-tuning the words until they are perfect. Writers thus shut off their creativity by insisting on perfection.

Remember: *The first draft is a working draft.* Write it quickly without too much thought to elegant expressions or final order and paragraphing. Your objective is to get the material on paper and to expand the structure of your outline. Let the words flow. Start wherever you can — in the middle, even near the end. You can complete the opening or introduction later. You can correct any weaknesses in logic, gaps in information, or points that are out of place in the final version.

Write the first draft, keeping your audience in mind. This will help you stay focused on the purpose of your work. Keep writing until you have completed the first draft.

Step Three: Revising

When you begin to revise your material, you are reading it primarily from the reader's point of view, not the writer's. If possible, give the draft to others and ask for their comments and suggestions. Let a few hours or days go by before you read your draft again. By allowing the material to cool off, you can spot inconsistencies and errors more easily.

Read the draft several times. Refer to Chapters 4, 7, and 9 for revision hints. Don't try to correct everything the first time through. Check the facts and data in your draft. If you change a set of figures in one place, be sure you change the same set of figures elsewhere. Make sure your ideas flow smoothly from paragraph to paragraph, leading the reader from one step to the next. The lead sentence or *topic sentence* in the paragraph should give the reader the substance of what is discussed. Following sentences should support the idea and develop it fully. Refer to Chapter 2, "Style in Business Writing," and the Appendix, Part B, for a review of sentence patterns.

Ask yourself if the text is clear. Do you need to define special terms or phrases? Are your explanations complete or do they skip steps? Have you packed too many ideas into one paragraph? Have you fully developed your argument or explained your proposal so the basic objectives are clear to the reader?

Check your work for errors in style and grammar referring to Chapters 2, 3, and the Appendix when necessary. Perhaps you can eliminate overused words and phrases. Make sure you write in the active voice rather than the passive voice. Vary your sentence structure to avoid a series of short, choppy sentences or long, complex ones. Read your draft for errors in spelling and punctuation.

Finally, revise your work for awkward phrases and lapses in tone. Awkward writing will sound clumsy and over-written, as though the words were stumbling over one another ; for example, "We would like you, if you could, to look into the delay and readvise us of certain aspects of the situation which we have not been able, at this end to ascertain." The writer meant to say, "Please investigate the delay and let us know why it happened. We have not been able to discover the reason ourselves."

Tone in writing is the same as tone of voice in speaking. It always reflects your attitude towards your reader. Your tone may be friendly or unfriendly, serious or humourous, formal or informal depending on the subject and the situation. In a letter to a financial institution, company officer, or board of directors, for example, you would adopt a formal, conservative tone. In a sales letter, you may want to use a more casual, humourous tone to engage the reader at a more familiar and friendly level. You can recognize lapses in tone by the appearance of inappropriate words or phrases in your material. You would not, for instance, want to use slang or jargon in the letter to your conservative client, nor would you insert a formal discussion of product specifications in a casual, light-hearted promotional piece. Consistency of tone will help you establish and maintain the appropriate relationship with your reader.

After you have rekeyboarded your revised draft in final form, be sure to proofread the material carefully. It is your last opportunity to catch any errors that you have inadvertently overlooked. You do not want the reader to catch your mistakes. Proofreading your work carefully can save you considerable embarrassment.

SUMMARY

Below is a brief checklist for the three basic steps to effective writing.

Step One: Prewriting

1. Identify and state your purpose.
2. Know your audience.
3. Define the scope of your subject.
4. Conduct research and gather data.

Step Two: Writing

5. Organize the data and devise a rough plan.
6. Outline your writing project.
7. Write the first draft.

Step Three: Revising

8. Edit and rewrite the draft for clarity, tone, accuracy, brevity.
9. Check for grammar and spelling errors and other careless mistakes.
10. Make sure the final copy is neat and free from erasures, strikeovers, smudges, and other marks.

You may use the three steps of effective writing — prewriting, writing, and revising — for any type of business communication. As you practise them and become more skilled in the writing process, you will be able to work through each step more quickly. Throughout this book, you will see how to use these steps to develop the various types of letters, reports, memos, and proposals used in business.

CHAPTER

2 STYLE IN BUSINESS WRITING

Effective business writing speaks to the reader's needs and interests in readily understood language. Whether you are writing a letter, a memorandum, or a report, you will always begin by considering the purpose of your writing and your audience.

The most effective business writing is concise, vivid, and clear. It does not waste the reader's time, and it is free of clichés, jargon, and awkward phrases. You can learn to be more aware of your language and avoid outworn and stilted expressions, wordy sentences, vague terms, and other lapses in style. Through practice and attention to the language you use, you can develop a clear, concise style to your business writing.

Pronouns

In business writing, there are two distinctive styles which are frequently used. The *objective style*, where the writer uses the third person (*he, she, it, they*), and the *subjective style*, where the writer uses the first person (*I, we*). You should use the objective style when preparing reports and the subjective style for letters and memos. Whenever possible, you should begin a letter or memo with a *you* reference, bringing in *I* and *we* after you have addressed the needs of the reader. It is important to strike a balance in favour of *you*. A good use of personal pronouns can add warmth to your letter and memo writing while at the same time letting readers know how you can meet their needs.

Active Language

Business writing does not have to be dull, stiff, or lifeless. You can use active verbs, nouns, adjectives, and adverbs, such as *debate, challenge, intricate, rapidly*, to create vivid images in your readers' minds. Active language is particularly important in sales or promotional letters where you want to attract and hold the reader's attention.

Another aspect of active language is voice. The term *voice* refers to whether the subject of a sentence acts or receives the action described by the verb. If the subject acts, the sentence is in the *active voice*. If the subject is acted upon, the sentence is in the *passive voice*.

Active voice: Mrs. Chong *wrote* this letter.

Passive voice: This letter *was written* by Mrs. Chong.

You should use the active voice to give your writing vitality, emphasis, and directness.

Passive Voice

There are instances when you should use the passive voice. These are:

1. When you wish to be diplomatic.

Passive: The information *has not been received.* (Diplomatic)

Active: You *did not send* us the information. (Not diplomatic)

Passive: Your credit application *has been reviewed* carefully. Unfortunately, it did not meet the criteria established by our company for first-time credit accounts. For this reason, a charge account *cannot be opened* for you at this time. (Diplomatic)

Active: We *have reviewed* your application and find that we cannot *extend credit* to your account at this time. (Not diplomatic)

2. When you know the receiver of the action is more important than the doer.

Example: The ambassador *was greeted* by the mayor.

3. When you do not know, or it does not matter, who or what is the subject of the sentence.

Example: The Hudson's Bay Company *was chartered* on May 2, 1670.

Except in the above cases, you should not use the passive voice because you will reduce the effectiveness of your message. In addition, you should not weaken your writing by shifting from the active to the passive voice.

Clarity

Clear writing involves choosing the best words to express your ideas and arranging those words in such a way that they are easily interpreted by the reader. It is important to remember that the meaning of a word depends on the context in which you use it and the understanding of the person who reads it. Because each one of us has slightly — or even widely — different interpretations of what words mean, you can never assume that what is clear to you is equally clear to your reader. You must determine exactly what you want to say and choose the simplest, clearest way to say it. The more abstract and vague your language, the less clear your message will be.

Edit

The best way to clarify your language is to edit ruthlessly. Ask yourself the question, "Is there a simpler way to say this?" Consider the following paragraph:

> Re your inquiry of October 30, please be advised that the item to which you refer (i.e., the 127-A Executive Model) has been removed from our catalogue as of the present writing. The optimum solution would be to select the most appropriate substitute and resubmit your order.

What the writer meant to say was:

> Thank you for your October 30 letter asking about our 127-A Executive Model. We removed this item from our catalogue November 22; however, the 128-A Trimline Model listed in our current catalogue should do the job equally well. Just submit a new order for the 128-A Trimline Model, and we will ship it promptly to your address.

The first paragraph is less clear and gives the reader less information. The second paragraph uses simpler language and tells the reader how to solve the problem.

Use Concrete Words

Concrete words refer to something specific, often something we can see, hear, touch, taste, or smell. Vague or abstract words refer to concepts or generalities, philosophies, or ideologies. The more abstract the word or phrase, the more removed from our ordinary experience and the more likely we will misunderstand the term. The more concrete the word, the less room there is for misinterpreting the message.

Vague: Management has admitted the need for greater levels of productivity in the assembly area.

Concrete: Management agrees that assembly workers need to increase their productivity by 20 percent.

Vague: In view of the company's current economic situation...

Concrete: With company sales up 10 percent and inventory reduced by 12 percent...

Vague: Market conditions dictate that we take a more prudent course...

Concrete: Over forty firms currently are producing computer accessories. The risk for a new company is high so we must target our products carefully.

Vague or abstract words often leave questions like "How much?" "What kind?" "Which one?" unanswered. It is important to check your letters, memos, and reports for abstract words and phrases that appear to say something but actually say little. By using concrete words, you answer readers' questions with specific information.

Keep the References Clear

When you use words to modify or refer to other words, be sure your train of thought is clear. The reader should be able to tell easily which word or words the writer has modified. You may provide some unintended humour if you are careless about your references; for example, consider the following:

Incorrect: You will be able to recognize the director. He is a tall, gray-haired man with a tan briefcase named Howard Guerson.

Correct: You will be able to recognize Howard Guerson, the director. He is a tall, gray-haired man with a tan briefcase.

Incorrect: If you cannot hang the sheet metal yourself, please ask for assistance in hanging it from the shop steward.

Correct: If you cannot hang the sheet metal yourself, please ask the shop steward for assistance.

You can use a variety of methods to correct confusing references: breaking one sentence into two or more sentences, rearranging word order, restating the sentence, or filling in the missing reference. Here are some basic guidelines for keeping your references clear:

1. Keep modifiers close to the words they modify. The reader should not have to guess at your meaning.

Poor: He visited over a period of six weeks each new plant the company had opened.

Better: Over a period of six weeks, he visited each new plant the company had opened.

Poor: An executive order she received recently managed to confuse the entire staff. (Is it *recently received* or *recently managed*?)

Better: An executive order she recently received managed to confuse the entire staff.

2. Place the adverb only in the correct position. When you are writing, place the word *only* immediately before the word or phrase it modifies in order to avoid confusion. Misplacing *only* can distort your meaning.

Poor: Our deluxe models only have a one-year guarantee. (Do only the deluxe models have a guarantee? or do the deluxe models have a guarantee of only a year as opposed to five years?)

Better: Only our deluxe models have a one-year guarantee.

(See Appendix, Part A, page 297)

3. Keep the subject and verb together. This arrangement helps the reader follow your thought and understand the sentence more easily.

Poor: The merger of Apco and Sunnex, which was one of the largest and most bitterly contested in the history of the oil industry and which involved a staggering $250 billion in assets, was approved on Friday, April 2.

Better: The merger of Apco and Sunnex was approved on Friday, April 2. The $250 billion venture was one of the largest and most bitterly contested mergers in the history of the oil industry.

Poor: Among the first to recognize the problem as a mechanical rather than an electrical one were Smith and his assistant Powell.

Better: Smith and his assistant Powell were among the first to recognize the problem as a mechanical rather than an electrical one.

Often the best solution to this problem is to break the sentence into two or more shorter sentences that allow you to convey the information without separating the subject and verb.

4. Make sure the references are correct. Words such as *who, that, which*, and *it* refer to the preceding noun in the sentence. You must ensure that your pronouns refer to *one* word in your sentences. If your references are not clear, your sentences may be ambiguous or unintentionally humourous.

Humourous: We will paint any car for only $559.95. Our offer is good for this week only. Have your car repainted before it expires.

The intention of the message is that *it* refers to the offer, not the car. The image of a rusted car expiring adds an inadvertent comic twist to the message.

Correct: We will paint any car for only $559.95. Our offer is good for this week only. Have your car repainted before the offer expires.

Keep the Structures Parallel

Parallelism is a technique used in writing to combine several statements into one. Thus, ideas in a sentence that are of equal importance should be expressed in parallel form. Using similar forms for similar ideas helps your reader understand how the ideas are related (see Appendix, Part B, Sentence Structure).

Incorrect: Mr. Thompson was not only *kind* and *generous* but also a very *efficient person.* (The word *person* destroys the parallelism.)

Correct: Mr. Thompson was not only *kind* and *generous* but also very *efficient.*

Phrases and clauses in a series or sentence should be parallel in structure. In the following example, the writer used prepositional phrases and switched to a clause at the end of the sentence.

> We should aim for production levels that are above last year's rate, on par with industry norms, *and should achieve our basic marketing objectives.*

You are apt to confuse your reader when structures in your sentences are not parallel. You have established an expectation on the reader's part that each item in the series will be similar. The sentence above should read:

> We should aim for production levels that are above last year's rate, on par with industry norms, and *in line with our marketing objectives.*

Another common mistake writers commit is mixing verb tense forms within the same sentence; for example,

> Ted Roberts looked into the Morgan contract, talked with Hays and Ventura and *finds* no conflict with the former client.

The verb *finds* is in the present tense while the other words are in the past tense. You can rewrite the sentence in two ways:

> Ted Roberts looked into the Morgan contract, talked with Hays and Ventura, and *found* no conflict with the former client.

or

> Ted Roberts looked into the Morgan contract and talked with Hays and Ventura. He *finds* no conflict of interest with the former client.

Another common mistake is for the writer to be inconsistent in the use of the infinitive; for example,

Wrong: The corporation's objectives are *to* increase productivity, *to* reduce costs, and improve employee morale

Right: The corporation's objectives are *to* increase productivity, *to* reduce costs, and *to* improve employee morale.

Make sure your series or sentences are parallel to help your readers understand the ideas you are communicating. Check over your writing to be certain you have not switched from parallel phrases to clauses within a series or changed verb tense forms in the middle of a sentence or paragraph.

Brevity

Many of us have acquired wordy expressions that we use without thinking. We often use unnecessary words and phrases to give our writing a more dignified, polite, or professional tone. When you eliminate such expressions your message is more concise. In addition, concise writing will save your reader time and effort in understanding what you have written.

Wordy: We urge you to be forthcoming with any information you may have about the current situation and you may be certain we will treat this information with the utmost confidentiality.

Concise: Please give us the information you have. We will consider it confidential.

Eliminate Unnecessary Words

1. Avoid empty phrases.

Wordy: The desks are blue *in colour*.

Concise: The desks are blue.

Wordy: ...thinking *on a theoretical basis*.

Concise: ...thinking theoretically.

Wordy: In *about* a week's *time*...

Concise: In a week...

Wordy: It is a *matter of prime* importance...

Concise: It is important...

Wordy: *The reason* I take the train *is that*...

Concise: I take the train because...

2. Avoid using there is or there are at the beginning of a sentence. Although you may need to use these words in order to avoid awkwardness, you can eliminate them most of the time.

Poor: *There are* several flights that make the round trip from Vancouver to Montreal.

Better: *Several flights make* the round trip from Vancouver to Montreal.

Poor: Whenever we achieve a new goal, *there is* a rise in morale.

Better: Whenever we achieve a new goal, *morale rises*.

3. Condense clauses beginning with <u>which</u>, <u>that</u>, or <u>who</u> into fewer words. When you are revising, look for these phrases and e-liminate them wherever you can.

Poor: The consultant, *who was hired from McKinsey*, gave a speech that was long and boring.

Better: The *McKinsey consultant* gave a long, boring speech.

Poor: The Preston report, *which was in two volumes*, outlined the responsibilities that each executive was to assume.

Better: The *two-volume Preston report* outlined executive responsibilities.

4. Eliminate the article <u>the</u> wherever you can to improve the flow and readability of your sentences.

Examples: ~~The~~ staff recommendations from the Finance Department will eliminate ~~the~~ need for outside consultants.

The October meeting will give us ~~the~~ two plans for ~~the~~ future office designs.

You can determine if you need *the* by crossing it out and reading the sentence for meaning. If the sentence is not clear, restore the article.

5. Avoid wordy phrases. Compare the following list of wordy phrases with their more concise alternatives. Eliminate wordy phrases wherever you find them in your own writing.

Wordy	**Concise**
at this point in time	now
consensus of opinion	consensus
meet together	meet
during the course of	during
few in number	few
personal in manner	personal
in the vast majority of cases	in most cases
on a weekly basis	weekly
refer back to	refer to
square in shape	square
until such time as	until
due to the fact that	because
very necessary	necessary

in spite of the fact that	although
engaged in a study of	studying
depreciates in value	depreciates
opening gambit	gambit (a gambit is an opening move)

Use Adverbs and Adjectives Sparingly

When you need to use modifiers, make sure they work for you and do not simply add words to your sentences. With a well-placed adverb or adjective you can heighten the impact of what you say. Overused modifiers can weaken your meaning or give your writing a flat, shopworn tone. Consider the following examples:

Poor: We will have to give the recommendation the *acid test*. It is *extremely* important that we find the best alternative, for in the *final analysis*, the *very* future of the company depends on our decision.

Better: We will have to test the recommendation against our own standards. Finding the best alternative is critical since the future of the company depends on our decision.

Poor: She gave a *quick and highly emphatic* reply.

Better: She gave a quick, emphatic reply.

You should avoid the following modifiers. They clutter your sentences and add little to the message.

absolutely necessary	final analysis
bitter end	acid test
perfectly clear	straightforward manner
quick glance	basically right
past experience	

Accuracy

Any piece of business writing — letter, memo, or report — must convey accurate information to the reader. In addition to its costliness, inaccurate information can be worse than no information at all. Mistakes in ordering parts, purchasing supplies, billing customers, and answering inquiries cost businesses millions of dollars a year. Inaccurate information costs time, money, and goodwill — three things no business can afford to lose.

The following guidelines will help you check your accuracy:

1. Double-check figures, dates, specifications, and other details. Being pretty sure or fairly certain that something is correct may be fine for your golf score but not for policy numbers, dates of shipments, price lists, and the like. Do not rely on your memory — it is too easy to reverse numbers or remember the wrong sequence. Put this motto on your desk: When in doubt, check it out.

2. Make sure you have spelled all names correctly. Your letter, memo, or report will not impress readers favourably if you misspell their names or the names of their companies. You should also verify the spelling of product names, titles of articles or books, or any other proper names you may use.

3. Check for clarity in presenting your ideas. Clarity is essential to accuracy. Learn to spot ambiguous statements, muddled expressions, and poor development of ideas. This step is particularly important when you are negotiating with a client. If you are to convey your terms accurately, you must state them in clear, unambiguous language.

4. Keyboard your letter, memo, or report neatly. Neatness is a part of accurate writing. If you fill your finished copy with strikeovers, erasures, or handwritten corrections, the reader may easily misread or misunderstand what you have written.

Tone

Tone is the emotional content of your writing. It can be formal, informal, positive, negative, persuasive, humourous, or argumentative. Each tone has its use; for example, you would use a formal tone in a letter to your local city council and an informal tone in a letter to your colleague. The tone you select will depend on the purpose of your writing and your audience.

The following guidelines may assist you in selecting the appropriate tone:

1. Formal tone. You should use this approach for most of your business correspondence.

Main features: Formal sounding words
Use of *we* as opposed to *I*

Example: We shall be presenting our proposal on artificial intelligence at the January meeting.

2. Informal tone. You should only use this approach if you have done business with your reader for a considerable length of time and have established a close relationship.

Main features: Informal, warm words
Use of *I*
Use of first names

Example: I will be in Europe on vacation during July; however, I'll be back in time to help you install your new computer system. My warmest regards to Sara and the children.

3. Positive tone.

Main features: Positive words
Use of *you*
Introduction of positive aspects before negative ones
Reasons for decisions provided

Examples: Your order will be mailed on Friday. If this timing is not convenient to you, please let me/us know.

Even though your job performance rating was in the top ten percent, Morgan's recent losses in earnings and revenues have forced us to lay off 20 percent of our staff.

4. Negative tone. You should avoid using a negative tone whenever possible. Never send any communication written in anger. If you are annoyed, write your message and then leave it for a couple of days until you have calmed down and can think objectively. Goodwill is difficult to recover.

Sentences

Sentences in business writing tend to be short: about twenty words or fewer. Language experts state that shorter sentences are easier to understand and communicate information more effectively. It seems we like to digest facts in small bits.

When we start putting thoughts on paper, however, we may end with either one of two extremes: long, complex sentences or short, choppy ones. Part of the problem may stem from the fact that a sentence must be a complete thought. As we add a qualifier here, a modifier there, or an incidental fact, our complete thought is likely to become a verbal maze for the reader. On the other hand, we may write our thoughts in brief, staccato sentences that leave the reader short of breath.

The following guidelines can help you write sentences that move the reader gracefully from one point to the next. (See also Appendix, Part B, and Chapter 1.)

1. A sentence must represent or express a complete thought and be grammatically correct. Build understanding step by step, with each sentence contributing to the main point of the paragraph.

2. A sentence must have unity. It is important that you emphasize and clearly state the main idea. Occasionally, writers attempt to include more than one unit of thought in a sentence with the result that the reader is confused.

In the following example, one sentence contains several thoughts. The writer appears to be thinking out loud rather than writing to someone else.

> Our discussion of the new product division has given me a chance to reconsider obtaining the Trenton plant which has always been an attractive prospect, even in the recession because of its location and local labour supply, and it might be a good time to bring the purchase proposal before the board when it meets on Thursday.

The conjunctions *and* and *but* often signal where a new sentence can be made. You can write the above in shorter sentences as follows:

> Our discussion of the new product division has given me a chance to reconsider purchasing the Trenton plant. I've always felt the plant was an attractive prospect, given its prime location and the local labour supply. I'd like to propose that we purchase the plant. Perhaps we can bring the idea before the board at its Thursday meeting.

3. A sentence must flow. Avoid short, choppy sentences. Vary your sentence structure to lead the reader from one sentence to the next. Read aloud the two versions below. Notice how the change in rhythm affects your perception of the material.

Choppy: I received your order for 25 office chairs on October 4. I regret to inform you that a labour strike has delayed production. We recently hired new workers. We expect to be back in production within one week. I apologize for the delay. We will offer a 10 percent discount on all back orders. Your patience is appreciated in this matter.

Varied: I received your order for 25 office chairs on October 4. We have a delay in the production of new chairs because of a labour strike in our factory. Recently, we hired new workers and expect to be back in production within one week. We sincerely apologize for the delay and would like to offer you a 10 percent discount on your back order. We appreciate your patience in this matter.

Short, choppy sentences tend to mimic a curt, unemotional tone. Varied sentences convey a more relaxed and friendly delivery. To vary your sentences, you may need to break one sentence into several, combine two or more sentences into one, or rearrange the word order within sentences.

For further assistance on sentence structure, refer to the Appendix, Part B, Sentences and Sentence Patterns.

Paragraphs

Paragraphs, like sentences, should lead the reader from one step to the next. The purpose of a paragraph is to develop each point in enough detail to give the reader a complete understanding of what you are trying to say. The degree to which you develop a paragraph depends on its aim or purpose. A good, well-written paragraph will have continuity and tend to be specific rather than general.

Breaking a piece of writing into paragraph form will make what you say easier to read and understand. A report may seem overwhelming to a reader if you do not paragraph it and lay it out properly. Similarly, a solid block of type is discouraging to someone who has only a few minutes to read, digest, and respond to your letter.

While there are few hard and fast rules about paragraph length, the guidelines below will help you write effective paragraphs.

1. Use key sentences — called topic sentences — to introduce or summarize your paragraph. Topic sentences highlight the essential point in a paragraph. The remaining sentences support or elaborate that point. A topic sentence at the beginning introduces the subject you will discuss, while at the end it summarizes the preceding information.

Topic sentence at the beginning: Our survey indicates that a chain department store located in Eden's Plaza would be successful. Over 70 percent of plaza shoppers indicated they would shop at the store. All the adjacent and surrounding small businesses supported the location of such a store in the plaza.

Topic sentence at the end: Twenty percent of the retailers have responded using the business reply card. Fifteen percent replied by phone, 10 percent by postcard, 14 percent by personal note, and 7 percent by third parties. The remaining 34 percent have not yet responded. In all, the business reply card elicited the largest response from retailers.

2. Determine where new paragraphs begin by looking at how sentences group around your ideas. As you write, you will be developing various ideas or points you want the reader to understand. You will find that, in general, sentences will fall into a natural grouping around these points. Proper paragraphing will help you draw attention to each topic and move the reader from one topic to the next. You can emphasize specific points more strongly with short paragraphs; however, you should use longer paragraphs to explain an idea or give more detailed information.

3. Avoid extremes of lengthy or choppy paragraphs. If you use one-sentence paragraphs, each covering a different point, your letters or memos will be disjointed and staccato in tone and appearance. In a report, a series of short, disjointed paragraphs will indicate to your reader that you have not developed a central concept but provided a list of ideas. On the other hand, your reader will likely skim or not read lengthy paragraphs. Ideally, a paragraph should be about eight or ten lines long, covering only a few points and presenting the main point quickly; however, the paragraphs in your letters should be only four to six lines long.

4. Keep in mind that your primary concern in paragraph division is the overall organization of your writing. Paragraphs will follow the same basic order regardless of whether you are writing a letter, a memo, a report, or a proposal. In the *opening* paragraph, you should indicate your subject and purpose in writing. You should develop the main points and indicate the goal you would like to achieve in the paragraphs in the body of your writing. You should use the *closing* paragraph to indicate the action you wish the reader to take, or, in the case of a report, provide a summary of what you have said and recommendations for the future.

ACTIVITIES

1. Rewrite the following sentences with a more positive tone:

(a) We cannot repair your broken printer for two days.
(b) We are unable to ship the supplies you ordered because of an unforeseen delay.
(c) I cannot mail your certificate until Friday.
(d) It is important to us to get your renewed subscription immediately. Everytime we have to remind you, it costs us money.
(e) We are closed from 6:00 p.m. to 9:00 p.m.
(f) I need the enclosed questionnaire returned by January 20, otherwise I can't use it.
(g) We cannot hold your reservation past 6:00 p.m. without a deposit.
(h) We will give overdraft protection to our preferred customers only.
(i) We don't feel your qualifications match our job needs.
(j) You claim that we did not enclose all the parts in your order.
(k) This is to inform you that as of January 5, 19—, your job with Triad will be terminated.

2. Rewrite the following with appropriate paragraphs and in a less condescending tone:

We have received your letter in which you ask us to sell you our Jones line awning products. We are one of the largest awning manufacturers in Canada and we have achieved this enviable position by choosing our licensees very, very carefully. According to our information, you do not qualify to sell our products although you have done quite well for yourself as a retailer. We are sorry we cannot sell to you directly. We can suggest that you contact Dean Kozak at 736-6869 who is one of our licensees in your area. Perhaps he could retail our products to you. Please let us know if we can be of help to you again.

3. Change the following phrases to make them more concise:

As regards your payment	Kindly remit

At your earliest convenience
Pending receipt of
Arrived at the conclusion
In many cases
During the time that
She is a person who
Subsequent to
We regret to inform you
Owing to the fact that
In the near future
In the event
A long period of time
At an earlier date

4. Correct the following sentences:

(a) The treasurer proposed an amendment to the bylaws, which the financial director opposed.
(b) At the age of forty, the computer was overwhelming according to the office manager.
(c) The assistant to the sales manager, who was hired recently, will assume responsibility for month end reports.
(d) Opening the meeting on a positive note, the agenda circulated among the committee members.
(e) Several items in a customer's order were out of stock, and it delayed shipment by two weeks.

5. Rewrite these wordy sentences:

(a) In consequence of the fact, that the item you have requested in your recent letter of March 17 is currently unavailable and out of stock, we regret to inform you that your order will be delayed.
(b) At their monthly meeting last Thursday, it was recommended by the board that the conclusions your group suggested be adopted.
(c) Owing to the fact that we feel obligated to make some adjustments in our policy with your company, we are taking this opportunity to write to you.
(d) In this connection, it may be observed that our losses to date this year are less than those to date last year.
(e) Despite what is being done, however, the fact is easily observed that the absentee rate amongst ten-year employees has continued to rise at an alarming rate.

6. For each of the following topics, write one paragraph using the active voice only:

(a) Appropriate dress in today's business office
(b) Prosecution of computer hackers

(c) Women in management
(d) Designing a company logo
(e) Management by crisis
(f) The importance of face-to-face communication in business.

7. Write a paragraph on the following topic using a diplomatic style. Imagine that this paragraph will be circulated to personnel in your office.

Morale in the workplace.

CHAPTER

3 CHOOSING THE RIGHT WORD

Throughout much of your business career, you will use the written word to communicate with co-workers, managers, customers, suppliers, and creditors. Your message must speak for you; you cannot stand at the reader's shoulder and explain what you mean. In addition, your letters, memos, reports, and other communications represent not only you but your company. As a result, you must choose your words with care.

In this chapter, we look at some of the guidelines you should use in business writing, including business vocabulary, words frequently confused, and gender-inclusive language. We provide only an overview here. We have dealt with more detailed discussions of style in the chapters on writing various business communications. For specific grammar questions, see the Appendix.

Business Vocabulary

Business vocabulary is more than simply knowing some of the special terms used in various professions and industries. It is understanding the difference between everyday language and the language we adopt for more formal communication. Our casual conversational style is generally too vague and imprecise for most business writing.

Avoid Slang and Buzz Words

Avoid the use of slang in your writing. It not only weakens your message but often leaves the reader wondering what you meant to say.

Avoid: The Purchasing Department considered the price from Allied a rip-off.

Better: The Purchasing Department considered the price from Allied much too high. (Explains more precisely what is wrong with the price.)

Avoid: I think Carla's analysis is a little far out in this case.

Better: I think Carla's analysis doesn't take into consideration the long-term impact of the problem. (Explains in specific terms the speaker's objections to Carla's evaluation.)

Avoid: The requirements for this job are unreal.

Better: The requirements for this job include having a Ph.D.

Some of today's slang and buzz words include:

expandability
at this point in time
megabucks
taxwise (or anything-wise)
portability
type of thing
you people
hassle
eyeball
bottom line
view point
sure thing
right on
basically
orchestrate
no way
state of the art

Avoid Unfamiliar Terms

Avoid using overly technical terms, unfamiliar abbreviations, or terms that relate to a particular profession or specialty when you are writing to someone who may not be familiar with such terms. Like slang, these terms can confuse the reader and obscure your message.

Avoid: We place a great deal of emphasis on employee participation through our QWL and MBO programs.

Better: We place a great deal of emphasis on employee participation through our quality of worklife and management by objectives programs.

Avoid: After analyzing your software program, we found an error that produced an infinite do-loop in the run.

Better: After analyzing your software program, we found an error that instructed the computer to repeat a step endlessly.

Unless you work in a legal office or are a lawyer, you should not use the following for everyday business letters:

aforementioned
duly
per, as per
pursuant to

herein
hereto
herewith
notwithstanding the above
re
therein
whereas

Avoid Clichés

In general, avoid the use of clichés including worn-out phrases such as *big as a house*, *nose to the grindstone*, and the like. Instead, choose words that convey more precisely the particular condition or situation you are describing.

Avoid: To reduce costs, we've got to keep our eye on the ball.

Better: To reduce costs, we've got to keep accurate records of all expenditures and look for ways to cut our overheads.

Avoid: Roald has heard from only one of two clients and is waiting for the other shoe to drop.

Better: Roald has heard from only one of two clients but is expecting a reply shortly from the second.

A good dictionary and a complete thesaurus (a reference book for locating synonyms and opposites) are your best sources for finding the right word. Use these references often. They can enhance your business vocabulary and help you express yourself clearly and accurately.

Words Frequently Confused

Many people confuse the meaning and spelling of the following words: Practise using them until they become familiar to you.

accept accept — to take, agree. *I accept the offer.*

except except — to exclude, omit. *It's correct, except for this.*

advice advice — opinion, counsel. *(Noun) He needs your advice.*

advise advise — to counsel. *(Verb) Please advise him.*

affect affect — influence, change. *Inflation always affects our level of income.*

effect effect — impression, results; to cause. *The computer has had a profound effect on communications. It has effected a real change in office procedures.*

already	already — even now. *They are already here.*
all ready	all ready — all prepared. *We're all ready to leave.*
assent	assent — to agree; permission. *Did you assent to the request? She gave her assent to the project.*
ascent	ascent — advancement. *He made the ascent up the corporate ladder.*
capital	capital — seat of government; wealth. *Our sales force is in the capital city. We need more capital.*
capitol	capitol — United States government building*. *We are in the capitol.*
	*Note: Not used to denote Canadian government buildings.
cite	cite — refer to. *He cited new sales figures.*
site	site — location. *The new building site is in Toronto.*
sight	sight — scene. *The skyline is a beautiful sight.*
consul	consul — foreign embassy official. *Check these trade arrangements with the West German consul.*
council	council — official body. *The city council met.*
counsel	counsel — legal advisor. *The corporate lawyer will act as counsel in this matter.*
	counsel — to advise. *Older employees often counsel younger workers about their new job duties.*
continuous	continuous — uninterrupted, unbroken. *A continuous water supply is essential.*
continual	continual — repeatedly. *Our productivity is low because of the continual breakdowns of our equipment.*
dissent	dissent — disagreement. *Voice your dissent at the meeting tonight.*
descent	descent — a decline, fall. *Sales made a steep descent.*
descend	descend — to come down. *Commands descend from the top management.*
fewer	fewer — used for numbers, individual units. *We require fewer salespeople.*

less less — used for quantities. *Net income was less than last year.*

formerly formerly — previously. *She was formerly at St. Andrew's Hospital.*

formally formally — officially. *She joined formally today.*

knew knew — understood. *I knew from the look on her face that the contract had been rejected.*

new new — recent. *The new personnel manager made some drastic changes in policy.*

know know — understand. *I know the procedure for filing an income tax return.*

no no — not any. *There were no volunteers for the work party on Saturday.*

later later — after a time. *I'll deal with that later.*

latter latter — last mentioned of the two. *If I'm offered a raise or a promotion, I'll take the latter.*

lie lie — to rest or recline. *I lie down. I lay down this morning. I should have lain down earlier.*

lay lay — to put or place something. *I lay the book on your desk. I laid it there a minute ago. I have laid it there many times and never lost it.*

lose lose — misplace. *Don't lose that address.*

loose loose — not fastened down; release. *The pressure plate seems loose. Turn loose your imagination.*

of of — used to show possession. *The office of the plant manager was located far away from the assembly line.*

off off — suspended, not on. *The power was turned off to allow maintenance of the computer system.*

past past — preceeding. *Our past record is good.*

passed passed — to go by. *Production this year passed last year's high. We passed the factory this morning.*

personal personal — individual. *I jog for personal reasons.*

personnel personnel — workers; a department. *The personnel office knows what motivates company personnel.*

precede	precede — to come before. *Hard work precedes recognition.*
proceed	proceed — to go ahead. *We can proceed with the talk.*
principle	principle — rule, standard. *Values are principles that guide our lives.*
principal	principal — main, chief; superintendent. *His principal goal is quality. The principal taught us well.*
quiet	quiet — silence. *The office is quiet after five.*
quite	quite — completely; to a considerable degree. *I am quite sure she'll come. He's quite a person.*
rise	rise — to go up, to get up. *I rise early each day. I rose a little late yesterday; however, I have risen on time today.*
raise	raise — to lift, bring up. *If you need help, raise your hand. I am raising this issue for a good reason. No one raised an objection before. You have raised your hand three times in the past half hour.*
sit	sit — to assume an upright position. *I sit at my desk. I sat here yesterday. I have sat here for years, it seems.*
set	set — put or place something down. *I set your lunch on the table. I set the coffee there a minute ago. I have set it all in front of you.*
stationary	stationary — still, fixed. *The chair is stationary.*
stationery	stationery — letter paper. *The company stationery is printed on gray paper.*
their	their — belonging to them. *Their responsibilities were clearly outlined in the job description.*
there	there — in or at that place. *We went there directly after the meeting.*
they're	they're — they are. *They're the best company reps we've ever had.*
than	than — after a comparison; when. *I'm taller than Ted. The copier no sooner started than it broke down.*
then	then — next; in that case. *They spoke, then left. If you want more pens, then I'll order some.*

weather weather — climate. *The crop needs good weather.*

whether whether — if; regardless. *I'm going, whether you're coming or not. Do you know whether she's at home?*

Gender-Inclusive Language

In today's business world, you will find both men and women in all types of occupations and at all levels in an organization. As a result, it is important not to assume that your readers are all male or all female. Increasingly, business firms are phasing out the use of *he, his, man, mankind*, and other exclusively masculine terms to refer to both sexes. The modern business writer uses language and references that are gender-inclusive, that is, not biased toward either sex but include both. Below are some practical guidelines for using gender-inclusive language in your business communication.

Avoid Stereotypes

Avoid thinking in stereotypes — the manager is male, the secretary female — in your writing.

Avoid: Our course is designed to help your assistant or secretary reach her potential. (The person could be a man.)

Revised: Our course is designed to develop the full potential of your assistant.

Avoid: The prudent executive needs to know where his money goes. (More women are reaching the top of their professions, and companies and advertisers are recognizing them as a new market.)

Revised: Prudent executives need to know where their money goes. As a prudent executive, you need to know where your money goes.

Avoid Awkward Constructions

Rephrase sentences to avoid awkward constructions. The constant repetition of *his or her*, *he or she*, *him or her* can call attention to gender rather than subordinate it to the message. When possible, rephrase the sentence by using the plural form, changing word order, using *I, we, you, they*, and the like.

Avoid: If the employee is late, give him one warning.

Revised: An employee who is late receives one warning.

Avoid: If the manager files his or her report by Wednesday, he or she will have the revised copy returned to him or her on Friday.

Revised: Managers who file their reports on Monday will have a revised copy returned to them by Friday.

Avoid: Don't judge someone simply on the basis of his sex or colour.

Revised: Don't judge someone simply on the basis of sex or colour. Don't judge people simply on the basis of their sex or colour.

Use Non-biased Titles

You can also make titles, names of positions or occupations, and common references gender-inclusive. Some non-biased titles for occupations and positions include the following:

Avoid	**Revised**
salesman	salesperson
chairman	chair, chairperson
craftsman	craftworker
draftsman	drafter
fireman	firefighter
watchman	guard, security officer
newsman	reporter, newsperson
foreman	supervisor
repairman	repairer
mailman	mail carrier, letter carrier
policeman	police officer

man-hours	staff-hours
man-made	artificial, synthetic
mankind	humanity, people, human race
man the office	staff the office
saleslady	clerk
gal Friday	assistant

Use Gender-inclusive Salutations

Salutations in business letters should also be gender-inclusive when you do not know the name of the person addressed. Many companies use the following salutations:

Dear Supervisor:	Dear Customer:
Dear Executive:	Dear Subscriber:
Dear Manager:	Dear Investor:
Dear Colleague:	Dear Friend:
(to those of the same rank or occupation)	(letter written as an appeal or to inform)

ACTIVITIES

1. Select the correct word from the two noted in parentheses.

(a) The chairperson was annoyed by the (continuous, continual) interruptions of one of the members of the committee.
(b) He travelled across the country in an attempt to (cite, site, sight) the perfect location for the new plant.
(c) When she went to (lay, lie) her book on the desk, she found the missing keys.
(d) A (principle, principal) of business letter writing is the *you* attitude.
(e) The choice of company (stationary, stationery) is important.
(f) (Whether, weather) or not the interview has gone well, you must always say thank you for the interviewer's time.
(g) The president made his decision to expand the office after consulting with the (personnel, personal) manager.
(h) Before he can (precede, proceed), he must have the approval of the vice president.
(i) We will not know the (affect, effect) of the budget cuts for six months.
(j) The board gave its (ascent, assent) to the proposal for an expansion into the Atlantic region.

2. Write sentences containing each of the following frequently confused words:

who's; whose
your; you're
raise; raze
cues; queues
incite; insight
leased; least
fiscal; physical
eminent; imminent
disburse; disperse
correspondence; correspondents
access; excess
allude; elude
waive; wave
addition; edition

3. Provide gender-inclusive titles for the following:

usherette
housewife
lady lawyer
cleaning lady
manmade
businessman
manpower

4. Rewrite the following stereotypic sentences:

(a) I'll have my girl telephone you tomorrow.
(b) We will select the best man for the job.
(c) The average businessman drinks his coffee black.

5. Rewrite the following sentences:

(a) If it's O.K. with you, I'll give the agent a buzz tomorrow.
(b) We enclose herewith a cheque in the amount of $500.
(c) I think you people should be able to handle this mess up.
(d) The LAN will be installed by next Tuesday for sure.
(e) The kid was as good as gold all afternoon.
(f) His sales technique was as smooth as silk.
(g) She entered the CEO's office as bold as brass.
(h) The sales projections are right on.
(i) As per the aforementioned matter, we are enclosing herewith our proposal re: Merrill Construction.
(j) From our viewpoint, it is basically wrong.

SECTION

2 EFFECTIVE LETTERS AND MEMOS

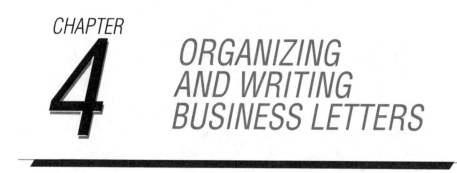

CHAPTER 4 ORGANIZING AND WRITING BUSINESS LETTERS

Effective letters are the result of good thinking and careful planning. In this chapter we take a look at the functions of business letters and consider ways of organizing and developing messages. The three steps introduced in Chapter 1 will help you plan your letters, outline them, and write polished final versions.

Functions of Business Letters

Business letters are an indispensable part of business communications. They are used to sell products or services, request material or information, answer customer inquiries, maintain good public relations, and serve a variety of other business functions.

You may ask if one could better handle some of these activities over the phone or in person. In some cases, these two methods may be the best way to get your message across. In reality, though, few business people have time to visit clients personally, and long-distance phone calls can be time-consuming and expensive. In addition, most people retain only about 25 per cent of what they hear and thus there is a chance your message will be forgotten or misunderstood. Putting it in writing remains one of the best ways to ensure that another person has accurately received your message, particularly if you are discussing technical or highly detailed information.

Business letters serve as part of a company's permanent records. They will verify bookkeeping and inventory entries. If you have a question about a customer order, the details of an agreement, or whether you answered someone's query, you can check your file copy of the letter. You cannot do the same with a phone conversation unless you record verbatim every outgoing and incoming call.

Letters also function as written contracts, fully recognized by the courts. Companies often draw up letters of agreement between themselves and independent suppliers or consultants. Job offers made through the mail are regarded as legally binding on the sender. If you accept a job in writing, your letter is a binding contract of employment.

Letters can act as formal or informal public relations material: They can help build goodwill between you and your clients, creditors, suppliers, and other public groups. Your letter represents you and your firm to people you may never meet personally or call on the phone. How you express yourself and the appearance of your letter form an impression in the reader's mind of you and your business.

Every letter that leaves your office fulfills several purposes. As a result, your business letters deserve considerable care and attention.

Step One: Prewriting

As you begin to plan your letter, keep in mind the questions every letter must answer.

1. What is the *purpose* of this letter? Why am I writing it?
2. Who is the *audience*? Whom do I want to influence?
3. What do I want to say? What is the *scope* of my subject?

Stating Your Purpose

Clarify your reason for writing the letter by jotting down the purpose in one or two sentences. It may be as simple as granting or refusing a request or as complicated as explaining a controversial company decision.

If you cannot state your purpose in a brief sentence or paragraph, talk the matter over with another person or give yourself time to rethink your reasons. In a sales letter, for example, is your purpose simply to tell the customer a product is available or to solicit an order by providing a business reply card? In a collection letter, do you want to extend the payment date or let the reader know payment is due immediately?

You should be able to state the purpose of your letter clearly and concisely before you begin the planning stage.

Knowing your Audience

Knowing your readers is as important as knowing your purpose for writing. You need to identify who they are and what motivates them.

You can gather facts about your readers fairly easily. A little research about their companies will tell you their positions, responsibilities, decision-making powers, as well as their budgets, types of business, and customers served. These facts will give you a good profile of your readers.

The art of writing effective letters, however, involves knowing something about what motivates people. Why do they decide to expand into a new market, develop a new line of products, cut back on services, move to a new location, upgrade or downgrade services? In business, certain common concerns drive people. Here are some examples:

Profit	improving it
Saving	spending less
Prestige	position and pride
Security	confidence in the future
Comfort	feeling of well-being
Convenience	saving time, boosting efficiency
Health	maintaining or improving it
Productivity	increasing it
Loyalty	fidelity to others and one's self
Curiosity	a sense of wonder, willingness to take risks

Knowing what motivates readers will help you decide what tone to adopt in your letters; for example, someone strongly motivated by saving would respond to a letter that promised to reduce the cost of office supplies by 20 percent. An executive motivated by prestige would be in the market for high-quality accessories or club memberships that offered special privileges to executives.

If you can identify your readers' motivations, you have a better chance of gaining their attention, cooperation, and compliance. You can establish goodwill and assure them that you are sensitive to their particular problems and interests. Put yourself in your readers' place, and you will begin to streamline your letters almost automatically. You can tailor each letter to the individual recipient.

Determining the Scope of Your Letter

Once you have identified your purpose and your audience, you will need to decide what you should cover in the letter. How much of the subject will you need to include? Will you require background material or research? Even before you make an outline, you can begin planning the content of your letter.

For a short, simple letter, your plan may be nothing more than a brief list of items you wish to mention. You may want to make notes in the margin of a letter you have to answer: "Request latest catalogue from this company" or "Interested in products offered but not now." For more complex letters, you will need to do more planning. If you know the subject well, you can jot down a list of topics that you want to cover; for example, suppose a client has asked you to explain your company's approach to convert a standard office to a computerized system, your list might look like the following:

Converting Client Office to Computer System

Survey office staff-attitudes, experience
Analyze work flow
Check on office colour scheme
Research best computer system
Develop data forms for computer
Research history of office automation
Do cost analysis
Establish installation and training schedules

Such a list will help you determine what you need to include in the letter and what you can eliminate. For example, "Check on office colour scheme" and "Research history of office automation" are not necessarily appropriate topics to cover; however, you may want to add "Do follow-up study" to the list.

Researching

When you have identified the scope of your topic, you will know whether you must do some research. Perhaps you can fill in the information from memory; on the other hand, you may need to check price lists, update your knowledge of suppliers, or investigate a customer's background.

Try to gather all the data you will need before you sit down to write your letter. You want to avoid having to stop in the middle of your first draft to check your facts or fill in missing information.

Step Two: Writing

By this time you have completed your preparation work and are ready to begin the actual writing. You will need to organize your material in the most logical and effective manner. Letter formulas and a good outline can help arrange your ideas and clarify your thinking.

Organizing with Letter Formulas

Over the years, people have developed formulas for organizing letters. Along with outlining, you can use these formulas to develop your ideas before you begin.

One widely used formula for sales letters is **AIDA**, an acronym for:

Attention: Getting the reader's eye

Interest: Arousing the reader's curiosity or interest in what you have to say

Desire: Making the reader want what you have to sell

Action: Showing or telling the reader what to do

IDCA is a variation on the AIDA theme and stresses conviction or the believability of your presentation. The object of this letter is to convince the reader to act on your message.

Interest: Catching the reader's eye

Desire: Creating a need for your product or service

Conviction: Convincing the reader of your message, some action is required on the reader's part

Action: Showing or telling the reader what to do

Another formula, **OFAC**, is used to inform a reader of a service or product you are offering, to solicit funds, or to convey information.

Occasion: Telling why you are writing to the person or company

Facts: Giving information needed for action on the reader's part

Action: Making a request, suggestion, statement, demand, appeal

Closing: Offering additional help or information, mentioning how the reader benefits

Formulas make it easy to keep your purpose in focus and to concentrate on essential information.

Outlining

Your outline may consist of a few main points you wish to cover or a more detailed breakdown of each point. Suppose, for example, an office manager from another firm asks you to explain how your company analyzes work flow among clerical workers. Your outline for a reply letter might look like the following:

I. On-site observation of work flow

II. Analysis of observation data

III. Recommendations

IV. Monitoring and follow-up

or

I. Observation of work flow

   A. Conducting one-week, on-site study of workers

   B. Compiling detailed data

II. Analysis of observation data

   A. Identifying strengths/weaknesses

   B. Comparing data with similar office surveys

III. Recommendations

   A. Drawing up new work schedules

   B. Describing new work methods

IV. Monitoring and follow-up

   A. Checking on staff progress every two weeks

   B. Adjusting recommendations as needed

Your outline will include more detail as your subject becomes more complex. Below are a few guidelines for developing effective outlines.

1. List the major topics in the order you feel they should appear. Assume for a moment that each major topic will be a paragraph. Take your time with this step. Write two or three lists if necessary. The major topics are the framework on which you will build your letter.

2. Arrange supporting ideas under each main topic in their order of importance. You may want to put the most important items at the beginning or end of each paragraph. If you find you are putting too many subtopics under each major topic, you should probably break each major point into two points.

3. Ensure everything in your outline is relevant. Keep in mind the purpose of your letter as you check through your topics. Do you have any trivial or irrelevant information? Have you left out data that would support your topics?

4. Check the order of your topics again. In light of the complete outline, would you change the way you plan to present the information? Should you start your letter with a question and then build to your solution? In most cases, your letters will follow a simple chronological or narrative order, building up to the main points. In special cases, you may want to vary the order and present the main idea in the first paragraph and use succeeding paragraphs to support it.

Lengthy letters will call for an extensive outline. To explain in detail how you would automate a standard office, for example, you might write the following outline:

I. Survey office staff
   A. Poll attitudes toward computers, automation
   B. Determine skill level and experience
   C. Determine staff abilities to learn new procedures
II. Analyze work flow
   A. Conduct one-week, on-site observation
   B. Analyze individual job responsibilities
III. Research best computer system
   A. Determine software needs
   B. Determine best hardware for office
   C. Survey plant outlets, power lines, electrical capacity, lighting, ventilation
IV. Do cost analysis
   A. Analyze costs of hardware/software
   B. Determine cost of maintenance, supplies
   C. Estimate insurance and service costs
   D. Estimate cost of training staff
V. Establish installation and training schedule
   A. Determine set-up and installation time

   B. Establish training schedule for staff
   C. Estimate time for conversion from manual to computerized system

VI. Develop data-entry forms
   A. Devise new forms for each job
   B. Devise forms for general office procedures
   C. Compare with industry forms

VII. Do monitoring and follow-up
   A. Debug hardware and software
   B. Monitor time and cost schedules
   C. Evaluate worker progress and attitudes

VIII. Reassure client
   A. Outline benefits of computerized office
   B. Assure client of continued support

Rather than to develop the perfect outline, remember your goal is to organize your thoughts and data in the most effective way possible. The outline should be a guide to your writing, not a rigid structure. You may find as you write that you need to add or delete information or rearrange the order of your topics. Your goal is a letter that influences the reader. A good outline can help you achieve that end. Refer to page 49 for a sample letter based on the above outline.

Writing the First Draft

No matter what type of letter you are writing — sales, credit, collection, acknowledgement, refusal — all three parts including the opening paragraph, body, and closing paragraph must enhance your message. You may find it better to begin in the body of the letter and write the opening paragraph later. The best rule of thumb is simply to begin and complete the first draft without being too concerned about which paragraph you write first.

Each part — the opening, body, and closing — has a different purpose. The following guidelines will help you develop concise, attention-getting paragraphs.

The Opening. Your opening paragraph must catch the readers' interest and get them to read your entire message. Keep the opening concise and fresh. Avoid repeating information the reader already knows. If you need to refer to previous correspondence between you, do so unobtrusively.

Poor: I have before me your letter of July 16 in which you list your computer accessory requirements for a surge protector, serial cable, dust covers, copyboard, and printer table. You would like each of these shipped by the 23rd and billed to your home office.

Better: We will ship the computer accessories you ordered July 16 and bill to your home office as requested. We are enclosing an invoice listing the items you ordered. As you will note the shipping date is July 23.

If you are selling a product or service, you may wish to open your letter with a question or bold statement.

Examples: We'd like to build the best customer service record in the industry.

How long has it been since you had a real vacation?

Why buy from Tango when you can get Centrex for less?

Ninety percent of Canadian executives pay too much for their insurance. Do you?

Not all readers will respond favourably to a bold or innovative opening. They may believe it is merely a gimmick to attract their attention. You must use your best judgment after analyzing your target audience.

Whether you adopt a conservative or innovative approach, make your opening paragraph an active one. Plunge right into your subject, whether it is providing information, expressing regret or pleasure, asking or answering a question. Your reader has little time and needs to know why you are writing.

Make sure your opening sets a positive, direct tone, appropriate to your subject and reader. It will help create a favourable impression of you and your letter.

Examples: Most insurance companies won't cover businesses your size. We're the exception.

We are pleased to inform you we have increased your credit limit from $1 000 to $1 500 as of April 25. Congratulations on your excellent credit record.

We are offering a February *white sale* on all letter-sized bond paper for your office needs.

Avoid openings which make use of the following:

1. A restatement of the obvious. e.g. "We have received your letter of March 30 in which you state..."

2. A negative tone. e.g. "Your failure to comply with our request for payment has forced us to close your account..."

3. Clichés. e.g. "Good banks are a dime a dozen, but finding a full service bank is like looking for a needle in a haystack..."

4. Participial Phrases. (See Appendix, Part A, Parts of Speech) e.g. "Regarding your order of June 24, we have..."

The Body. The body of the letter will develop your main points and move the reader toward the closing. The greatest consideration you can show your readers is to say only what is important. Separate what they *need* to know from what is merely *nice* to know.

Poor: Our file cabinets come in four colours: blue, red, black, and beige. Beige is the most popular colour among our customers, accounting for 45 percent of the file cabinets ordered.

Better: Our file cabinets come in red, blue, black, and beige. The colours are baked-on enamel, scratch-resistant, and easy to clean.

Your readers don't need to know that beige is the most popular choice; they do need to know the colours are durable.

Keep your paragraphs brief and to the point. Brevity is the result of using simple language and discussing only a few points at a time.

The Closing. In the closing paragraph you are bringing your letter to a courteous, businesslike conclusion and indicating what action you would like the reader to take. The specific action will vary according to the purpose of your letter. Here are a few guidelines for writing your closing paragraph:

1. Use positive words — when not if.

Poor: If you would like more information...

Better: I would be happy to provide more information...

Poor: I will call you next week to see if we can get together.

Better: I will call you next week to see when we can arrange a meeting.

2. Indicate what specific action you would like the reader to take. The amount of pressure you apply will depend on the nature of your letter. In the examples below, the closings range from a simple expression of goodwill to a high-pressure call for immediate action.

Examples: Please let us know when we can be of further assistance.

May we have our field representative Karla Petsky call on you next week?

Fill out and mail the enclosed postcard. We will send you our free 20-page booklet on tax tips that could save you hundreds of dollars.

Our sales offer ends in ten days. Send in your order today to secure this exceptionally low price. Hurry! Supplies are limited.

Your neglecting to send us a payment by August 25 will force us to turn your account over to a collection agency. Please send your cheque or money order in the enclosed envelope. Do not let such a small amount jeopardize your credit rating.

3. Avoid closing paragraphs that diminish the effect of your letter. A weak ending can ruin an otherwise well-written message. Your closing paragraph should not apologize, begin with a participle, add trivial after-thoughts, or use clichés.

Your final paragraph should leave the reader with a clear understanding of what you want done or what you have to offer.

Step Three: Revising

In revision you switch roles from writer to reader. Review what you have written as if you had never seen it before. If possible, let the first draft cool off for a while. Put it away overnight so that you can read it with a fresh eye in the morning. Use the following check list in revising your letters.

1. What is the purpose of this letter? Have I made it clear?

2. Are the points developed logically and completely?
3. Have I used clear, simple language? Have I avoided clichés, jargon, overly complex technical terms, and abstract or vague nouns?
4. Have I used the active rather than the passive voice?
5. Are modifiers close to the words they modify?
6. Have I expressed myself in the fewest possible words?
7. Are the sentences an average of fifteen to twenty words long.
8. Are paragraphs no more than eight to ten lines long?
9. Do sentences and paragraphs flow smoothly from one to the next?
10. Do my nouns and verbs agree in number?

Pay particular attention to opening and closing paragraphs. As you review, ask yourself the following questions:

1. Is my message tailored to the reader's interests and motivations?
2. Does my message begin with information important to the reader or in answer to the reader's request?
3. Did I adopt the correct tone?
4. Does the closing paragraph state specifically what action I want the reader to take?
5. Do I make it easy for the reader to act?
6. Have I given the reader one action to take rather than several?

Revision is essential to good writing. As you revise, remember three key terms — *clarity, brevity, simplicity.*

Proofreading

Once you have revised your letter, proofread it carefully. Whether you sign the letter or have someone else sign it for you, you are responsible for the accuracy of its content. Check for spelling and grammatical errors, inversion of numbers, mistakes in format, and errors in paragraphing.

The proofreading marks listed below will help the word processing operator to correct the letter. Learn to use these symbols, which keyboard operators and printers universally accept.

Delete	Insert comma
Close up space	Insert apostrophe
Delete and close up	Insert quotation marks

Leave space #

Begin new paragraph ¶

Run paragraphs together no ¶

Transpose ⌒⌣

Spell out ○

Let it stand ..... stet

Lowercase letter / lc

Insert period ⊙

Insert question mark ?

Insert semicolon

Insert colon

Insert hyphen =

Insert dash $\frac{1}{M}$ or $\frac{1}{N}$

Insert parentheses ( )

Sample Letter Based on Outline on Page 44

I am happy to suggest the following approach as one you may wish to implement in converting your office to a computerized system.

It would be most useful to begin by undertaking a survey of your office staff to determine their attitudes towards computers, their skills level and experience, and their abilities to learn new equipment and procedures. Simultaneous with conducting this survey, you will want to analyze individual job responsibilities and make a detailed study of current work methods. We would be pleased to undertake both of these tasks for you, if you wish. We would conduct a one week on-site observation with our personnel.

After you have collected this data, you will want to research the best computer system for your office. You should consider your software needs as well as determine the most appropriate hardware. Such factors as plant outlets, power lines, electrical capacity, lighting and ventilation will affect your final decision.

Once you have gathered this information, you can proceed to a cost analysis. You will want to analyze the costs of the hardware/software and determine the cost of maintenance and supplies. In addition, you must estimate the costs of insurance, service, and training your staff on the new system.

The actual changeover requires that you establish an installation and training schedule. You will want to determine the actual set-up and installation time required and establish an appropriate training schedule for your staff. It would be wise to estimate the time required for the actual conversion and to set dates for its completion.

As you begin your surveys and research, you will want to start developing data entry forms for the computer system. It would be useful for you to see forms which other businesses such as yours are using and I'm sure the computer supplier can give you some help in this regard. You will have to devise new forms for each job within your company as well as develop forms for general office procedures.

The last step in the move to computerize your office occurs after the new system is in place. You will want to make a plan for monitoring and following-up on the effectiveness of the system. You will have to debug the software and hardware and monitor time and cost schedules. It will also be important to evaluate worker progress and attitudes.

I hope these suggestions have been helpful to you. I am sure that you will be more than satisfied with your decision to computerize once the system is in place and your staff familiar with it. As I have indicated to you in our earlier meetings, the benefits of such a system are numerous and lead to a more efficient office and happier staff. If you have any further questions or would like to involve our staff in your changeover, please feel free to contact me.

ACTIVITIES

1. Based on the checklists given on pages 47 and 48 of this chapter, revise the following letters.

(a) Dear Ms. Dupuis:

We have completed our preliminary study for Carroll & Associates, Inc. and have submitted our initial report under separate cover.

As I mentioned in our phone conversation of October 5, your distribution department is the primary cause of your firm's decline in sales volume. Serious thought must be given to replacing the head of this department.

If you would like to discuss this matter further, please call me at your earliest convenience.

Sincerely yours,

Frank G. Towers
Associate

(b) Dear Ms. Quinn:

We are about to sign a contract to develop Confederation Plaza, and we would like to know if you are still interested in managing the TGIF Lounge in the Algonquin Building. You mentioned that your firm would consider renovating the lounge if we secured the lease.

I am enclosing a copy of the lease agreement. I will call you next week to arrange a time for us to discuss the TGIF Lounge and Conferderation Plaza.

Yours truly,

Marilynn C. Brighton
Realty Agent

(c) Dear Mr. Janda:

This the third and last time we are going to warn you about your overdue car payment. You now owe us $232.50 and if we don't get it within 7 days, we will be sending the sheriff over to repossess your vehicle. At that point, we will commence legal action with no further notice to you.

You must live with your head in the sand if you think you can do business like this and never get caught.

Yours truly,

Eliza Swartz
Finance Manager

CHAPTER

5 BUSINESS LETTER FORMATS

In this chapter we take a look at the different parts of a letter and various formats used to create professional, attractive communications. Whether you keyboard the letter yourself or have someone else prepare it, you should be familiar with the mechanics of producing a business letter. When you sign any letter, you are advising your reader that you assume responsibility, not only for what the letter says, but also for how it looks.

Parts of a Business Letter

Most business letters, regardless of their purpose, have the following basic parts:

Figure 5.1 Parts of a Business Letter

	Standard	**Optional**
1 Heading	A Letterhead/Return address C Date line	B Reference notations D Mailing notations E Special notations
2 Opening	F Inside address H Salutation	G Attention line
3 Body	J Contents	I Subject line
4 Closing	K Complimentary closing M Identification line N Reference initials	L Company name O Enclosure notation P Copy notation Q Postscript

See the following page for an illustration of the above parts of a business letter.

Figure 5.2 Sample Business Letter showing Standard and Optional parts

1. HEADING

REGINA OFFICE EQUIPMENT LTD. A

1904 HAMILTON STREET
REGINA, SASKATCHEWAN
S4P 3N5
TELEPHONE: (306) 548-8723
FAX: (306) 548-8724

B Reply to the Attention of: A.Macht
File No: 8,432/1

C October 15, 19--

D PRIORITY POST

E

2. OPENING

F Sedgwick & DeWitt Ltd.
400 - 1975 Scarth Street
Regina, Saskatchewan
S4P 2H3

G Attention: Ms. S. Marcus

H Gentlemen

3. BODY

I Re: Acoustical covers

J In your October 10 letter, you mentioned that your company was purchasing an office system with a mainframe computer and several terminals and printers. You asked for a quotation on our acoustical covers for microprinters.

I am happy to report we can offer you a substantial discount on a lot order of 20 - 25 acoustical covers. These covers will fit any microprinter and you may adapt them to fit printer options such as single-sheet feeders and track feeders. They will reduce printer noise levels by 80 percent. Studies have shown that lower levels of noise in the office increase productivity and worker efficiency.

The discount offer will expire November 30. You can take advantage of our discount by phoning in your order, using our toll-free number, or completing and mailing the enclosed order form. I would be happy to arrange for shipment directly to your home office or warehouse.

4. CLOSING

K Yours truly,

L REGINA OFFICE EQUIPMENT LTD.

M Angie C. Macht
Sales Manager

N ACM/CT

O Enc.

P Copy to: Joel Dusenberry, Area Sales Representative

Q

The following is an overview of the purpose, placement, and style choices of the basic parts of a business letter.

Heading

A. Letterhead / Return Address

- Most companies have printed letterhead stationery. Use this for all your letters.
- If you do not have company stationery, keyboard the name, address and telephone / fax numbers of the company at the top of the page. There are no hard and fast rules for placement; just make sure the appearance is attractive.
- If your letter is more than one page long, use continuation paper (of the same colour and quality as your letterhead paper) for the second and subsequent pages. The heading contains: the name of your company; the name of the addressee; the page number; and the date.
- Style choices for continuation paper are:

Block style

REGINA OFFICE EQUIPMENT LTD.

Sedgwick & DeWitt Ltd.
Page 2
19— 10 15

Alternate style

REGINA OFFICE EQUIPMENT LTD.

Sedgwick & DeWitt Ltd. 2. 19— 10 15

B. Reference Notations

- Some letterhead stationery is printed with reference notation guide words such as: *Reply to the Attention of; File No.* Use these when applicable to your letter.

C. Date Line

- Place the date line either two lines below the last line of your printed letterhead or approximately 13 lines from the top of the page. Use your judgment.

- Follow your company policy regarding the style of date to be used. Either of these styles is acceptable:

  Numeric: 19— 06 04 (Year, month, day)

  Standard: June 4, 19—

D. Mailing Notations

- The purpose of mailing notations is to ensure that you have a record of how the letter was sent, e.g. PRIORITY POST; SPECIAL DELIVERY; REGISTERED MAIL; BY COURIER .
- Place mailing notations two lines below the date line or at the bottom of the page after the copy notation.
- Keyboard the notations in all capitals.

E. Special Notations

- The purpose of special notations, such as PERSONAL and CONFIDENTIAL is to ensure that only the recipient will open the letter.
- Place the notations two lines below either the date or the mailing notation, if there is one.
- Keyboard the notations in all capitals or with initial capitals and an underscore.

Opening

F. Inside Address

- Place the inside adress at the left margin two or three lines below the date or mailing/special notations.
- The inside address should contain the name, title, company division or department, company name, mailing address and postal code of the addressee.

Mrs. P. McDonald	(Name)
Vice President	(Title)
Marketing Division	(Company division / department)
Johnson Terminals	(Company name)
1435 Main Street	(Mailing address)
Vancouver, B.C.	
V7H 3H9	(Postal code)

- Indent continuation lines by two spaces:

  Mr. F. Senior
  Alliance of Canadian Cinema, Television
    and Radio Artists

- Use the following style choices for titles:

  Mr. C. Timmins, Vice President
  Calgary Imports Ltd.

  Mr. C. Timmins
  Vice President
  Calgary Imports Ltd.

- Always use a social title, e.g. *Mr., Mrs., Ms., Miss, Messrs.* (plural male); *Mesdames* or *Mmes.* (plural female):

  Mr. D. Neumann; Mrs. C. Sebastian; Ms. V. Ebersberg;
  Miss Q. Deneuve; Messrs. Garahy & Goetz; Mmes. LaPlaca & Seeger.

  Note that initials are not used with *Messrs., Mesdames,* and *Mmes.*

- You should find out what form of address a woman prefers. These guidelines may help you:

Marital status unknown	Use *Ms.*
Married woman	Use *Mrs.*, woman's initial, husband's family name (Mrs. S. Nightingale)
Widow or divorcee	(see Married woman above). Check to see if woman has reverted to her maiden name.

- Address couples according to their perference. Here are some examples:

  Mr. D. and Mrs. P. Giallonardo
  Dr. and Mrs. Richard Snow (Husband has a title)
  Dr. Sylvia and Mr. Peter Bartoshewski (Wife has a title)
  Drs. Janet and Marc Grodin; Drs. Marc and Janet Grodin; or
    Drs. Marc Grodin and Janet Grodin (Both have titles)
  Mr. D. Morrissette and Ms. V. Chan

- You may use *Esquire* (abbreviated Esq.) when addressing *male* lawyers or diplomatic consuls. It replaces *Mr.* and is placed after the name: Stanislaw Miloch, Esq.

- Use either a title or a degree, not both: Dr. Robert Block or Robert Block, M.D.
- When you do not know the gender of the person you are addressing, you may use the single letter M: M. Jan Voyce.
- When the abbreviation *Jr.* or *Sr.* follows a name, you have an option to use a comma: George C. Hayes, Jr. or George C. Hayes Jr. Drop both titles when either the father or son dies.
- Place suite, room, or apartment numbers on the same line as the street address. They appear either before or after the street name and are separated with either a hyphen or a comma:

  Suite 204, 8932 Saskatchewan Drive
  Edmonton, Alberta
  T6B 1R4

  8932 Saskatchewan Drive, Suite 204
  Edmonton, Alberta
  T6B 1R4

  204 - 8932 Saskatchewan Drive
  Edmonton, Alberta
  T6B 1R4

- When compass directions precede a numbered street, use cardinal numbers (1, 2 ...). When they follow the street, use ordinal numbers (1st, 2nd ...);

  375 North 78 Street
  622 104th Avenue NW

  Periods in the compass direction are optional, i.e. NW or N.W.

- Place postal stations after post office box numbers:

  P.O. Box 1445
  Station "D"

- For faster delivery, use a post office box number as opposed to a street address.
- When street names consist of numbers, use words for one to ten and numbers for over ten. Insert a hyphen between the building and street numbers:

Sixth Avenue
33rd Street
40 Sixth Avenue
1435 3rd Street

- Separate the town from the province with a comma: Brandon, Manitoba.
- Keyboard province names either in full or use the abbreviated form (see Appendix, Part D, for provincial and state abbreviations):
- Keyboard the postal code as the last line of the address or at least two spaces after the province name.

G. Attention Line

- An attention line guarantees that someone at the address will open your letter even if the addressee is absent.
- Keyboard the attention line two lines below the inside address.
- Use any of the following style choices:

Attention Mrs. R. C. Kozinski
Attention: Ms. R. C. Kozinski
Attention: Ms. R. C. Kozinski
ATTENTION MS. R. C. KOZINSKI
ATTENTION: Ms. R. C. Kozinski
Attention of the Sales Department

H. Salutation

- Place the salutation two lines below the inside address or attention line.
- Follow the salutation with a colon if you are using a two-point or closed punctuation style (see pages 65 and 66).
- Capitalize the first word and all nouns.

Dear Mr. Culver:	(Name known)
Dear Dr. Purdy	(Name known)
Dear Sir:	(Gender known, name unknown)
Dear Madam	(Gender known, name unknown)
Dear Members:	(Group)

Body

I. Subject Line

- The subject line summarizes the topic of your letter in a few words.
- Place the subject line two lines below the salutation, centred or at the left margin, depending upon the style of your letter (see letter styles, pages 64 to 67).
- Use of the guide words *Subject* or *Re* is optional.
- Place file numbers in the subject line, if you wish.
- Keyboard your subject line in either upper or lower case, with or without an underscore.

SUBJECT: PURCHASE OF NEW TELEPHONE SYSTEM

Subject: Purchase of New Telephone System
Purchase of New Telephone System
Re: Purchase of New Telephone System.
Re: Culver v. Warburg — File No. 34,567/8

J. Contents

- Start the body of your letter two lines down from the salutation or subject line.
- Keyboard paragraphs in single spacing with double spacing between paragraphs.
- Follow business letter style formats as far as paragraph indentations are concerned (see letter styles, pages 64 to 67).

Closing

K. Complimentary Closing

- Place the complimentary closing two lines below the body of the letter.
- Capitalize the first word only, e.g. Yours truly; Yours sincerely; Sincerely; Sincerely yours.
- Use the complimentary closing preferred by your company.

L. Company Name

- Place the company name in full capitals two lines below the complimentary closing.

M. Identification Line

- Place the identification line four to seven lines below the complimentary closing or company name.
- Place the name and / or title of the sender on one or two lines.
- A female sender may wish to include her social title:

  Shari Leung (Miss); (Ms.) Holly Jenks.

N. Reference Initials

- Place reference initials two lines below the identification line.
- If the originator's name is in the identification line, you need not keyboard the originator's initials.
- Show the originator's initials first, then the operator's.
- Select any style choice:

  FJ/RS (Both originator's and operator's initials)
  FJ:RS
  FJ/rs
  FJ:rs
  RS (Operator's initials only)
  rs
  RS 14 (Operator's initials and assigned number)
  FJoel:rs (Originator's initials and name and operator's initials)

- Place word processing reference numbers either after the reference initials or underneath them.

  SGR:RS (Disk 98; Document 3456)
  SGR / RS
  (WP/98/3456)

O. Enclosure Notation

- Use this notation when you are enclosing material with your letter.
- Place the notation one or two lines below the reference initials.
- Select any style choice: Enc., Enclosure, Encl., Enc. 2., Enc. (2), Enc. 19— catalogue.
- If you are attaching materials to your letter, use the attachment notation: Att., Attachment.

P. Copy Notation

- Use this notation to indicate to the reader who is receiving a copy of the letter.
- Place the copy notation one or two lines below the enclosure notation at the left margin.
- Select any style choice:

  Copy to: Mr. M. Regalbuto
  c.c. Mr. M. Regalbuto
  cc Mr. M. Regalbuto
  C.C. Mr. M. Regalbuto
  p.c. Mr. M. Regalbuto
  c. Mr. M. Regalbuto
  (c.c. = carbon copy; c = copy; p.c. = photocopy)

- For multiple copies, list the names in order of seniority or the alphabet.

Copies to:	**Copies to:**
Mr. W. Howse	Mrs. C. Tobin
Ms. S. Lauter	Mr. S. Lauter
Mr. D. Senna	Mr. W. Howse
Mrs. C. Tobin	Mr. D. Senna

- If you do not wish the reader to know who you have sent copies to, place a blind copy notation on the *copies* of your letter: bcc Mrs. E. B. Van Valkenburgh; b.c.c. Mrs. E.B. Van Valkenburgh.

Q. Postscript

- Use a postscript to add emphasis or to include something omitted from your letter.
- Place the postscript two lines below the copy notation.
- Avoid the use of postscripts whenever possible except in sales letters. A postscript may indicate that you have not planned your letter carefully.

Formats for Business Letters

Format styles you will most often use in business letters include *Full Block*, *Block*, *Semi-block*, and *Simplified*. The main differences are the placement of the date, complimentary closing and identification lines, and the use of paragraph indentations. Whichever format you use, you must be consistent and avoid mixing styles. The appearance of your letter on the page will influence your reader's perception of your message.

Punctuation Styles

Just as there are different formats for laying out your business letters, so are there different punctuation styles within them. The three styles are *two point* (also known as mixed or standard); *open*; and *closed.* Closed punctuation is rarely used. You may use any style of punctuation with any style of letter.

Figure 5.3 Full Block Style; Open Punctuation

2775 Matheson Blvd. East
Mississauga, Ontario
L4W 4P7

Telephone
(416) 238-6074
Fax No.
(416) 238-6075

19-- 05 07

PRIORITY POST

Mr. O. J. Hamlin
Rightway Printers, Inc.
437 Inverhouse Drive
Mississauga, Ontario
L5J 4B4

Dear Mr. Hamlin

Re: Office Systems

I received your quote for printing the book Office Systems. I am pleased to tell you we have accepted your bid and will be sending you copyboards by 19-- 05 19.

We would like you to complete the job by 19-- 06 25 as we have very tight deadlines to meet on this project.

We look forward to working with you on this book and others in the future. Your reputation among your clients for fast, reliable service is outstanding.

Sincerely

Bruce C. Kaplan
Production Editor

rs

Full Block Style Features

- All lines start at the left margin
- Paragraphs not indented

Open Punctuation Style Features

- No punctuation at end of lines in the inside address
- No punctuation following salutation and complimentary closing

Figure 5.4 Block Style; Mixed, Two-Point or Standard Punctuation

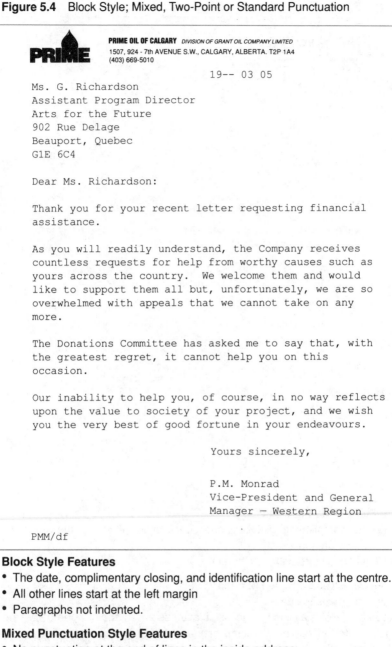

PRIME OIL OF CALGARY *DIVISION OF GRANT OIL COMPANY LIMITED*
1507, 924 - 7th AVENUE S.W., CALGARY, ALBERTA. T2P 1A4
(403) 669-5010

19-- 03 05

Ms. G. Richardson
Assistant Program Director
Arts for the Future
902 Rue Delage
Beauport, Quebec
G1E 6C4

Dear Ms. Richardson:

Thank you for your recent letter requesting financial assistance.

As you will readily understand, the Company receives countless requests for help from worthy causes such as yours across the country. We welcome them and would like to support them all but, unfortunately, we are so overwhelmed with appeals that we cannot take on any more.

The Donations Committee has asked me to say that, with the greatest regret, it cannot help you on this occasion.

Our inability to help you, of course, in no way reflects upon the value to society of your project, and we wish you the very best of good fortune in your endeavours.

Yours sincerely,

P.M. Monrad
Vice-President and General
Manager – Western Region

PMM/df

Block Style Features

- The date, complimentary closing, and identification line start at the centre.
- All other lines start at the left margin
- Paragraphs not indented.

Mixed Punctuation Style Features

- No punctuation at the end of lines in the inside address
- A colon follows the salutation
- A comma follows the complimentary closing

Figure 5.5 Semi-Block Style; Closed Punctuation

THE HERALD

A POPHAM NEWSPAPER
Box 913
Dartmouth, Nova Scotia. B2Y 1C5
Telephone (902) 429-5100

November 27, 19--.

Mr. S. Stevenson, Producer,
Hurricane Films Ltd.,
202 - 111 Ilsley Avenue,
Dartmouth, NS
B3B 1S8

Dear Mr. Stevenson:

The Herald recently received your letter and forwarded it on to me for a reply to your request.

Unfortunately, although we receive many requests such as yours, we cannot publish them because of the volume.

I suggest that you contact the local Hall of Aviation located on the mezzanine level in the Halifax Convention Centre. They may be able to help you.

Sincerely,

(Ms.) S. A. Saito,
Director of Promotions.

SAS/nl

Semi-Block Style Features

- The date, complimentary closing, and identification line start at the centre
- Paragraphs are indented.
- All other lines start at the left margin.

Closed Punctuation Style Features

- A period follows the date
- A comma follows all lines in the inside address except the last one *before* the postal code, as well as the complimentary closing, the company name, and the identification line.
- A colon follows the salutation
- A period follows the last word of the identification line.

Figure 5.6 Simplified Style; Open Punctuation

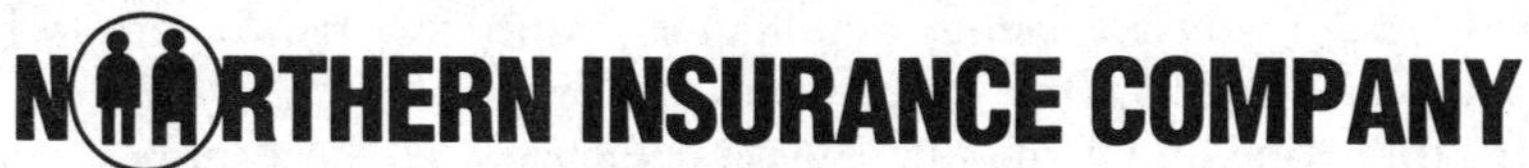

205 PRECAMBRIAN BUILDING, BOX 2641, YELLOWKNIFE, NORTHWEST TERRITORIES. X1A 2P9
(403) 873-4915

19-- 01 05

Mr. R. R. Barrigar
Barrigar & Associates
308 Main Street
Whitehorse, Yukon
Y1A 2B5

PROTECT YOUR COMPUTER INVESTMENT!

Buying a computer such as yours represents a sizable investment--$10 000 to $20 000. Yet you can lose that investment through fire, theft, or natural disaster.

For only $17 per month, you can purchase our complete COMPUTER PROTECTION PLAN. Our coverage will give you 100% reimbursement on the list price of your computer in the event of damage or theft.

To find out more about our PLAN, fill out the enclosed card and mail it today.

HELGA R. ALCHIN - CONSUMER PRODUCTS DIVISION

Simplified Style Features

- No salutation or complimentary closing.
- Subject line essential and in full capitals.
- Subject line three lines below inside address and three lines above the body.
- All lines start at the left margin.
- Identification line in full capitals, preferably on one line.

Addressing Envelopes

Do not jeopardize your message by careless mistakes in addressing envelopes. If you are using a computer, reduce the risk of errors by copying the inside address on to your envelope.

By following a few guidelines, you can ensure the best service from the post office and guarantee that your letter will reach the right person on time.

Figure 5.7 Sample Envelope

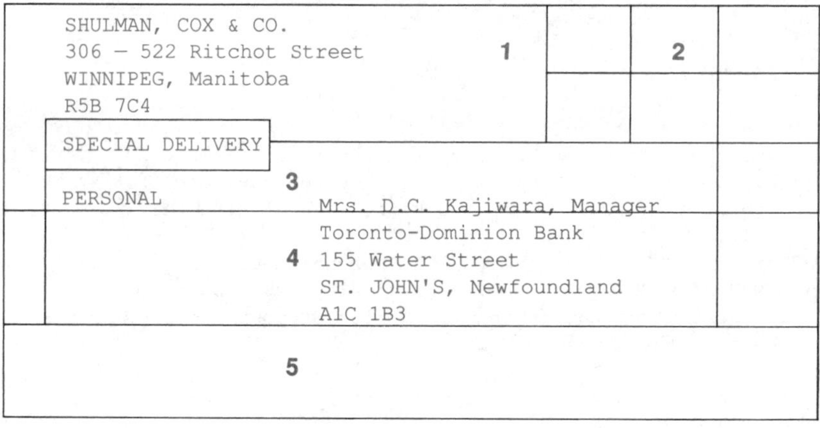

1 Return Address: This space is reserved for your return address and postal code. Place mailing and special notations about 7 mm below the return address and within section 1 and 3.

2 Postage stamps or meter impression

3 & 4 The Address: Place the address anywhere in sections 3 & 4. Place attention lines in sections 3 or 4, either under the special notations or as the first or second line of the address. You must place the postal code Section 4, on the last line of the address. If this is not possible, because of addressing limitations, place the code on the same line as the city and province, at least two spaces after the province. For overseas mail, place the country name in full capitals on the last line of the address.

5 For post office use: Do not write in this space.

Note: See Appendix, Part D, for provincial and state abbreviations.

Some operators keyboard addresses using initial capitals and punctuation while others type them in all capitals with no punctuation. Whichever style you use, be consistent. Do not mix the two. Avoid italic, script, or other unusual type faces that make if difficult to distinguish numbers or letters.

```
Mr. Jacob W. Andrews
Vice President
Telecommunications WorldWide, Inc.
13204-118 Avenue
EDMONTON, AB
T5L 4N4
```

OR

```
MR JACOB W ANDREWS
VICE PRESIDENT
TELECOMMUNICATIONS WORLDWIDE INC
13204 - 118 Avenue
EDMONTON AB
T5L 4N4
```

ACTIVITIES

1. The following letter contains numerous errors in format, style and punctuation. With reference to the information in Chapter 5, correct and re-write the letter.

Brown's Building Supply and Plumbing
2321 Linden Ave, Prince Albert, Sask.
Area 386-427-7978   S6V 6Z4
22/6/-

George C. Chapman, Inc.,
26 10 street n.v.
Calgary, Alta. T6W1X4

Dear Sir;

As per your request which you have stated in your letter of July 27, we are sorry but we cannot fill your entire order. We also cannot charge the bill for the items we do ship because your company doesn't have a Charge account. But we can send it COD if that's o.k.

Next time if you gave us a bit more warning we could probably fill your hole order at once. We surely do appreciate your business.

Yours Truly

Brian C. Boyce.

BCB:KYD

2. Check the following full block style letter for these component parts:

Date line
Mailing notation
Inside address
Salutation
Subject line
Body
Complimentary closing
Identification line
Reference Initials
Copy Notation

Correct all errors in letter style, spelling and punctuation. Prepare a final corrected version of the letter.

March 4, 19–

PRIORITY POST

Ms. Georgia Patterson
Vice President
The Royal Bank of Canadian
Place Ville Marie
Box 6001
Montreal, Quebec H3C 3A9

Dear Ms. Patterson:

Subject: Report on Montreal Customers

Enclosed is the report on customer demographics in the greater Montreall area completed for your Marketing Department. We concentrated on the 24 to 45 age bracket as requested in your Janary 6 letter.

Our study revealed a growing affluent customer base in the 24 to 45 age group. This group should respond particularly well to your investment and savings instruments, mortage financing, and consumer loan programs. According to our findings, your institution is moving into the consumer financial market at the right time.

If you have any questions regarding our findings, please call me at the office or my home. It has been a pleasure to assist your institution in its continued growth.

Yours truly,

MACOMB MARKETING
CONSULTANTS, INC.

Lucille (Mrs.) Tuskey
Senior Marketing
Consultant

LT/eb
Enclosure

CHAPTER

6 SAMPLE BUSINESS LETTERS

During your business career, you will write various types of letters to respond to customers' complaints, answer requests, sell products or services, grant or refuse credit. This chapter provides not only sample letters but brief, practical tips on how to compose letters to get results. You will find the samples in full block, block, semi-block, or simplified format, with various reference lines. There are models included for each of the following types of letters:

1. Acknowledgement
2. Adjustment (responding to a claim)
3. Claim (making a claim)
4. Collection
5. Credit
6. Goodwill or public relations
7. To government officials, agencies, the press
8. Inquiry (asking for information)
9. Refusal
10. Request (replying to a request)
11. Sales
12. Social business
13. Transmittal or cover

Chapter 10, "Types of Business Reports," also discusses letters of transmittal. You may find letters relating to employment — application for a job, recommendation, resignation, and follow-up — in Chapter 17, "Résumés, Applications, and Employment Letters," and Chapter 18, "The Job Interview."

Acknowledgement Letters

You may be required to write a letter of acknowledgement in response to a letter sent to your company. Such an acknowledgement lets the writer of the original letter know that you have received and acted upon the message. You will write acknowledgement letters in response to orders, to requests for information, to messages of congratulation, and to letters where you will have to delay the action requested for one reason or another. You should write an acknowledgement letter in such a way as to promote the goodwill of your company.

The following letter is an acknowledgement of the inquiry letter on page 97.

Acknowledgement Letter

Full Block Style

19-- 11 26

Ms. G. Carlson
1339 - 9th Street N.W.
Calgary, Alberta
T3H 0R4

Dear Ms. Carlson

Thank you for your recent letter to Ms. Kathleen Horowitz, our chief archivist, regarding archival war footage.

Ms. Horowitz is absent from the museum until 19-- 12 08. Upon her return, I will advise her of your inquiry. I am sure she will be in touch with you at that time.

Sincerely

Larry Jackson
Assistant to the Chief Archivist

LJ/CQ

Adjustment Letters

Adjustment letters handle customer complaints and problems while being fair to all parties involved. A reputation for handling customer claims quickly and fairly is a powerful public relations tool for any firm.

Most companies tend toward generous settlements whenever possible, giving the customer every benefit of the doubt. A company must walk the thin line between preserving a client's goodwill and maintaining the firm's integrity. Customers should not feel shortchanged, yet at the same time they should not believe they can take advantage of a company's desire to maintain good customer relations.

In writing adjustment letters you should make the claimant feel that telling you about the problem was the right thing to do. Convey an understanding attitude, even if the customer is initially angry or hostile. By sympathizing with the client's problem, you establish the basis for a just settlement. To accept responsibility for the problem will reinforce your firm's integrity in the customer's eyes.

At times the claim may involve a third party, such as a distributor or carrier. Your company may have a policy that simply replaces the goods or services and obtains an adjustment from the third party. In other cases, when the customer may not know how to get an adjustment from the third party on his or her own, you would act as go-between for the client. You may offer customers legal assistance to make their claim.

The format for an effective adjustment letter generally follows these steps:

1. Assure the customer that telling you about the problem was the right step to take.

2. Explain your policy of handling customer claims.

3. Describe the results of your investigation into the matter as clearly and concisely as possible. You can itemize your findings, particularly if they lead up to a refusal of the customer's claim.

4. State your decision on the basis of your investigation. Avoid giving the decision before you state the facts. The reader may become so irritated by the decision that the rest of the letter is ignored.

5. Close with a positive statement. If you have had to refuse the claim, offer an alternative solution: A new service or product or a substitute may solve the client's problem. If you are granting the adjustment, close with a statement expressing the hope that the customer will continue to enjoy the services and products of your firm.

6. Refrain from judging or accusing the customer. Avoid negative terms that cast the customer in the role of complainer or troublemaker.

Poor: We received your *complaint* about the damaged shelves...

Better: We received your *report* about the damaged shelves...

To grant any reasonable adjustment and maintain good customer relations is your objective in writing such a letter.

Adjustment Letter

Block Style

June 30, 19--

Ms. D. W. Markle
10054 Williams Road
Chilliwack, B.C.
V2P 5H2

Dear Ms. Markle:

We deeply regret that you received the bulbs and flowers you ordered in early March too late for spring planting.

We have enclosed a refund cheque for $43.56, which covers the purchase amount plus your shipping costs for returning the order.

You mentioned that you had to purchase your bulbs and flowers from a retail florist since you did not receive the order you placed with us. We understand that you spent $10 more for the retail order.

Although we cannot reimburse you for the added expense you incurred by purchasing at retail, we are including two complimentary lilac bushes, perfect for fall planting.

Thank you for your patience in this matter. We hope you enjoy the lilac bushes.

Sincerely,

WESTERN GARDENS LTD.

A. Jane Reid
Customer Relations

AJR:iw
Enclosure

Claim Letters

Delayed shipments, damage to goods, misunderstandings, errors in filling orders, and other problems occur even between well-run companies. When these problems arise, you will need to make a claim against another firm. You have two objectives in writing a claim letter: to settle the claim to your satisfaction and to preserve the cordial relations between you and the other firm.

Make your claim accurately and tactfully. Assume in your letter that the other firm will grant your claim and will attempt to make a satisfactory adjustment. Avoid threats, accusations, or veiled hints about what you will do if the other firm does not settle.

If possible, address your claim to a specific person in the company: the head of customer relations or customer service, the salesperson who took your order, the executive who heads the department where you bought the merchandise or service. You may even want to send your complaint directly to the president of the company. This tactic is often an effective strategy, particularly if the company is small. Go directly to the source that can provide the most help. In reporting your claim, give the company accurate and complete information so they can investigate the matter and offer a fair adjustment. Make sure you include the following:

1. **Provide all pertinent dates.** Indicate purchase and shipping dates and a record of any conversation or correspondence with the company about the item or items in dispute. Include copies of proof-of-purchase such as invoices or receipts.

2. **Describe the problem.** State your points one by one, giving all the details such as model number, type of service, and the like.

3. **Explain the implications of the problem for you.** Does it mean a loss of business, interruptions in service or operations, inconvenience, injuries, and so on?

4. **State what adjustment you would like.** Should the company replace the merchandise, perform the service again, refund your money, compensate you for your loss of business? Make your claim realistic in light of your injury and the other company's resources.

5. **State your confidence that the company will respond favourably and fairly to your claim.** Be open to negotiation. The company may not be able to grant everything you request. Decide

which points you are willing to negotiate. Always keep in mind your second objective, that of preserving cordial relations with the other firm. You may need to do business with them again.

Claim Letter

Full Block Style

19-- 01 15

Mr. James Jordan
Envision Design Ltd.
737 Lanark Street
Winnipeg, Manitoba
R3N 2L6

Dear Mr. Jordan

Our company has had an excellent working relationship with Envision Design for a number of years. You have developed many imaginative materials for us of very high quality. After receiving 10 000 copies of our Summer brochure from the printer, however, we discovered several typos and a major content error in the text.

We feel that these errors resulted from a mutual oversight. While we gave final approval to the graphic design and copy that your staff developed, we would consider careful proofreading of the text your responsibility.

The brochure must be corrected and reprinted at an estimated cost of $3 000. We believe that your firm and ours should share the cost of the correction. As a result, we will deduct one half of the printing charges ($1 500) from the invoice you submitted to us.

Should you differ with our solution or have an alternative suggestion, please call me. I will be happy to discuss the matter with you.

We realize that mistakes can happen. This situation will not affect the fine relationship we have enjoyed in the past nor prevent us from using your services in the future.

Sincerely yours

Alice Davis
Creative Director

lw

Collection Letters

Companies often use a series of collection letters that range from polite, friendly reminders for payment to stronger requests, to termination of credit accounts. You want to show your customers every consideration while letting them know that they should also show you the same respect.

The tone of your initial letter should encourage a delinquent customer to say why he or she has delayed payment or to pay even the overdue amount. You should reserve stronger messages for those times when all your friendly letters have failed to produce results. The guiding rule for collection letters is: be *firm but fair*.

1. Polite reminders for overdue payment. Send the first collection letter to a customer after an account is 60 to 90 days overdue. It informs the customer of the overdue amount and suggests that perhaps he or she has already made payment. The letter is polite but seeks to jog the customer's conscience about the unpaid bill. You can remind the person of his or her excellent payment record of the past. Few customers will want to damage your good impression of them.

Use the following pattern for your first polite reminder.

1. Appeal to customers' self-interest. Show how paying the amount due benefits them as well as you.
2. Show customers that you are confident they can and will respect their business obligations. Express your concern for their interests and situation without being overly sympathetic or patronizing.
3. End with an action statement for the reader. A collection letter is selling customers on the idea of paying an overdue amount promptly. Indicate whether you want clients to send in a cheque, notify you when you can expect payment, make a partial payment, or other action.

2. Stronger collection letter. If the first appeal does not work, send a more-pointed, but still friendly, second letter. You are pressing the customer to take immediate action. Statements like, "We urge you to take care of this matter promptly" or "Please do not jeopardize your fine credit standing with our company" can help motivate readers to respond.

Often, second collection letters ask customers to explain why they have not made payment or to suggest their own plan for paying the amount due. The tone of the letter is still polite, with the expectation that customers can and will pay. You have left the initiative up to them.

3. Final collection letter. For the final letter in the series, you assume a tougher tone. Your letter is courteous but more blunt and warns of actions that you will take if payment is not made. You want to leave no doubt in the reader's mind that you intend to collect the amount due. This letter is a no-nonsense approach that states clearly what steps the reader needs to take to prevent your further action.

If the customer still refuses to pay or even to notify you that your previous letters have been received, you can choose between two alternatives. You can send another tough letter, giving the reader the benefit of the doubt that the first letter did not arrive. Second, you can simply send a final notice stating what action you plan to take.

If you decide to send another tough letter, you should:

1. Review past attempts to collect the amount.
2. Hold the customer responsible for damaging a good credit standing.
3. Give the customer a final opportunity to pay and to prevent an unfavourable credit record.
4. Restate the consequences of failure to pay the amount owed or at least to respond to your letter.

If you choose to send a notice stating what action you will take, explain precisely what you have decided to do. The actions open to you may include turning the account over to a collection agency or terminating the customer's credit. Your letter should express regret at the necessity for this action but emphasize that the reader's lack of response has given you no choice.

Throughout the collection process, avoid scolding customers or judging them. You may try creative or off-beat approaches in the earlier letters to catch the customers' attention. If these approaches do not work, you can return to a more business-like tone.

Your letters should be courteous but firm at all times. If you must sever relations with a customer, express your regret at the loss.

Always try to preserve your customer/client relationship and recover the amount due. Well-written collection letters that treat customers sensitively yet state your own position with firmness can help prevent the loss of both customers and revenue.

Collection Letters — First Letter

Semi-Block Style

August 1, 19--

Mr. M. S. Jensen
Box 275
Charlottetown, P.E.I.
C1A 7L1

Dear Mr. Jensen:

Probably it's just an oversight on your part...but our records show that you have an overdue balance of $114.50.

We realize this is a small amount and could easily have escaped your notice. In case you have misplaced your bill, we have included a copy of the invoice.

Please remit the amount due in the enclosed return envelope. We look forward to your continued business.

Sincerely,

GOLDEN-C JEWELLERS

Len Stroder
Accounting Department

LS:pm
Enc.

Collection Letters — Second, Tougher Letter

Semi-Block Style

September 15, 19--

Mr. M. S. Jensen
Box 275
Charlottetown, P.E.I.
C1A 7L1

Dear Mr. Jensen:

We have appreciated your business in the past and would like to keep you as a customer; however, the current balance of your account, $114.50, is now 120 days overdue.

We have sent two reminders requesting payment or an explanation for the delay in clearing your account. So far, we have had no response from you regarding the overdue balance.

Please do not jeopardize your fine credit record over so small an amount. Send a cheque or money order for $114.50 in the enclosed return envelope or notify us when we may expect payment.

We value our customers and make every effort to accommodate their needs. Please take care of this matter so we may restore your credit account to its former excellent standing.

Sincerely yours,

GOLDEN-C JEWELLERS

Len Stroder
Accounting Department

LS:hs
Enc.

Collection Letters — Final Notice

Semi-Block Style

January 6, 19--

Mr. M. S. Jensen
Box 275
Charlottetown, P.E.I.
C1A 7L1

Dear Mr. Jensen:

We have attempted to contact you repeatedly over the past four months regarding your overdue balance of $114.50. You have not responded to our letters or phone calls.

Your account is now eight months overdue. At this point, we have no choice but to cancel your credit privileges immediately and pursue legal action to collect the $114.50 balance due.

We are reluctant to take this step since it means a black mark on your credit record.

You can still, however, preserve your credit standing by discussing repayment of your account with us. Please contact us immediately.

If we do not hear from you within three (3) days, we will turn your account over to a collection agency.

Sincerely,

GOLDEN-C JEWELLERS

Len Stroder
Accounting Department

LS:pm

Credit Letters

Credit represents a trust extended by a seller to a buyer. The seller has the confidence that the buyer can and will pay what is owed within a reasonable time, usually fixed by agreement. Credit can encourage spending and foster a strong buyer-seller relationship among firms and customers.

Credit letters may grant or refuse credit to individuals and businesses. As a result, it is essential that your letters convey consideration, fairness, and tact. You will need accurate information about your customer's financial circumstances to make your decision. You must request additional information tactfully, without appearing to pry into personal affairs. Refusing a customer credit also demands the utmost tact and diplomacy to retain the person's goodwill.

Granting credit privileges is a fairly straightforward matter of letting the customer know the good news. You can also take the opportunity to restate conditions of credit terms and include a list of benefits, such as bonus buys, coupons, discounts, and special privileges credit customers earn.

Refusing credit is more difficult. Here are a few guidelines to help you write successful refusal letters:

1. Show, in the opening paragraph, that you care about the reader's situation. Put yourself in the reader's shoes.
2. Explain the credit policy and the reasons for the refusal before stating your decision.
3. Offer an alternative solution, if possible, or a time when the customer can apply for credit privileges again.
4. End on a positive note. Suggest that the customer buy on a cash basis until another application for credit can be considered. Offer to discuss the matter further in person or over the phone. Always be able to back your refusal with objective reasons and facts.

Refusal of credit is a sensitive issue and may even lead to customers taking legal action if they feel that any type of discrimination influenced the decision. Make sure you state your case clearly and keep the door open for future applications.

Credit Letters — Acceptance of Credit Application

Block Style

19-- 12 10

Mrs. Mary Koerner
1840 Lorne Street
Prince Albert
Saskatchewan
S6V 6Z2

Dear Mrs. Koerner:

Congratulations! We have approved your application for an Alben's Department Store charge card. You are the proud owner of a credit card that you can use for all your household and clothing needs.

As a special welcome to new cardholders, we invite you to accept our money-saving offer:

> *If you purchase more than $50 in merchandise from any of our stores within 30 days, you can deduct $15 from your February statement.*

To make it easy for you to take advantage of this offer, we've enclosed a list of our many fine stores.

Remember, you can order any of our catalogue items by phone and simply charge the order to your Alben's card. The special offer above includes catalogue purchases.

We are pleased that you selected Alben's as your store and look forward to serving you. Welcome to Alben's credit card family.

Sincerely yours,

Carol Whittaker
Customer Service

CW/pm
Enclosure

Credit Letters — Refusal of Credit Application

Semi-Block Style

19-- 05 15

Mr. Carl Johnson
712 Main Street
Andover, NB
E0J 1V0

Dear Mr. Johnson:

Thank you for applying for our Canor Oil Company credit card. Our Credit Department has carefully reviewed your application.

Based on the financial information you have provided, your expenses/income ratio is slightly below the level we have established for our credit accounts. As a result, we cannot at this time approve your application.

If, however, you have additional information that would improve this ratio--other assets, savings accounts, extra earnings--we would be happy to review your application again. We are including an Additional Financial Information form for your convenience. Please complete the form and return it to my attention.

Thank you again for your interest in our Canor credit card. We hope we can approve your application, and we look forward to serving you.

Sincerely,

CANOR OIL COMPANY, INC.

Debra Santini
Credit Advisor

DS/ts
Enclosure

Goodwill or Public Relations Letters

Goodwill or public relations letters are often an important part of a company's and an individual's correspondence. While you will not use these letters to transact business or to communicate strictly business matters, they do help build the personal and community relations that make good business possible.

You may have many occasions in your business career to write goodwill or public relations letters. You will write them to show appreciation, acknowledge achievement, provide information, propose solutions to community problems, offer support or assistance, and establish committees or philanthropic organizations.

Such communications are part of a firm's outreach and strengthen the company's reputation as a firm that cares about people and the community in which it does business. Today, more companies are realizing the importance of building good public relations with the many people they serve.

A simple, effective plan for writing goodwill letters follows these three steps:

1. State the purpose of the letter clearly and briefly in the opening paragraph. Perhaps you want to congratulate the local Little League team on winning a provincial championship.

2. Provide specific details in the body of the letter and stress their significance and benefits to the reader; for example, if you are welcoming a new employee into the firm, you might list the advantages of working for your company.

3. Close by stressing your confidence, appreciation, or concern on behalf of the reader. You may be congratulating a colleague on a promotion and stating your confidence in his or her ability to perform the new job.

Focus on the *you* approach and make the reader the central consideration of the letter. Your goodwill letters will be most effective if you appeal to the reader's loyalty, honesty, persistence, excellence, or other positive characteristics when phrasing your message. Study the sample letter to see how the writer accomplished the letter's purpose.

Goodwill Letter

Semi-Block Style

July 10, 19--

Mr. Len Ashton
6530 rue Boyer
Montreal, Quebec
H2S 2J4

Dear Mr. Ashton:

Just a personal note to thank you for your participation in our recent Dental Health Institute Conference at the Place Royale.

Your seminar on report writing interested all of us in a particular way. Each of us has many such reports to write in the course of a year and your information on organizing and designing reports was useful.

It was a successful meeting, and your presentation was a very valuable contribution. I do appreciate it and want you to feel the satisfaction that the dental staff has conveyed to me.

Yours sincerely,

A. S. Gray, D.D.S.,D.D.P.H.,
M.Sc., F.R.C.D.(C)
Acting Director
Division of Dental Health
Services

ASG/bk

Letters to Government Officials, Agencies, and the Press

You may have to write to a government official, an agency, or the editor of a newspaper or journal to express an opinion or ask for help. You may be doing research on a particular issue, preparing a proposal, responding to an editorial, or asking for more details regarding a story or report you have seen.

Many companies wish to make their positions on issues known and will ask representative members of their management staff to write a statement. The relationship of business, government, and the media to one another is traditionally dynamic with the individuals alternately confronting and cooperating with one another.

Government officials are often sensitive to the opinions and positions of their constituents, particularly when important policies or legislation are being developed. Likewise, newspaper and magazine editors and radio and television managers need to know their readers' or viewers' reactions to articles or programs. If readers and viewers express those views in a clear, courteous, and persuasive manner, they are likely to impress editors and managers.

Whether your message is a request, protest, or word of support, you must clearly state it. Your opinions or requests will be more effective if you plan your message to make your points carefully and convincingly. If you are writing on behalf of your company, you will want to make doubly certain that you have represented your firm's point of view accurately.

Keep the following guidelines in mind as you write your next letter to a government official, editor, or station manager:

1. State the subject of your message and your reason for writing in the first paragraph.

2. Explain your interest in the matter and support your position with facts, statements from well-known spokespersons, or other pertinent information to show your concern.

3. Suggest ways to improve the situation or solve the problem. You may offer a plan of your own or support the plan of someone else. The important consideration is to be helpful. You are not simply raising an issue but offering some action step that officials can take. You can shoulder your share of the responsibility while holding government officials or the media accountable to the public.

4. Urge immediate action on your proposals or the proposals of others and indicate your willingness to help in whatever way you can.

By organizing your letter according to this plan, you will give readers the information they need to consider your message seriously. The attention your letter receives depends largely on how effectively you present your argument or appeal.

Letter to Government Agency

Simplified Style

19-- 04 10

Miss M. Renner
District Taxation Office
Revenue Canada
165 Duckworth Street
St. John's, Newfoundland
A1C 5X6

FILE 33 45 6778--McDONALD'S FISHERIES LTD.

I enclose copies of four cancelled cheques for our tax payments in 19--. In addition, I have attached photocopies of my previous correspondence with you.

We ask that you review the attached documents and verify that you have properly credited each of the tax payments to McDonald's Fisheries Ltd. We also ask that you advise us of our current tax status to date.

Should you require any further documentation or have any questions regarding the attached information, please call me. We would like to be sure that our tax records are in order as we enter the 19-- tax year.

MICHAEL CRAIN - ACCOUNTANT

sb

Letter to the Editor

Full Block Style

19-- 11 06

Editor
The Gleaner
Box 3370
Fredericton, NB
E3B 5A2

To the Editor:

Your recent feature story on the role of business in easing youth unemployment ("Business Gives Youths a Break," October 16) failed to mention the fine work of Ahlstrom Brothers.

This company, a small dry-cleaning establishment, actually introduced the innovative youth jobs program now so proudly publicized by the city. Interestingly enough, the city has neglected to include one important part of the Ahlstrom Brothers' program--day care for the children of teenage mothers.

Without day care, teenage girls with children cannot participate in the jobs program. Yet statistics released by the mayor's office in September 19-- showed that 72% of unemployed youth are young girls with preschool children.

The day care model proposed by Ahlstrom Brothers is simple. Retired people with nursery, elementary teaching, or related experience work at minimum wage to care for the children, often in a rented space or at one of the worker's homes.

Ahlstrom Brothers discovered that finding paid or volunteer workers was no problem. When they advertised for three day care workers, they received over 250 calls in one day from people eager to apply for the jobs.

The city could easily put this model to work, setting aside low-rental space or providing a small subsidy to help pay day care workers. It could also encourage other businesses to adopt the Ahlstrom Brothers' model.

Now that would be a feature story worth syndicating.

Sincerely,

Bernard Sterling
President
Fredericton Chamber of Commerce

Request Letter

You will write request letters for many purposes. You may be conducting research and need help locating sources or finding experts whom you can interview. You may need to know if a product is appropriate for your company's needs or if a price list is up to date. Your inquiry may range from a simple request for a catalogue to more complex matters such as the per capita consumption of sugar in Canada over the last ten years.

The principal weakness of many request letters is a lack of clarity. The writer fails to state the request clearly, fails to let the reader know precisely what information is desired, or fails to direct the request to the proper person. As a result, the writer may receive the wrong information in reply or a letter asking for more details about the request. Do not assume automatically that the recipient of your letter is at fault should this happen to you. You need to do your homework before writing a request letter.

First, make sure you have identified the proper source — is the person you are writing to actually the one who can fulfill your request? Second, include enough detail in your request to obtain the action or information you desire. Don't assume that the reader knows what you want. If you are writing in response to an advertisement or other promotional medium, mention the source or name in the letter. Companies change advertisements and promotions frequently and need to know which one caught your attention.

In some cases you will be writing on your own initiative to ask for help or to request information that may require some of the reader's time and effort. You will get the best response using the following guidelines:

1. State clearly the type of information or help you are seeking. For example, if you need to know the per capita consumption of sugar in Canada from 1980-1990, you should include this exact information in your request; otherwise, you may get yearly consumption rates, not per capita rates.

2. Pare down your questions to those that only the recipient can or must answer. List them in your letter to make them easier to read. Make sure that you phrase your questions clearly and concisely.

3. Explain why you need the information and why your reader should respond. Is the reader an expert in the field? Will the person receive acknowledgement for the work or a copy of the finished material? In this section of the letter, do a little selling to gain the reader's cooperation.

4. Express your appreciation for the reader's consideration of your request. Do not thank the reader in advance for help. The reader may not be able to assist you or may decline to do so. Rather, express your gratitude for the time taken to read and consider your request.
5. Include a self-addressed, stamped envelope where appropriate. Since you asked for the information or help, you should bear the cost of a reply.
6. Indicate your willingness to pay any fees or cover the cost of any materials that the reader may send to fulfill your request.

Request letters should accomplish two objectives: *state clearly what you need and persuade the reader to help you.*

Request Letter

Block Style

19-- 11 19

Ms. K. Horowitz
Chief Archivist
Winston Museum
1900 Heritage Drive S.W.
Calgary, Alberta
T2V 2X3

Dear Ms. Horowitz:

I am currently producing a documentary film on the Edmonton Fuseliers. For one particular sequence, I need archival footage of World War II soldiers training and en route to war.

Is such footage available through the Winston Museum? If so, would you advise me of the details and the costs and copyrights involved.

We will begin post production in the new year. I would appreciate hearing from you at your earliest convenience.

Sincerely,

(Ms.) Gillian Carlson

GC/ma

Refusal Letter

Knowing how to say "no" to a customer, applicant, or associate is an important skill. You must refuse someone yet preserve their goodwill, offer an alternative solution or course of action, and end on a positive note. The reader should know clearly that you cannot grant the request.

The basic principle of writing refusal letters is courtesy first and refusal second. This principle applies to any type of refusal letter, from turning down a customer's request for credit, to refusing an extension on a contract, to declining an offer to head the local charity drive.

The following guidelines should help you write tactful, friendly yet firm letters of refusal:

1. Respond immediately so the reader can seek help elsewhere. This action shows consideration of the reader's problem.
2. Open by assuring the reader you have given the request careful consideration. Do not mention in the first paragraph whether you will refuse or grant the request.
3. Give your reasons for the refusal. List them in a clear, straightforward manner so the reader will be able to understand them quickly. You are setting the stage for your "no" and preparing the reader to accept it. Even if your decision is unpopular, the reader will probably respect your reasons for making it.
4. Suggest an alternative course of action or solution to fulfill the original request; for example, if you must turn down a request for reservations because your hotel has no more vacancies, you can suggest alternative accommodations at other hotels nearby. Your primary message is that you care about the reader's situation and will offer whatever assistance you can.
5. Close with a positive statement. Don't overly apologize for your refusal; state that you hope you will be able to grant other requests in the future. Your closing paragraph can wish the reader success or provide encouragement to try other companies or institutions that may be able to help.

A refusal should not appear as a rejection. Readers should understand clearly that you are unable to grant their request yet at the same time feel that you have considered their needs, respected their feelings, and handled your "no" diplomatically.

Refusal Letter

Full Block Style

19-- 02 02

Mrs. G. P. Guerton
Central Heating & Air Conditioning Ltd.
2745 Sheppard Avenue E.
Willowdale, Ontario
M2J 1W8

Dear Mrs. Guerton

Centennial Plaza Project

Thank you for submitting specifications and a cost estimate for the heating and air conditioning work on the Centennial Plaza project. Your references and list of previous clients are impressive.

We received over fifty bids for the plaza work. We reviewed each bid carefully in light of our budget and the qualifications of each company.

Your firm was among five finalists that we considered. After careful deliberation, however, we selected Energy Systems Ltd. for the plaza project. Their bid was closest to our budget and their experience most in line with the variety of office and business sites we plan to build in the plaza.

We appreciate your interest in our project and the time and effort you took in preparing your bid. We hope you will consider bidding on future projects we supervise. Your firm's qualifications are excellent.

Sincerely

PLAZA DEVELOPMENT CORP.

Estelle Cheung
Project Supervisor

EC/dk

Response Letters

You should answer customers' letters of request in a manner that shows you care about their problems and needs. You have an opportunity to build goodwill by personalizing your replies. This in turn tends to make customers loyal to you as a supplier of goods and services. As a result, your responses to request letters can serve as public relations and sales pieces at the same time.

Use the following structure when answering letters of request. Remember that every contact with customers is an opportunity to strengthen their confidence in your ability to meet their needs.

1. Set a friendly, positive tone in the opening paragraph that tells the customers that you both value and appreciate them. For new customers you might begin by saying, "We are glad that you came to us for help..." You may address the long-time customer with, "It's good to hear from you again..."
2. Let them know how you are handling their request. If you are responding to an order, tell them when and how the order will reach them. "We will be shipping the cartons airmail. You should receive them by July 15..."

   If they requested information, give them all the data they need. "You will find a complete price list enclosed for all our paper products."

   Try to anticipate problems or questions the customer may raise and deal with them in your letter. Put yourself in the reader's position and ask what you would need to know from a company.
3. Show confidence in your product or service and invite further business contacts. Your closing should include a message that says, in effect, "We would like your continued business. How can we be of further service to you?" Your friendly tone will foster goodwill so that the reader remembers not only your product or service but also your attitude toward customers.

Look over the sample letter. Notice how the writer has conveyed the message "the customer is our major concern."

Response Letter

Block Style

June 8, 19--

Mrs. J. Klein
Tri-Products Limited
2829 Arlington Street
Hamilton, Ontario
L0R 1W0

Dear Mrs. Klein:

Thank you for your telephone order of June 6, 19--. As you requested, we have ordered the following items:

*10 packages of white, 3 x 5 pressure-sensitive labels imprinted with your company name and address.

*5 dozen yellow, 4 x 6 memo pads imprinted with your company name only.

We will ship the memo pads to your attention via Central Canadian Parcel Service by June 15, 19--.

Presently we have the pressure-sensitive labels on back-order but we anticipate receiving them by June 29, 19--. We will ship your order by air express at no additional cost. We apologize for the delay.

Thank you for your order. We appreciate your continued business.

Sincerely,

OFFICE SUPPLIES LTD

Mohammed V. Dhari
Order Department

MVD/rw

Sales Letters

The principles of effective sales letters are the same as those for effective personal sales. First, identify the reader's interests, needs, and motivations. Second, know your products and services thoroughly. Third, convince your readers that what you have to offer will satisfy their needs. The more creatively you can match products or services to the particular needs of your readers, the more successful your letters will be.

Two of the most effective formulas for organizing sales letters are **AIDA** and **IDCA**.

A	Attention	**I**	Interest
I	Interest	**D**	Desire
D	Desire	**C**	Conviction
A	Action	**A**	Action

Use either of these formulas when you begin writing your sales letters:

1. Start by capturing the readers' attention or interest. You may ask them a question about saving time, money, or work. You may start with an offer, free product or service, or discount. Your opening statement may be a startling fact about their business or industry, a testimonial from satisfied users, a promise, or a guarantee.
2. Create, in the second paragraph, a desire for your product or service. You can describe the product or service in terms of the readers' motivations for profit, comfort, convenience, leisure, savings, pleasure, or any one of a number of motivations you have identified for your readers. Choose the details carefully to appeal directly to the needs of the reader: do not give an exhaustive list of qualities and characteristics about your product or service. Every sentence should reinforce the reader's need for what you have to sell.
3. Next, support the desirability of your product or service by offering evidence to convince readers of your credibility. You might mention results from independent testing services, statistics from market tests, comments from satisfied customers, and a guarantee, refund or replacement for any defective parts. You want readers to believe your message.
4. Finally, motivate the reader to act. If your letter has done its job well, the reader is already eager to take the next step — order the product or service, give you a call, invite a sales representative to

call, or whatever action you indicate. Avoid giving two or three alternatives; the reader may decide to do nothing. Your action step should be easy — mark an enclosed business reply card, fill out and return an order form, telephone for further information.

Below is a quick checklist to help you write effective sales messages:

1. Attention (or Interest):

- Have you identified the reader's needs and interests?
- What benefits does your product or service offer the reader?
- Can you state the benefit in a question or arresting statement?

2. Interest (or Desire):

- What motivations are you addressing — profit, savings, comfort, convenience, prestige?
- If the reader has a problem you have identified, does your product or service offer a solution?
- Did you point out what emotional satisfaction the reader would gain from your product or service?

3. Desire (or Conviction):

- Have you supported your statement with interesting facts, statistics, tests, testimonials?
- Did you offer any warranty, money-back promise, or evidence of your support for your product or service?

4. Action:

- What specific action do you want the reader to take?
- Did you avoid alternatives or ambiguous choices?
- Have you made it easy for the reader to act?
- Is your desired action the last sentence of your letter?

Sales Letter

Simplified Format

9-- 04 07

Mr. Z. H. Kahn
Mail Room Supervisor
Kurtiss Manufacturing Co.
5258 Duke Street
Halifax, Nova Scotia
B8J 2P3

SEAL-IT...A SUPER-FAST, SUPER-STRONG TAPE!

SEAL-IT tape moves your mail system into the 21st century. Its one-step application lets you seal any size package or envelope quickly and securely.

SEAL-IT:

*Has a self-adhesive backing strong enough to withstand the roughest treatment.

*Meets all postal shipping requirements.

*Comes with a hand-held dispenser to seal boxes and envelopes quickly and securely.

*Guarantees no more shipping losses as a result of broken seals.

Try the sample SEAL-IT enclosed. Test its convenience and strength for yourself. Once you have tried it, we think you will want to order a supply for your mail room.

Simply fill in the enclosed order form or call our Order Department at our toll-free number: 1-800-243-5550.

CELINA EBERHARDT--MARKETING DIRECTOR

P.S. As an added bonus, we will send you a free portable tape dispenser with your first order.

Social Business Letters

Not all business letters deal directly with business. As in the case of goodwill letters, social business letters communicate on a more personal level.

You will use the social letter to write to business associates, colleagues, and friends. You may want to congratulate them on a promotion, console them for a loss, or request a contribution for a charitable cause. These situations call for a letter that is genuine, spontaneous, and warm.

Oddly enough, it is those qualities that often cause people the most trouble in writing social business letters. It is one thing to compose a letter summarizing a meeting or explaining a new product: It is quite another to write a personal letter in which you express your private thoughts and feelings. This is particularly true for most people when they write letters of sympathy to the friends and relatives of someone who has died, yet such instances are as much a part of business life as congratulating someone on their achievements. It is important for you to be able to express yourself in may ways.

The following guidelines are an effective pattern for writing social business letters:

1. Strike a conversational tone. The key to writing social letters is to sound as if you are speaking to the reader in person or over the phone. Engage your emotions as well as your thoughts.
2. Begin your letter with a statement that mentions the occasion that prompted you to write. If you are soliciting funds for charity, describe the reason you need the funds. If the letter is in response to a personal matter involving the reader, add your reactions to the occasion and your personal wishes; for example, if your reader has recently received a promotion, you may want to express your confidence in the person's ability to take on added responsibilites.
3. Close the letter with a statement that reinforces what you have expressed or states what action you would like the reader to take.

By following this pattern, you will write well-organized and sincere messages, even for difficult situations.

Social Business Letter

Semi-Block Style

October 5, 19--.

Ms. Irene Orlando,
Director of Sales,
Blomquist Industries Limited,
10807 Industrial Road,
Edmonton, Alberta.
T6J 4H3

Dear Ms. Orlando:

It was with deep sorrow that we learned of the sudden death of Mr. Sam Schroeder. We thought highly of Sam both as a salesperson and an individual of considerable integrity and charm.

I remember how many times Sam helped speed through rush orders for us or worked to fill an order to our satisfaction. He was a great favourite with the staff, and we looked forward to his visits.

Please accept our deepest sympathies for the loss of a fine man. We will greatly miss him.

Sincerely,

Louise Koenig,
President.

lk
(WP12/1350)

Transmittal or Cover Letters

Transmittal or cover letters perform a vital function in business communication. They accompany an item or document sent to a customer and identify what the writer is sending, the person receiving it, and the reason for delivering the item or document to the recipient.

The letters act as valuable references for sender and receiver, since they document accompanying items and the mailing date. If there is any question about either of these matters at a later time, the transmittal letter provides an accurate record of the transaction. Such documentation is particularly important in relation to legal claims.

Transmittal letters that accompany items such as a cheque, catalogue, brochure, or other material requested by a customer cover the following:

1. Describe the material being sent and number of copies or, in the case of money, the amount.
2. Specify any action the recipient might need to take.
3. Identify the purpose of the enclosed material. If you are sending money, your letter would state the use of the money.

Transmittal letters also accompany reports and proposals sent to a client. They often summarize the main points of the document or, in the case of a report, condense the findings and conclusions contained in the full document. When writing a transmittal letter of this type, keep the following guidelines in mind:

1. Make sure you focus your brief remarks. Do not rephrase the entire proposal or report.
2. Highlight some of the major points that you believe are of particular interest to the reader.
3. Express appreciation for any help the reader's staff may have given you during the proposal or report process.
4. Use the letter to help sell your ideas or recommendations.

You will find further detailed information about this type of transmittal letter in Chapter 10, "Types of Business Reports."

Transmittal or Cover Letter

Block Style

September 25, 19--

Mr. R. Bargowski
750 Lombard Avenue
Brandon, Manitoba
R4H 3J7

Dear Mr. Bargowski:

Thank you for your interest in our custom-made suits and fine evening jackets. The enclosed catalogue describes our tailored clothing line and current prices.

Our customers include some of the most well-known names in the entertainment and business worlds. We are proud to serve such a discriminating and exacting clientele.

We feel sure that we can meet your elegant evening wear needs to your complete satisfaction. When ordering any of our custom-made items, be sure to include all your measurements on the order form.

We look forward to serving you.

Sincerely yours,

Dina Vandenberg
Customer Service Consultant

DV/js
Enclosure

ACTIVITIES

1. Read the following letter. Write a revision based on clarity, brevity and simplicity using the hints offered in the margin.

19-- 02 04

Mr. Colin Graham
Director, Human Resources
Air Canada
Place Air Canada
Montreal, Quebec
H2Z 1X5

Dear Mr. Graham:

opening too wordy – what is the main point?

In this day and age, companies must focus on increasing the productivity of their employees. After all, productivity is the key to any company's survival in today's competitive environment. But to increase worker productivity, you must know what motivates people to work harder and take pride in their work.

body is too long and writer has not focused enough on reader's needs and writer's solution

As Director of Human Resources, you have been given the responsibility of discovering how to motivate workers and reward their efforts. I am sure that you find this a challenging task! In fact, 40 percent of the human resources managers in the country today stated that they felt their jobs were the most difficult and most underrated of any position in the company.

Finding out what motivates people is our specialty. We have developed a range of seminars to help managers like you determine what needs drive employees and how they seek to fulfill them.

language vague and abstract; need more specific facts about program

Our program – What Motivates You? – is a self-learning series that focuses on identifying individual needs and explores how to meet those needs on the job. There are four seminars in number, each one focusing on a different aspect of motivation and satisfaction. At the end, each employee will have a better understanding of his or her needs, and you will have a detailed map of employee motivations and how to satisfy them on the job.

closing is weak — what action does the writer want the reader to take?

Our program is offered at a discount for companies with 200 or more employees. You can earn an additional discount by indicating whether you would like to take a special introductory course for managers only. We would enjoy talking to you about our program — What Motivates You? — in more detail.

Sincerely,

(Ms. M. Shuel)
Program Director
University Learning Resources
McGill University
845 Sherbrooke Street W
Montreal, Quebec H3A 2T5

2. The following letter contains a number of errors which the writer must correct before she can sign and mail it. Referring to the list of proofreading marks on pages 48 and 49, indicate the necessary corrections.

19-- 05 20
Mr. Foster F D'John
Reservations
Ambassador West Hotel
55 W. State Street
Chicago, IL 60614

Dear Mr. D'John:
I would like to reser ve Guild Hall for Friday, November 7, from 7:00 pM to 10:00 PM for our group, the northshore Executive Women's Club. Is the hall available on that date?

You mentioned that catering is provided (on a first-come first serve bases) and that We could

receive a discount if we could guaranteed at least
100 paying guests.

We will have twice that number and would lik e
to order the catering service as part of our our
reservation for that evening.

Please list us on your activities roster as
"Northshore Executive Womens Club. We thank
you – and your staff for the help you have given us.

Sincerely yours,

Karen Christoffersen
Executive Director

3. Based on the principles of good letter writing, write a letter to the editor of your local paper about a social or political issue which concerns you. Perhaps you can judge the success of your letter by whether the paper publishes it.

4. You are employed as the assistant marketing director of a soft-drink beverage company. In the course of a week, you write letters for each of the following scenarios.

(Note: Your company uses the block format with two-point punctuation. You may create your own company name and letterhead.)

(a) You have received a letter from Mrs. D.P. Hoy, President of the local youth soccer association, asking you to supply soft drinks for an upcoming tournament. Because your company has traditionally accommodated such requests, you will respond favourably to this one.

(b) You are advised by one of your staff that some promotional brochures advertising a new product have come back from the printer. They have been badly prepared and your staff member finds the quality unacceptable. You agree. Write a letter of complaint to the printer explaining that you are dissatisfied and want the brochures reprinted at no cost to your company.

(c) A colleague of yours in another company has recently received a promotion to Vice President in charge of Sales and Marketing. Write a letter of congratulations to this individual.

(d) Two months ago, you were the keynote speaker at a convention of marketing directors in Halifax. You were promised an honorarium of $500 plus all your expenses. You submitted the receipts seven weeks ago but as yet have not received either your honorarium or your expense cheque. Write a letter to the President of the organization.

(e) A company similar to yours, operating out of Englewood Cliffs, New Jersey, has recently developed a new marketing strategy for soft drinks aimed at the over 65 age group. Write to the assistant marketing director asking for information about this new campaign.

(f) A letter has reached your desk from an individual in Ottawa who claims to have found a caterpillar in one of your company's soft drinks. The complainant suggests that he has suffered trauma and distress and that considerable compensation is in order. Write a letter handling this complaint.

(g) A old school friend has phoned you and asked you for a job. Although you can't personally help him out, you have offered to write a letter introducing him to an associate in the XYZ Company which has a large sales staff. Write the letter.

(h) You have received a request for your company's annual report from a marketing student at the University of Toronto. Write the letter which would accompany the report.

CHAPTER

7 ORGANIZING AND WRITING MEMOS

In business you will use memos as a form of communication within a company or among various branches or divisions of the same company. Because businesses regard them as internal business letters, they can become a permanent record of transactions within a company. You should, therefore, use the same standards as in preparing and writing external business letters. In this chapter, we will look at the functions and format of memos. The three step approach which you used in writing business letters will help you plan, outline, and write polished memos.

Functions of Memos

Memos provide a summary of important information and suggest action. They also route information, acknowledge receipt of goods or data, and inform recipients about various matters.

Memos can move in all directions in a company — up and down the management ladder or horizontally across department and division lines. You may send them to one person or to hundreds. Occasionally, they may even go outside the company to suppliers, customers, government agencies or officials, or the press. Although memos can be ten pages or more, shorter memos of a page or two are more common.

Keys to writing effective memos include:

- Having good organization
- Getting quickly to the point
- Supplying accurate information
- Indicating specific actions

Whether your memos are short or long, you can use the steps of business writing to prepare, write, and revise them. Most firms have printed forms for writing memos, although the format may vary slightly from company to company.

Step One: Prewriting

As with a letter or report, you must identify your *purpose*, determine your *audience*, and establish the *scope* of your subject. Your approach to memo writing will change slightly, depending on the situation and intended readership. You would use a different tone and include different information in a memo to the president of the company than in one to a line manager.

To determine who should receive a copy of a memorandum, ask yourself whether the person had an involvement in the project or issue and should receive information about the situation. If the answer is yes, then include that person on your distribution list. Copies of memos serve several purposes: they keep lines of communication open among all concerned individuals, they protect you in sensitive or highly political situations within a company, and they can prevent someone else from pirating your ideas.

Gather all references and data you will need before you start writing. Prepare a list of topics as a guide to the research you may need to do. Ask yourself what the reader must know from all the information you have gathered. What do you want the memo to accomplish?

Step Two: Writing

As you write your memo, keep the purpose and the reader's needs in mind. If you are informing employees about a company relocation, try to see the action from their point of view and anticipate their reactions or questions. What effect might the news have on company morale and efficiency?

Organizing

You can organize a memo in several ways.

1. **Chronological.** With this method, you tell the history of the situation beginning with the past and moving up to the present or starting with the current situation and bringing in past events to fill in the early history.

2. **Functional.** In this approach, you discuss the functions of products or people such as marketing researchers and product developers. You focus on the product or person without bringing in historical information.

3. **Cause and effect.** You can start either with the causes of a situation or with the effects, depending on which one you wish to

emphasize. An oil spill, for example, is the effect of an accident or natural catastrophe. You may want to discuss the implications of the effect — ecological or economic damage — or discuss the causes — an off-shore accident, a shipping collision, an earthquake, or a storm. This method focuses on the immediate situation and recommends immediate action.

4. Question and answer. In this approach, you anticipate the reader's questions and answer them or ask those questions that reflect the reader's point of view. You then proceed to answer them in the memo both to inform the readers and to persuade them to take the action you outline. For example, you may use this approach to persuade employees to work an extra shift or accept a change in benefits.

5. Statistical. Memos that report on statistics such as monthly sales figures or production levels use this method. You do not need to persuade or convince readers or bring a crisis or other type of situation to their attention. You are simply reporting information routinely.

You can also organize from highest sales figures to lowest, largest to smallest divisions, and the like. The important point is to arrange the data to meet readers' needs.

6. Problem, analysis, and solution. Here you are using the memo to give a capsule account of a situation, your analysis of it, and your solution. The purpose is to draw attention to an issue that needs a quick action. You are giving the reader important information on which to base a decision or call a meeting. By providing the reader with preliminary analysis and solution, you have saved the reader time and effort.

Organizing Long Memos

Memos longer than two typed pages generally have more formal structure than shorter ones, but the main point is still to apprise the reader of the topic quickly. The reader should not have to work through two pages to find the point of the memo or the essential information. A long memo should have the following sections:

1. Summary. The summary, placed at the beginning of the memo, should condense the subject to five or ten lines. It should not contain jargon or highly technical language but be a clear, simple account of the subject. The summary can help readers decide quickly if they should read the entire memo or only certain sections. Summaries usually contain findings, conclusions, or recommendations.

If you expect a hostile reaction to your memo, you may want to begin your summary with a statement of the problem, a brief analysis, and conclusions or recommendations. In this way, you may neutralize your opposition or at least get a fair hearing.

2. Introduction. The introduction orients the reader by stating the purpose and scope of the memo. You may add a paragraph or two of background material if the reader needs more information.

You may also use the introduction to ask or answer key questions, make a thank-you statement, or give good news such as the approval of a proposal. If you must refuse a request or reject an offer, use the introduction to establish your reasons before saying "no." If you are pointing out a mistake, avoid using statements that blame or judge.

3. Discussion. You may limit the main discussion to a few paragraphs or it may run to several pages of detailed analysis. The subjects may range from policy changes to reorganization of a department to a proposal for diversifying company holdings. Long memos usually discuss topics that will require considerable outlays of resources, time, and personnel. You need to support your arguments carefully and accurately identify and present the facts of a situation.

Your ability to outline and organize material will be crucial to this section of the memo. You can use various headings to separate your information into sections: Statement of the Problem, Approach to the Problem, Analysis, Evaluation, Conclusions, and Recommendations.

4. Closing or Concluding Remarks. The conclusion discusses what action you require of the readers. This section reviews and underscores the main points and problems your readers should keep in mind. The closing is also the place to acknowledge assistance, ask critical questions of the readers, or request a particular action or decision.

5. Attachments. Attachments provide supporting material for the subject of the memo. You may wish to include quotes or tables from attachments in the text. How much material to include will depend on the situation, but it is usually good to limit the amount taken from attachments. Make your text stand on its own with attachments providing support.

Writing the First Draft

Regardless of the organizing approach you use, there are three guidelines for writing the text of the memo. Keep them in mind as you develop your first draft.

1. Tell readers only what they need to know. Memos by nature are concise packets of information. Elaborate details will obscure your point and frustrate the reader.

2. Tell readers what the information means. You are not simply supplying information but interpreting it for the reader. If sales have declined by 20 percent over the past six months, give the reader a brief analysis of what that drop might mean. Is a product line failing? Has a division become a critical drain on operations? Interpreting the information leads to the next step.

3. Tell readers the action to take and when to take it. Should you close down or sell the failing division? When? Discuss ways of achieving the desired action, but keep it brief. Remember, a memo is like a telegram alerting the readers to a situation that demands attention.

The style of a memo emphasizes descriptive words and phrases, active voice, a positive, conversational tone, technical language, and accuracy.

Writing Style

Descriptive Words and Phrases. Ask yourself questions about the subject. What makes it important? What does the reader need to know about it? There is a problem, but what kind of problem? A product is for sale, but what is the height, weight, performance, and feel of that product? Use your words to create a vivid picture of what you are describing and why it is important. In a memo to persuade your office manager to buy new carpeting for the department, include photographs and explain the virtues of carpeting you have in mind. Instead of "The carpeting will last long" say, "The carpet's stain-resistant, nylon-wool blend will give us years of wear."

Active Voice. Use memos to urge readers to take some action. Use of the active voice will underscore the impression that your message is important and needs an immediate response. "A decision must be reached by Tuesday" does not carry the same imperative as "We must decide this matter by Tuesday." The active voice involves the reader directly.

Positive, Conversational tone. The style of most memos should approach that of natural conversation. Write as if the recipient were with you. Avoid stilted or artificial language like the following:

> It has come to my attention that the pronounced lack of worker attention to safety matters is jeopardizing all personnel in the docking and loading area. Effective June 4, instructions on safety gear and procedures will commence. All shifts are required to attend.

The writer meant to say:

> Our accident rate this year is 50 percent higher than it was for the same period last year. It is clear workers are not wearing safety gear nor following safety procedures in the loading and docking areas. Beginning June 4 we will conduct seminars in safety procedures and equipment for all shifts. Supervisors from each shift will see that all employees attend the seminars.

A positive tone in your memo can set the stage for cooperation and establish goodwill between yourself and your readers. If you must disagree with the reader's opinions or policies or criticize the reader's products or services, try to preface your remarks with a favourable comments. Look at these examples:

Poor: The new adhesive you recommended doesn't work. You must not have researched our products at all.

Better: Although the new adhesive works well in most fabrication plants, we have found that it does not hold up under the tests we give our products.

Avoid preparing a memo in anger; it is likely to provoke an angry reply in return. Read over your criticism carefully to make sure you are not letting a sarcastic, complaining, or demanding tone slip into your words. A negative tone would be:

> I realize that productivity matters more than the morale of the workers, so I am complying with the recent order to raise production output by 10 percent.

A more objective and pointed tone might be:

> The recent order to increase productivity by 10 percent does not address one of the major causes of reduced output. Worker morale is unusually low over employment cuts in the company. I propose that

we delay implementing the new level until we have talked with the workers about their job future.

In the second memo, the writer points out a problem and proposes an action step to address it while tactfully criticizing the new production levels.

A positive rather than a negative tone is more helpful to both reader and writer. It suggests the writer has something more to offer the reader than simply a demand or a judgment.

Technical Language. In memos, you will be able to use technical language more than in general business correspondence. One professional often writes memos to another. Instead of saying to a fellow computer analyst, "The new model has an expandable memory that should meet our needs," you would be more likely to say "The new model's 256K memory can be expanded to 640K, more than enough for our spreadsheet program." Since professionals do not write their memos for a general or lay reader, they use technical language to save time, to prevent misunderstandings or delays, and to clarify specific details.

Accuracy. Memos often urge immediate action or decision; as a result, the facts on which they base those actions must be accurate. Double-check facts, figures, events, cause-and-effect relationships, dates, time lines, and other information essential to the decision. Distinguish fact from opinion, particularly when you are interpreting or offering recommendations on the subject of the memo. Check your grammar, punctuation, spelling, and format. Do not send out a memo that has strikeovers, obvious corrections, or erasures that may obscure or distort data. An attractive, clean copy can help ensure that your memo gets a quick reading.

When you have determined what you want to say, begin writing your first draft. Review your memo to make sure that the tone is appropriate, the ideas clear and concise, the style natural and flowing, and the information accurate. Take into consideration the reader's personality and surroundings. How is the reader likely to react when reading the memo? Consider the total context in which he or she will receive the message, particularly if you are criticizing the reader's policies, products, or opinions.

Step Three: Revising

Look over your first draft and revise it for brevity, active language, and clarity. Make sure that you have explained technical or unusual terms adequately and that you have included only the most pertinent, essential information. Ask yourself what you would need to know if you were the reader.

Finally, proofread the memo carefully, paying particular attention to facts, dates, names, figures, and any other quantitative data. This step is your last chance to make any changes or corrections before the memo leaves your office. Double-check the distribution list, if you have one, to make sure you have not left out anyone who needs to see a copy.

CHAPTER 8 MEMO FORMATS AND OTHER MESSAGE FORMS

Memo Formats

Most firms have printed memorandum forms. The formats may vary from company to company; however, the two most common styles are: block and indented.

Figure 8.1 Block Style Memorandum


```
NORTH ATLANTIC AIRFREIGHT CO. LTD.

MEMORANDUM

TO:          All Support Staff Supervisors

FROM:        Parvis Kanani, Controller

DATE:        19-- 12 05

SUBJECT:     YEAR-END BONUS FOR SUPPORT STAFF

I am pleased to announce that we will be distributing a year-end
bonus to all support staff and middle management this year.  We
have increased sales by 25 percent in the past eight months and
are up 36 percent from the same period last year.

We will calculate bonuses according to employees' salary and length
of service as follows:

    Service                      Amount

    10 years or more             3/4 of monthly salary
    5 to 9 years                 2/3 of monthly salary
    Less than 5 years            1/2 of monthly salary

You have contributed to the rise in sales revenue this year.  The
bonus is one way of expressing our appreciation for your outstand-
ing effort.  We will issue your bonus cheques on 19-- 12 23 along
with your regular pay cheque.
RB
RB:ma
```

Figure 8.2 Indented Style Memorandum

MEMORANDUM

TO: See distribution list FROM: JMcA

SUBJECT: SAFETY AND SECURITY OF OFFSHORE OIL-DRILLING PLATFORM #45 DATE: 19-- 10 27

I have completed my investigation of the superstructure of offshore oil-drilling platform #45 as you requested. Several platforms sustained heavy damage in the 19-- 10 25 hurricane. Platform #45 is still operational but we must correct some serious structural problems before another storm hits the area.

The pylons anchoring the platform received severe torque in the hurricane and no longer meet current safety standards. In addition, the drilling shaft has cracks and could shear the cable as a result of undue pressure.

I recommend that we shut down the platform until we can make repairs. To delay them could jeopardize the lives of the 45 permanent crew members and 10 part-time workers on the rig. A major accident could also spill crude oil into the bay and destroy nearly fishing beds and beachfront.

We must make a decision on this matter as soon as possible. I realize the economic consequences of shutting down the platform and disrupting the flow of oil, but the safety considerations should be paramount. The firm cannot afford a major oil spill.

I will remain on site until I hear from you. Please let me know your decision as soon as possible.

J. McKenna
James McKenna

JMcK/sd

Attachments: Form 122A
Form 357A

Distribution: TG, GB, RY, NWP, CHY, VGW, HEE, OID, SA, DL, PR, BFD, MM

Figure 8.3 Variation of Standard Styles

MEMORANDUM

May 14, 19--

To: Joe Myers, Accounting Department Supervisor

From: Joanne Byron, Director of Personnel Services

Copies to: Henri Barbeau, Marina Putsep

Re: Laurie O'Brien's Long Term Disability Coverage

I attach a copy of the insurance company's response to my letter of April 19 (also attached). I agree with their position that the data I seek can only be released with the permission of each physician; thus, we can have Laurie:

1. request and authorize each physician to release data to us and the insurance company, or

2. obtain reports from each physician and forward them herself to us and the insurance company.

The insurance company suggests the latter route and I concur. Once achieved, we could assist Laurie to determine if anything is missing from the file and then approach the insurance company for a review of her application for benefits. I would appreciate your comments.

Joanne Byron

Joanne Byron

JB/dc
Atts.

Figure 8.4 Electronic Mail Memorandum

TO: ID109 (Sarah Werntz, Director of Planning)

FROM: ID202 (Claus Seiffert, Supervisor, Purchasing and Requisitions)

DATE: 19-- 12 02

SUBJECT: November Activities

I am forwarding this summary for your records.

Number of purchase orders issued 573
Number of purchase requisitions issued 518
Number of incomplete requisitions 17
Number of sales interviews 31
Number of meetings attended 5

I have been busy with the northern expansion tenders and the purchasing of the new equipment; as a result, I will need to hire an Assistant III to take over some of the more routine tasks of the department.

December will be a difficult month because of the holidays and the uncertainty of knowing which of our suppliers will be closed over the holidays. Our costs will undoubtedly be higher than we had planned because of the rush to complete the orders for the northern expansion.

Note: The computer will automatically insert the date and the names and titles of the recipients (once you have keyboarded the ID numbers). You need not keyboard a signature line or initials because you will not be physically signing the document. The document will be transmitted electronically to the recipient's computer terminal.

Parts of a Memorandum

1. Heading. The heading of a memorandum consists of the name of your company, division or department and a telephone number (all optional), the title *memorandum*, the guide words, and the guide word details.

The standard guide words are:
TO: FROM: DATE: and SUBJECT: or RE:

Optional guide words are:
COPY TO: and REF:

You may place the guide words in any order.

You may keyboard the readers' and sender's names in several ways:
TO: All Sales Staff (Group memorandum)
TO: See distribution list (Large number of recipients)
TO: Nissan Pushba, Corporate Counsel (Name and title)
FROM: NP (Initials only)
TO: ID107 (Computer identification number)

2. Body. Keyboard the paragraphs in single spacing if the memorandum is long; use double spacing if the memorandum is short or you need to balance the printing on the page.

3. Ending. Most memo writers initial or sign a memo to indicate responsibility for its content. Place your written signature over either the keyboarded initials or signature line which are usually placed four lines under the body of the memorandum.

If you are attaching photographs, charts, calculations, correspondence, or other types of documents to your memo, list them at the bottom.

If you are sending a memo to a large number of people, you may list the distribution at the end of your memo either in alphabetical or rank order.

Other Message Forms

Memos are only one kind of interoffice message used in companies. There are other forms such as snap sets, routing slips, and compliments slips which are adapted from the memo format. Many firms also make use of telegraphic services and with computerized office communications, messages can now be sent by electronic mail.

Snap Sets

These forms are often referred to as *three way memos*. Use them when you wish to write a brief memorandum and eliminate photocopying. The following illustration shows how information is organized so that it may be quickly understood and acted upon. The form has space for a reply to your request. Because the snap set is self-carbonning, no copying is necessary. Both you and the receiver retain a copy of the memo for your records.

Figure 8.5 Snap Set

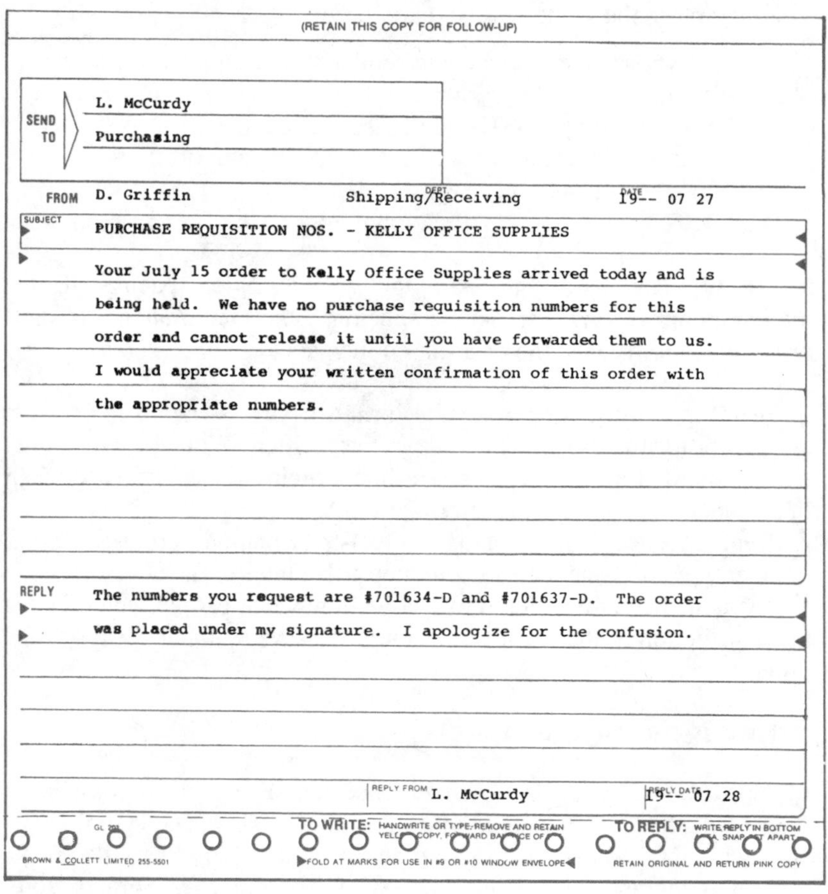

(RETAIN THIS COPY FOR FOLLOW-UP)

SEND TO: L. McCurdy
Purchasing

FROM: D. Griffin   DEPT: Shipping/Receiving   DATE: 19-- 07 27

SUBJECT: PURCHASE REQUISITION NOS. - KELLY OFFICE SUPPLIES

Your July 15 order to Kelly Office Supplies arrived today and is being held. We have no purchase requisition numbers for this order and cannot release it until you have forwarded them to us. I would appreciate your written confirmation of this order with the appropriate numbers.

REPLY: The numbers you request are #701634-D and #701637-D. The order was placed under my signature. I apologize for the confusion.

REPLY FROM: L. McCurdy   REPLY DATE: 19-- 07 28

TO WRITE: HANDWRITE OR TYPE. REMOVE AND RETAIN YELLOW COPY. FORWARD BALANCE OF SET.   TO REPLY: WRITE REPLY IN BOTTOM AREA. SNAP SET APART.

BROWN & COLLETT LIMITED 255-5501   FOLD AT MARKS FOR USE IN #9 OR #10 WINDOW ENVELOPE   RETAIN ORIGINAL AND RETURN PINK COPY

Routing Slips

Use routing slips when you send material to several people within a firm. The slips can be small (3" x 5"). They are attached to the first sheet of the material you are sending — a book, magazine, report, memo, minutes, and the like. The slip lists the sender and those who will receive the material (see Figure 8.6). Each person crosses his or her name off the list and forwards the material to the next person. This method of communication ensures that everyone who needs to read the information will do so.

Figure 8.6 Routing Slip

```
From the desk of Carol Saunders:

        ☐ E. Collins

        ☐ D. Johnson

        ☐ B. Galbraith

        ☐ R. Leung

        ☐ H. Sanderson

Please circulate and return
to C.  Saunders.
```

Figure 8.7 Routing Slip

```
From the desk of Carol
Saunders:

EC   _________  _______
     Signature   Date

DJ   _________  _______
     Signature   Date

BG   _________  _______
     Signature   Date

RL   _________  _______
     Signature   Date

HS   _________  _______
     Signature   Date

Please return to C. Saunders
```

You also use routing slips to send contracts or other documents that need the approval and signature of several people. The routing slip provides a record of all signatures and dates (see Figure 8.7).

Routing slips save companies time and money by eliminating the need to duplicate and send material to all concerned. After circulation of the original material, you can place it on permanent file.

Compliments Slips

Occasionally, you will send material to someone with your compliments. Instead of keyboarding a letter, you can attach a printed compliments slip (see Figure 8.8) to the material indicating that the material is forwarded by you for the interest and use of the receiver. Some companies will ask you to date the compliments slip, list the attachments, and make a copy for the file (see Figure 8.9).

Figure 8.8 Compliments Slip

```
With the compliments of Madison C. Katz
```

Figure 8.9 Compliments Slip

```
With the compliments of Madison C. Katz

                Katz, Arnheim & Co.
                Barristers and Solicitors
                Box 2628
                INUVIK, N.W.T.
                X0E 0T0

                Tel:  (403) 979-3366
                Fax:  (403) 979-3367

19-- 03 02:  Copy of Divorce Order dated 19-- 02 28
```

Telegraphic Messages

Several services for sending messages are available from telephone and telegraph companies. The most well-known is the **telegram**. Telegrams are also the most costly, which is the reason businesses seldom use them.

To send a telegram call CNCP, give the name and address of the recipient and an exact message. CNCP will send the message to the branch office nearest the recipient. Upon receipt of the message, the branch office will then telephone the recipient and, upon request, will mail a copy of the telegram as well. This telegraphic service is available virtually all over the world. The number of words and the location of the recipient determines the cost of the telegram. Because you are charged by the word, it is important that your message be as brief and to the point as possible. In other words, you should use the minimum number of words to produce the required action.

Many offices use **teleprinter equipment** to send messages directly to branch offices or divisions. A company with offices in Halifax, Montreal, Toronto, Winnipeg, Calgary, and Vancouver can install teleprinters in each office to speed up communications among the locations. The most common service is Telex. Offices use the Telex service so often it has given business language a new expression: **to telex** a message.

A telex must give a clear, unambiguous message in the minimum number of words. Because a telex message is charged by time, you may use abbreviations. A typical telex message might look like this:

Figure 8.10 Telex Message

```
THOMPSON     CHRYSLER     DETROIT

DELIVERIES V8 TRANSMISSIONS URGENTLY REQD. PLS

REPLY BY RTN.

CARSON     CHRYSLER     WINDSOR
```

FAX

The FAX machine is a vital means of communication in many businesses. Using this simple facsimile transmission system, you can send graphic and printed material instantly over telephone lines. The recipient will have the material within seconds of your sending it.

Electronic Mail

When it comes to speed, however, electronic mail has no competitors. You can send messages via electronic mail at the speed of light from one computer terminal to another or to several terminals via a telecommunications link. See Figure 8.4 for a sample message.

At that speed, communications are virtually instantaneous. Separated by a few blocks, a few miles, or an entire ocean, terminals can still receive messages immediately. Distance is not a problem. Cable or satellite relays can transmit messages from one coast to the other or from continent to continent.

Telephone lines and special communications hardware link computers in one location to computers in another or several locations. Both sender and receiver must have a telecommunications link in order to transmit and receive information. An operator can create any type of data on the computer screen — graphics, maps, diagrams, charts, figures, text — and send them from one site to another.

ACTIVITIES

1. Write the appropriate memo, to your supervisor, following this telephone conversation:

"Hello, this is Kim Manierka in personnel. Please ask Jennifer Kamel to send over the job description for the programmer I position. If she doesn't get it to me by Thursday, we'll miss the Saturday paper again. I don't know what the big problem is with your department. Anyone else would have had this done yesterday. Oh, and by the way, tell her that those reclassifications she asked for will be processed by the end of next week. I'll need a meeting with her then. Would you let her know? Thanks a lot."

2. Write an electronic mail message in reply to this note sent by Jason Quaid, one of your employees (ID109).

"I know its only March but everyone in this section is asking about summer holidays. All 10 of them want time off in July but obviously that will be impossible. Could you memo me with some direction specifically concerning company policies around seniority and previous procedures for granting holidays?"

3. Write a memo to your supervisor about the following request.

Your sister is getting married in June in Montreal. You are to be an attendant at her wedding but in order to do so, you will need five days away from work. You have had your holidays for the year so you are asking for a leave of absence without pay. Two of your co-workers have agreed to cover your job for you so it will not be necessary for the company to hire a replacement.

4. Write a memo to your office staff outlining routine procedures for answering the telephone. (Refer to Chapter 15, "Using the Telephone.")

5. Write a TELEX message for each of the following situations. (Note: Invent any additional information you may need).

(a) You have written a letter of complaint to a supplier for non-delivery of goods. Your letter has been mailed and the goods just arrived.

(b) You require immediate information on the availability of replacement parts for a video recorder your company needs.

(c) You wish to advise a construction firm of their successful tender for your new office building.

6. You need a list of all the user I.D. numbers on your company computer system. Write an appropriate message to the manager of Computer Services.

7. You wish to advise the president of your company that she has to attend the Eastern Region Business Conference dinner at 19:30 on Wednesday, April 30, at the Holiday Inn, 456 Water Street, Halifax.

8. The company secretary has asked you to draft a circular memorandum to shareholders advising them of the latest rise in share prices: April 10 - $3.10; April 11 - $3.25; April 12 - $3.70; April 13 - $4.64; April 14 - $5.20.

9. You wish to circulate a copy of *Office Automation* to everyone in your office/class. Select and prepare an appropriate form of message.

SECTION

3

SPECIAL WRITING AND RESEARCH PROJECTS

CHAPTER 9

ORGANIZING AND WRITING BUSINESS REPORTS

Functions of Business Reports

Your primary objective in writing any business report is to *inform* your reader. When you first start work, you will probably not be asked to write reports; however, as you progress in your career, your supervisor may ask you to prepare reports on such things as department procedures, future equipment requirements, and workflow statistics. Once you start working in a management position you will be asked to write reports for use by upper management. You may be involved in writing annual reports, monthly sales reports, quality production reports — all of which are routine; however, some of your reports may explore areas of concern to upper management.

Like any other business writing, report writing requires planning. The finished report must show that you have thoroughly investigated your topic and organized and written your material well. When writing routine reports check to see if similar reports are on file and whether you must follow any specific company format and style.

In this chapter we will focus on the report writing process and begin by a return to the three basic steps for effective writing.

Step One: Prewriting

As in the case of letters and memos you begin by establishing the *purpose* of your writing. You must analyze the problem and consider the scope and depth of the report. Your first task is to determine the exact objective of the report. Is it to convey information? Is it to make recommendations and suggestions? Is it to persuade or urge a particular course of action? If you are not sure about the purpose of your topic, ask questions until you can state the objective in a sentence or two.

Your second task will be to determine your intended *audience*. Will the report be written for your supervisor? top management? the government? other firms in the same industry? Will it be available to middle and line management or to workers at the support staff and production levels? The interest of the audience in the report and the background information they have on the subject will certainly influence both the content and language of your report. Once you have determined your audience, ask yourself what they need to know. Interview those who are requesting the report to find out what they would like included and use those answers to guide research. Put yourself as much as possible in the reader's place as you work.

Next you will determine the *scope* of your report. You will need to narrow down the subject to a list of topics you will cover. A useful technique is to draft an informal, preliminary outline noting the main points you wish to cover in your report. You can use the preliminary outline as a guide to your research and to help you crystallize your ideas. Later, you can develop a detailed outline from which you will write the report.

Researching

Your main research sources are libraries, industry and government data, other people, your company, and your own knowledge and experience. For a report on an assigned topic, you would probably institute a literature search of books, articles, and reports written on the subject. Your company librarian or the reference librarian in the business section of a public or private library can help you. You can save considerable time and effort by using computer-assisted research systems. You will receive printouts listing all the works published on your topic, giving you author, title, publication, year, and a synopsis of the work. (See Chapter 11, "Finding Business Information," for a discussion of resources.)

To gain information from other people, such as workers and managers, you will need to conduct interviews and use questionnaires. Questionnaires give you access to a large number of people in a short time, but the information you gather is limited by the number and type of questions you can ask. Devising unbiased, probing questionnaires requires professional skill. Most people are not willing to fill out a lengthy or detailed questionnaire. They may also be concerned that someone will place the results in their personnel records, particularly if their questionnaires are critical of the company.

Personal interviews generally yield more information but will also limit the number of people you can include in your survey. Interviewing is time consuming. You must win the confidence and trust of each person you interview and learn how to probe without offence.

Interviews can be well worth the time spent, however, in terms of the information and knowledge you gain.

You can also investigate industry and government sources for information on your topic. The government offers an astonishing array of free data. Industry associations also do surveys, reports, studies, and seminars on various topics or may publish the proceedings from a conference or convention. Again, the reference librarian can help you locate the specific material you need.

Your own company files and archives are often a fruitful research source; however, don't overlook your own knowledge and experience. Think back over your own career and see if you have resources you may have forgotten or simply put aside.

The important point is to obtain quality information on which to base your conclusions and recommendations. You want to gather the most reliable and up-to-date information possible.

You may need to go back to an information source more than once, particularly if your interviews, for example, yield widely different data. Part of the information-gathering process involves your analyzing and evaluating the data.

Notetaking

Because it is important to keep careful records of all sources used, you will want to develop a system of notetaking. When you begin to write your report, you will rely on your notes; therefore, they must be complete and accurate.

You may want to make use of notecards (either 4" x 6" or 5" x 7") to catalogue quotations, statistics, summaries or other data which will be compiled into your report.

Figure 9.1 Sample Note Card

SECTION IV

"Applications software programs most often used on microcomputers in the business office fall into these categories:

1. Word processing
2. Accounting
3. Spreadsheets
4. Database management
5. Graphics
6. Desktop publishing
7. Telecommunications
8. Programming"

p. 79 INFORMATION PROCESSING CONCEPTS. ELAINE MULLINS & MARG MELANSON. COPP, CLARK, PITMAN LTD., TORONTO, 1988.

Use a separate notecard for each item. It is a good idea to develop a numbering system where numbers on your notecards will correspond to numbers in your rough outline. When you develop your final outline, it will be easy enough to rearrange your notecards correspondingly.

There are two main methods of notetaking: summary and quotations. Although you will likely make use of some quotations, you will make greater use of summarized material. As you take notes, you should get into the habit of writing in your own words. When you are writing directly from the original source, use quotation marks and be sure to note the page number from which you take each quote. (See the Appendix for further information on handling quotations.)

Keep careful records of all sources you use. Document author, title, publication, publisher, date, and page number. Put each reference on a separate index card and keep your cards in a special file. You can save yourself considerable frustration when you are ready to keyboard the bibliography if you have documented all your sources. It can take hours, even days, to track down a missing reference. Make sure that you reference accurately any quotes, opinions, figures, or facts cited. You should know where all background information originated.

To summarize the pre-writing phase:

1. Establish the purpose of your report.
2. Identify the audience and its needs.
3. Determine the scope of your topic.
4. Draft a rough outline.
5. Plan and conduct research.
6. Document all reference material collected.

Step Two: Writing

Now that you have gathered the information you need, your next step is to organize it into logical sequence before you begin writing your rough draft. You can make this a two-step process: develop a plan from your preliminary outline and then write a final, more detailed outline of the report. This process can be especially useful if you have accumulated a large amount of data.

Organizing the Plan

You should consider the following items when organizing your plan.

1. **Subject of the report.** State the subject in one or two sentences;

for example, employee involvement in management decision-making.

2. Purpose of the report. State the purpose in a single sentence. Keep refining the purpose until you can state it clearly and briefly; for example, to establish whether employee involvement in management decision-making is suitable for our company.

3. Special terms. Define any special terms; for example, *quality circles*. Establishing your definitions will give your readers a common basis for understanding.

4. Data. Specify the kinds of information you will be using in the report — interviews, questionnaires, literature from public, industry and government sources, company data, personal experience, and the like. This will give your readers some idea of your methods in researching the subject.

5. Sources. Keep a working bibliography so that you will be able to compile your sources at the end of the report.

6. Rough outline and organizational approach. The preliminary outline from which you conducted your research will be useful in determining your organizational approach (refer to Chapter 7, "Organizing and Writing Memos.")

7. Conclusions and recommendations. Formulate possible outcomes of the report based on your information; for example, improved productivity, decision-making, profits, morale, and labour/management relations.

8. Estimated budget and time line. How much will printing and binding cost? When can you deliver the finished report? Setting budgets and schedules will help you move from one step to the next without getting caught at any one stage.

The rough plan paves the way for the next step in the organization process, preparing the detailed outline.

Outlining the Report

Once you have had a chance to go through your data and organize it, to evaluate what you will include and discard, what the information means, and what conclusions and recommendations you can make, you are ready to prepare the detailed outline that will serve as the basis for writing the report.

The outline should be detailed enough to help you develop each section of the report, yet flexible enough so that you can change it if necessary. The outline is your way of thinking through the structure and content of the report in detail. You can make final adjustments and corrections when you write the first draft. It is important to remember that you are writing the outline as a guide to help you.

Sample Outline

Topic: *Employee Involvement in Management Decision - Making*

I. Summary or synopsis (summarizes major points of the report and conclusions)

   A. Employee involvement can be used in medium-sized companies to improve labour-management relations, develop human resources within a firm, improve productivity and efficiency, develop better decision-making processes, and increase overall company performance.

   B. Employee involvement needs to be introduced carefully. Management and employees must receive adequate training in employee involvement procedures. The success of the method depends on employee commitment and education.

II. Introduction (explains the reason for writing the report)

   A. Purpose of the report: to determine if employee involvement is suitable for our company.

   B. Scope of the topic: definition of employee involvement and its application. Description of what you plan to cover in the report.

   C. Methodology: how you gathered and analyzed the data.

    D. Structure of the report: the organizational approach chosen.

III. Historical review of employee involvement in Canada

    A. Introduction of employee involvement in Canadian firms.

    B. Overall success and failure rate of the method.

    C. Comparison of Canadian and foreign programs, focusing on the U.S., Japan and Europe.

IV. Evaluation of employee involvement in medium-sized firms

    A. Description of firms chosen and explanation of their programs.

    B. Interviews, questionnaires, and data from published literature revealing characteristics of successful and unsuccessful programs.

    C. Summary of findings.

V. Evaluation of our firm and employee involvement

    A. Current structure and organization of firm.

    B. Ways in which employee involvement would impact firm – pros and cons.

VI. Conclusions and recommendations

    A. When instituted and administered properly, employee involvement improves a company's productivity, decision-making process, profits, morale, labour-management relations, and development of human resources.

    B. Recommend that employee involvement be instituted in our company.

    C. List of conditions for instituting and administering program successfully:

```
         commitment from management and labour
         leadership, selection of training and
         education programs, means of administering
         and phasing in new system, follow-up and
         monitoring.

      D. Estimate of time and cost to institute
         program and get it running effectively.

 VII. Bibliography

VIII. Appendices

      A. Charts of four companies showing increase
         in productivity, morale, revenue; decrease
         in absenteeism, turnover, labour-
         management conflicts.

      B. Questionnaires used and transcripts of
         selected interviews with workers and
         management in four companies.

      C. Summary of historical data from government
         reports.
```

Writing the First Draft

After developing and refining the outline, you are ready to write. In order to accomplish your task efficiently, you may wish to divide your report into manageable units. Write one section at a time. It does not matter where you begin. The trick is to start with a section you find easy or manageable and carry on from there. Within each section, develop your arguments or observations clearly and logically with good topic sentences and effective transitions. As you complete your first draft and the report begins to take shape, read it in its entirety, inserting appropriate headings and sub-headings to divide your report into logical sections. You should also check your draft against the outline to be sure that you have not overlooked anything. An important thing to remember is that you are only writing a draft. You will come back to it later to refine and revise it.

Step Three: Revising

If possible, put aside your first draft for a few days. When you are ready to revise, read it through several times, keeping in mind the following questions:

1. Did I achieve the purpose defined in my working plan and outline?
2. Does the introduction establish the scope and methods of the report?
3. Is the presentation of data in the body of the report logical? (In the process of writing your first draft, you may discover that you need to rearrange paragraphs or sentences.)
4. Is the information presented complete? Does the reader have all the data necessary to understand the situation? Are my facts well documented and supported?
5. Have I presented the information concisely? (Read through your material carefully and see where you can cut unnecessary words and phrases, condense information, or eliminate repetition. Such editing can make your report more effective. Keep the reader in mind as you work.)
6. Have I separated opinions from fact? (Where you need to express an opinion, label it clearly with such phrases as "In my judgement..." "These facts suggest that..." "The situation seems to be...")
7. Have I chosen the precise word to convey my meaning?
8. Have I checked my facts? (Accuracy is essential in any report. The company may make major decisions on the basis of your information. Double-check statements, figures, charts, and sources for accuracy.)
9. Do my titles accurately reflect the material discussed? (Edit your headings to make sure they indicate precisely the subjects that follow. Avoid general headings.)
10. Have I checked for errors in spelling and grammar? (Read through your report for grammar and spelling errors. Such mistakes will detract from your credibility. In one report, for example, the writer did not notice that he had misspelled *values*. His report title read, "Reviewing Company Valves.")
11. Have I asked someone else to read through the report? If possible, have another person read your manuscript. (Carefully consider their questions or suggestions. False pride as an author will not help you produce the best report possible. Good writing is often a joint project.)
12. Is the report neat? (Neatness will enhance your report's credibility and influence readers in your favour.)

CHAPTER 10 TYPES OF BUSINESS REPORTS

In your business career, you will undoubtedly write several types of reports. Some may only be a page or two, much like a detailed memo, long letter, or government report. The content and forms of these documents are usually set beforehand as in the case of monthly sales reports, inventory reviews, and the like. Other reports are more detailed and elaborate, requiring considerable research and a more formal presentation. In this chapter we will look at the characteristics of several reports, specifically the memorandum report, the letter report, the form report, and the long report.

The Memorandum Report

You may best handle a report less than four pages in length as a memorandum report. This style of report writing is common when you are writing to readers within your company and when you can cover the contents in one to three pages.

Examples of this type of report include assessment reports, monthly reports, travel reports, inventory reports, staff and equipment utilization reports, and so on. As with all business writing, it is important that you consider your readers, analyze the information you have to present, and plan carefully.

Most memorandum reports follow a specific pattern which begins with the heading (see Chapter 8, "Memo Formats and Other Message Forms.") Assign each major topic of your memorandum report a heading. Place this heading at the left margin and underscore it.

The report itself usually begins with an *introductory statement* limited to two or three sentences. This statement will give the reader the reason for the report and indicate its function.

The longest and most important part of the memo report is the *findings or results* section which follows the introduction. This section is the heart of a memo report. You may wish to make use of side headings for each major topic to prepare your reader for the information that follows. You will want to select a concise, direct method of presentation and attach supporting material only if it is absolutely necessary.

The last section of the memo report deals with *conclusions and recommendations.* After you have presented all the data, you may wish to draw conclusions and make recommendations. Obviously, it is important that you base your conclusions on sound reasoning and the data which you have presented in your report.

Figure 10.1 Memorandum Report

DE JONG MANUFACTURING LTD.

TO: J.W. Lim, Chief Administrator
FROM: Joyce C. Campbell, Personnel Liaison Officer
DATE: 19--08 10
RE: Results of Evaluation of Empathy and Interpersonal Relationships Workshop

---

Introduction

Participants at both sessions completed an evaluation form. Although not all forms were returned, there is still considerable validity in the results.

Findings and Results

The main criticisms of the workshop, as seen in the results of the evaluation, was insufficient time. Everyone wanted it to be longer. Although the workshop ran 15-20 minutes overtime, the speaker covered all of the material stated in the objectives. The criticism is actually a positive reflection of the workshop.

There are several important positive outcomes as seen in the results; namely, the participants learned a very beneficial skill, they enjoyed learning the skill, they will pass the information to others, and they feel the workshop should be repeated for other company personnel. They even felt that they would like another session in empathy training. James Archibald made a great impression on the participants.

Attendance at the workshop was not as good as expected. A limit of 15 persons was set for each session. Fifteen registered for the first session, 14 attended. Fourteen registered for the first session, 12 attended. Several of the registrants could not attend because they neglected to check about getting the time to attend.

2.

Conclusions and Recommendations

I would like to suggest three possible reasons for the low registration:

1. Time: Many people are on holidays in July. People are more reluctant to come in on their days off in the summer months.

2. Advertising: There was not enough advertising and advance information.

3. Lack of Knowledge: Few people understand the concept and need for empathy.

I would like to stress the success of the workshop in terms of what the participants learned. Empathy has become more important to those who attended because they used it and witnessed it at the workshop.

I attach a copy of the empathy handbook used in the workshop. You may find it interesting.

Joyce C. Campbell

Joyce C. Campbell

JCC/MC
Att.

The Letter Report

When you are writing a brief report for a business or individual outside your organization, you may write a letter report. Essentially, all the criteria for memorandum reports apply to letter reports, although the format will be that of a business letter (see Chapter 5, "Business Letter Formats"). As with the memorandum report, assign each major topic a heading. Usually you will centre the headings if the letter has indented paragraphs. State clearly your objective and purpose along with your findings and recommendations. If the letter report exceeds three pages, you should write a letter of transmittal and handle the report as discussed later in this chapter.

Figure 10.2 Letter Report

August 10, 19--

Mr. D. H. Smithson
Employee Safety Coordinator
Mariposa Mines Ltd.
Box 3704
Sudbury, Ontario
T6J 1A4

Dear Mr. Smithson:

In this letter, I will summarize my findings and recommendations concerning your proposed upgrading of Employee Safety Awareness Week.

FINDINGS

The quality of the various programs delivered during Safety Week last year differed greatly. The difference in quality was largely as a result of two factors.

1. The objectives for the program were not drawn up with enough care and forethought. Not enough consideration was given to the type of audience for whom these programs were devised.

2. The instructors were not briefed thoroughly or prepared for the audiences to whom they would be lecturing.

Mr. D.H. Smithson 2. August 10, 19--

RECOMMENDATIONS

Based on my investigation, I would recommend that:

1. The Safety Committee draw up a specific set of Mr. D. H. Smithson objectives with regard to safety education in the mine.

2. The Safety Committee choose the instructors for Employee Safety Awareness Week based on the instructor expertise in specific safety related areas.

3. The Safety Committee should choose all instructors at least one month prior to the program to allow for preparation.

4. If instructors are using films as part of the program, members of the Safety Committee should preview the films and assess their suitability.

5. Fire Safety should be a separate program held at a different time than the other safety programs.

6. If you deem any safety programs designed for supervisory staff necessary, you should implement them at a time other than during Employee Safety Awareness Week.

CONCLUSIONS

I believe that if you incorporate the above recommendations into your plans, this year's Employee Safety Awareness Week will be a success without any of last year's difficulties.

Sincerely,

Helaine A. Urata
Management Consultant

HAU/DP

The Form Report

Many people, especially those working in the medical profession, prepare their reports on printed forms. You can use a form report whenever you have routine situations and content. You merely complete the form.

Figure 10.3 Form Report (Medical Report)

ST. MARY'S HOSPITAL
MEDICAL REPORT

Patient:

Address:

Medical Plan No:

Date admitted:

Attending physician:

Physical symptoms:

Diagnosis:

Treatment:

The Long Report

You will usually write a long or formal report on an assigned topic at the request of management. The topics might include evaluating the communication skills of employees or determining the best marketing strategy for next year. For these reports, you will need to determine the content for yourself.

Although the format may vary from company to company, all reports are keyboarded in double spacing with ample margins. You will want to make your report as attractive and easy to read as possible. You should not hesitate to make use of white space and of headings and sub-headings to divide your material into condensed packages. Most long or formal reports have eleven elements. Not every report will contain all eleven parts. You may want to omit some parts, depending on the kind of report and your reader's needs; nonetheless, you should be aware of the purpose and function of each part.

The eleven elements can be divided into *preliminary materials, body of the report*, and *supplemental materials.*

Preliminary Materials

1. Title page. The title page contains all the identifying information — title of the report, company, recipients, date, and writer's name. Each company usually has its own format for the title page. Check copies of previous reports to see which format your company uses.

Figure 10.4 Title Page

RETAIL STORE ANALYSIS

Prepared for

TAYLOR'S FINE FOODS LTD.

April 5, 19--

Presented by

RICHARD NEAL

Figure 10.5 Title Page

RETAIL STORE ANALYSIS

Prepared for

TAYLOR'S FINE FOODS LTD.

April 5, 19--

Presented by

RICHARD NEAL

2. Letter of authorization. This letter follows a blank sheet of paper after the title page and is keyboarded according to the company's format for business letters. The person who authorized the report should write the letter. It should outline the purpose or importance of the material.

Figure 10.6 Letter of Authorization

TAYLOR'S FINE FOODS LTD.
Purveyors of Fine Foods Established 1923

402 – 100 Park Royal, West Vancouver, B.C. V7T 1A2 **Tel: (604) 925-6443; Fax: (604) 925-7632**

February 22, 19--

Mr. Richard Neal
Marketing Consultant
2645 Portage Avenue
Winnipeg, Manitoba
R3J 0P9

Dear Mr. Neal:

Marketing Analysis

Further to our conversation of February 15, 19--, I am pleased to authorize your marketing analysis of Taylor's Kerrisdale store.

I hope you will include in your analysis the demographics of our primary market as well as the distribution systems, the pricing structure, and the promotional activities we are presently using. You are free to expand your analysis to include other relevant areas.

As we agreed in our earlier discussions, I will expect to receive your report and recommendations on April 5, 19--.

Sincerely,

TAYLOR'S FINE FOODS LTD.

Josephine S. Taylor
President

JST/am

3. Letter of transmittal. This letter, in the form of a regular business letter or memo, indicates the audience for the report. It may contain a checklist of all persons who will receive a copy of the report.

Figure 10.7 Letter of Transmittal

2645 Portage Avenue
Winnipeg, Manitoba
R3J 0P9

April 5, 19--

BY COURIER

Miss Josephine Taylor
President
Taylor's Fine Foods Ltd.
402 - 100 Park Royal
West Vancouver, B.C.
V7T 1A2

Dear Miss Taylor:

Marketing Analysis - Taylor's Kerrisdale Store

I am enclosing the report on the above store which you requested.

The report presents an analysis of the Kerrisdale store in terms of product selection, distribution systems, marketing strategies, pricing structures, and promotional mix. I have also included my prediction of the store's future prospects, as well as a few suggestions which I believe would benefit the store.

I appreciate the valuable assistance you and the Store Manager, Annette Detwiller, have provided. I also wish to acknowledge the assistance of the Advertising Director, Hugh Lalji. The data provided has been extremely useful to me.

I look forward to working with you again in the near future.

Yours truly,

Richard Neal

RN
Enc.

4. Table of contents. The table of contents lists all the topics and materials in the report. Use lower-case Roman numerals to number all preliminary materials, except the title page. Number the body of the report with Arabic numerals. Each company may have a slightly different format for the table of contents. Check previous reports to establish the format.

You may keyboard the table of contents in upper/lower case or in all capitals. You may want to list the titles of appendices by letter (A. Charts of Four Medium-sized Companies). You will indent the Appendix titles under the heading Appendices.

Figure 10.8 Table of Contents

TABLE OF CONTENTS

Figure 10.8 Table of Contents (Continuation)

2.

5. Synopsis or summary. Other terms you can use for this section of the report are *preface, introduction, abstract, forward,* or *digest.* This section gives the reader a quick, concise overview of the report. It is usually one-half to one page long and does not include data or figures. A good summary (1) provides enough information to specify the aims and results of your project; (2) is brief without omitting essential information; (3) is written in a fluid, easy style; (4) is consistent in tone and emphasis with the body of the report; and (5) makes use of accepted abbreviations to save space but does not include any tables or illustrations.

Figure 10.9 Synopsis

SYNOPSIS

The following report presents an analysis of the market and marketing strategies of Taylor's Kerrisdale Store.

The report considers the history and markets of the store (including marketing strategies and market segmentation). It also considers the product selection, the distribution systems, the pricing structures, and the promotional activities. The report concludes with recommendations of how to expand the market and marketing potential of Taylor's Kerrisdale Store.

Body of the Report

The body of the report contains the introduction, body, conclusions, and recommendations. You may not always have both conclusions and recommendations, but generally you will have one or the other.

6. Introduction. The introduction describes the reason for the report. It contains the purpose, methods of gathering data, sources, definitions, and a brief plan of the report. A good introduction arouses readers' interest and gives them some background information on the subject, preparing them for the contents of the report.

7. Body. Include in this section all the pertinent data you have gathered and analyzed. State your case and substantiate your points, presenting the results of your research and analysis. You may also include illustrations — charts, graphs, pictures — to support or enhance your discussion.

You will organize the report under various headings. Major headings indicate the main points of the report. Subheadings and sub-subheadings indicate subordinate and supporting ideas. Where you place the various categories of headings will depend upon your company's preference; however, the following is a guide for you:

First category	Centred, in capitals
Second category	Left margin, in capitals
Third category	Left margin, initial capitals, underscored
Fourth category	Indented five spaces from left margin, initial capitals, underscored
Fifth category	Left margin, initial capitals, run in

Generally three categories of headings are sufficient; however, you may use additional headings if necessary.

See Figure 10.10 for an annotated extract from the body of a report to see how it is organized.

Figure 10.10 Annotated Body of Report

Page numbers	10.
Major heading	MARKETS
Subheading	MARKETING STRATEGY
Margins **Body**	Taylor's Fine Foods' decision to expand the Kerrisdale Store was based upon a market growth strategy. Taylor's hoped to increase their market share by offering new gourmet services and products designed to appeal to the middle and upper class consumer. Since the expansion, management has taken steps to appeal to additional market segments (see Promotion section).
	MARKET SEGMENTATION
Sub-subheading	Geographic Segmentation
Long quotes etc.	The primary market area for Taylor's Kerrisdale store is the area bounded by 57th Avenue to the south, Broadway to the north, Oak Street to the east and Marine Drive to the west (Census tracts 20, 25, 26, 28, 35, and 49). The secondary market area is east of Oak Street to Cambie Street and north west to the University Endowment Lands (see Figure 2). The primary market area includes Shaughnessy, Kerrisdale, and Point Grey.

Page numbers: Number second and succeeding pages either at the top centre or top righthand side, four lines from the top of the page. Alternatively, you may place page numbers at the bottom centre or righthand side, approximately four lines from the bottom of the page.

Major heading: Centre and capitalize major headings.

Subheading: Keyboard subheadings in capitals and place them at the left margin.

Margins: Allow 2.75 cm (1 1/2") left margins; 2.5 cm (1") right margins; and 2.5 to 2.75 cm (1" - 1 1/2") bottom margins.

Body: Keyboard the body of the report in double spacing.

Sub-subheadings: Keyboard sub-subheadings with initial capitals, underscore them, and place them at the left margin.

Long quotes etc: Keyboard long quotes, end/footnotes, displayed information (tables), and bibliographies in single spacing.

Make sure the wording of your headings is parallel; for example, if your first major heading is COMPUTER HARDWARE, your second major heading could be COMPUTER SOFTWARE but not SELECTING COMPUTER SOFTWARE. Similarly, if your subheading is BUYING PRINTERS, then the next subheading could be BUYING MODEMS but not BUY MODEMS.

You may wish to use footnotes or endnotes in the body of your report to provide additional information on the main text or to cite bibliographic references.

There are two styles of footnotes: *A.P.A. (American Psychological Association) style* and *traditional style*. The A.P.A. style is the most commonly used format because it is the easiest to keyboard and your page looks less cluttered. You keyboard the name of the author and the year of the publication in the body of your report and then place the full bibliographical reference in the bibliography. In the case of a traditional style footnote, you keyboard a superscript number in the body of your report and then place the full bibliographical reference at the bottom of the page.

Example of an A.P.A. Style Footnote:

Body of Report:

Peter Drucker was the first person to use the term management by objectives (Drucker, 1954).

Entry in Bibliography:

Drucker, Peter. *The Practice of Management*. New York: Harper & Row, 1954

Example of a Traditional Style Footnote:

Body of Report:

Peter Drucker was the first person to use the term *management by objectives*.[1]

Bottom of the Page:

---

1. Drucker, Peter. *The Practice of Management*, Harper & Row, New York, N.Y., 1954, page 87.

Use endnotes when you are writing articles for magazines and trade journals or authoring books. Throughout the chapter, use superscript numbers, just as you do with traditional footnotes; however, instead of placing the bibliographic reference or additional information at the foot of the page on which you have keyboarded the superscript number, prepare a set of endnotes on the last page of the chapter or article.

Example of an Endnote:

ENDNOTES

1. The ASCII code is the electronic code by which letters, numbers, and symbols are represented.
2. There would be other options as well.
3. BASIC is a programming language.
4. A communications port is the place on your computer into which you plug a modem.
5. Kavouras, Gustav. *Introduction to Computers.* Toronto: Copp, Clark, Pitman, 1989.
6. Hayes, Debbie. "Modems and All That Stuff." *Computing Today*, January 4, 19—, pp. 56 — 59.

8. Conclusions. Readers may skim through the body of the report to get to the conclusions section. They want to know what the data and supportive materials mean. What patterns, trends, or observations did you find in your research? You should state your conclusions briefly and clearly, preferably in a series of numbered statements. You should make sure that your conclusions are logical outcomes of your data, supported by the information and research you have completed.

Figure 10.11 Conclusions Section of a Report

CONCLUSIONS

The future for Taylor's Kerrisdale Store looks very promising. Kerrisdale has two characteristics which other gourmet food retailers envy: an ideal location combined with minimum competition.

The expansion in September 19—, brought with it many short-term problems: temporary construction closures and stock shortages as well as high customer and staff frustration; however, most of the problems have now been rectified. Although a few customers deserted Taylor's during the expansion, most have since returned. When the proposed renovations are completed, many new customers should be won over.

Taylor's has taken positive steps in order to maintain its loyal customer following. The things for which Taylor's has always been famous still exist: quality, selection, and service. Taylor's also has recently emphasized low price in its recent gourmet catering service promotions in order to bring in new markets.

Store manager, Annette Detwiller, stated that when she first joined Taylor's Kerrisdale store in 19—, in many ways it was like walking into the past. She was referring primarily to the distribution systems and manpower allocation. There have been big improvements in these two areas. The current distribution system is superior to the old one, in terms of practicality and cost efficiency. Manpower allocation is much more logical now than previously. At one time, there would often be four people in at 7:00 a.m. to do work which two people could easily do. There are now more staff scheduled during peak selling hours.

9. Recommendations. Your employer may ask you to develop recommendations for further study or action in your report. You will be taking your conclusions to the next step and answering such questions as: What should be done? How do we achieve the desired outcome? How can we persuade people to agree with our plan of action? Your recommendations will be action steps or suggestions for action that give the readers a starting point for the next phase in the process. In some cases, when the situation is urgent, you may want to place your recommendations at the beginning of the report in the introduction. Usually, however, you will place them at the end of the report after you have presented your findings and conclusions.

Figure 10.12 Recommendations Section of a Report

RECOMMENDATIONS

While the expansion will give the store a much needed facelift, the lack of space in the store is still a major problem. There are no foreseeable plans to expand the store further. There had been rumours about Taylor's moving the gourmet catering service into separate facilities, thus creating additional selling space in the main store. Taylor's should consider this facilities alternative.

Taylor's should also re-examine its policy on advertising in *The Tribune*. Taylor's advertising director, Hugh Lalji, questions how many people actually read *The Tribune*; however, several customers have told the author that *The Tribune* is a very popular community newspaper. Some market research should be undertaken to determine the extent of the readership. Taylor's may be missing an ideal method of reaching its target market.

Supplementary Materials

This section lists the sources of your information and any supporting data that did not appear in the body of the report but that you wish to include.

10. Bibliography. List in the bibliography all sources used in writing your report. You should also list the names of people you interviewed or with whom you corresponded. You will need to give complete information on all books, reports, articles, documents, and other references so that readers can locate and review these materials if they wish.

You must include in all bibliographical entries the author or authors, title of the material either underscored or in quotation marks, the publisher's city and province/state and the publisher's name, and the date and year. For a sample bibliography see Figure 10.13.

Alphabetize entries in the bibliography by the author's last name or by the document's title if there is no author. Articles *an, a*, and *the* are not used as the first word. Single-space each entry with a double space between entries. Place the first line at the left margin and indent run-over lines five spaces. Your company may have its own style for keyboarding bibliographic entries. If not, a common style used in many business reports follows: notice the spacing and punctuation.

Books with one author:

Alder, Alfred. *Six Great Ideas*. New York: William Morris, 1978.

Books with two authors:

Morgan, John H. and Rachel C. Haynes. *Corporate Culture in the '80s*. Chicago: Contemporary Books, 1981.

Magazines and newspapers:

"Getting Management and Labor to the Round Table." *Business Week*, January 6, 1982, pp. 15-17.

Smith, Hedrick, "Giving Labor Authority in the Workplace." *New York Times*, April 10, 1983, pp. 1, 17.

Unpublished materials:

Dunne, Michael. "Effectiveness on Productivity of the Consultative Employee-Employer Management Model." Masters' Thesis, University of Toronto, Toronto, Ontario. 1982.

Government documents:

Ministry of Tourism, Government of British Columbia. "Film Opportunities in B.C." Victoria: Queen's Printer, 1984.

Institutional/Company Materials:
Air Canada. Annual Report 1988. Montreal, Quebec. September 20, 1988.

Figure 10.13 Bibliography

BIBLIOGRAPHY

Beckman, Dale, David Kurtz and Louis Boone. Foundations of Marketing - Third Edition Essentials. Toronto: Holt, Rinehart and Winston of Canada, Ltd. 19--.

"Taylor's Will Expand into the Gourmet Catering Business." Globe and Mail. December 24, 19--, p. B4.

Detwiller, Annette. Interview. Taylor's Kerrisdale Store, February 22, 19--.

"Food Store Inflation Seen at 4% to 6% for '87." Canadian Grocer, April 19--, pp. 20, 52.

"Food War Flares." Vancouver Province, November 29, 19--, p. B4.

"Fourth Quarter, 19--: Situation and Outlook." Food Market Commentary, March, 19--, p. 3.

Lalji, Hugh. Telephone Interview. Taylor's Fine Foods Ltd. February 20, 19--.

"Statistics of Canada - Census Tracts Vancouver: Part 1." Census Canada, 19--. #1 Ministry of Supply and Services, January, 19--.

Taylor, Josephine. Interview. Taylor's Fine Foods, West Vancouver, B.C. February 12, 19--.

11. Appendices. Include in this section information that supports the data in the body but is too lengthy or detailed to include in the text. You can also include in the Appendices charts, questionnaires, short reports or documents, photographs, explanations of statistical methods or computer programs used to gather data, transcripts of interviews, or any other data you feel the reader would find valuable.

Figure 10.14 Appendix to a Report

Appendix A

FOOD EXPENDITURE SHARES AND PERCENTAGE CHANGE 1982-84

Item	1982	1984	Change 1982-84 (%)
Food prepared at home	69.0	69.4	0.6
Dairy products	10.9	11.2	2.8
– Fluid milk	4.9	4.7	-4.1
– Other dairy products	6.0	6.5	8.3
Eggs	1.2	1.0	-16.7
Bakery products	5.9	6.0	1.7
Cereal products	2.7	2.9	7.4
Meat	16.7	15.6	-6.6
– Beef	8.0	7.1	-11.3
– Pork	4.4	4.3	-2.3
– Other meat	4.2	4.2	0.0
Poultry	3.2	3.3	3.1
– Chicken	2.6	2.7	3.8
– Turkey	0.5	0.5	0.0
– Other Poultry	0.1	0.1	0.0
Fish	2.2	2.3	4.5
Fats and oils	1.8	1.9	5.6
Beverages	4.1	4.4	7.3
Miscellaneous groceries	4.7	4.9	4.3
Canned and dried fruit	1.7	1.8	5.9
Canned and dried vegetables	1.6	1.5	-6.3
Fresh fruit	4.5	4.4	-2.2
Fresh vegetables	4.4	4.5	2.3
Frozen food	1.9	2.1	5.3
Prepared food	1.5	1.6	6.7
Food eaten away from home*	31.0	30.6	-1.3

* Includes food and beverages in eating places, board paid by family members and food expenditures while away from home overnight or longer.

Sources: Statistics Canada, Family Food Expenditure in Canada, 1982, Catalog No. 62-554, Ottawa, September, 1985
Statistics Canada, Family Food Expenditure in Canada, Selected Cities, 1984, Catalog No. 62-55-4, Ottawa, March 1986

Illustrations

You can use illustrations to add impact to your report by showing readers, not simply telling them, about a situation. You can use many forms of illustrations — graphs, tables, drawings, charts, and the like. Since many offices have computers with graphics capabilities, creating illustrations is relatively easy. Make sure you have a clear need for an illustration. Readers will find it difficult to follow your line of reasoning if you lose it in a forest of charts and tables.

Make sure illustrations stand on their own, enhancing what you have stated in the text instead of merely repeating it; for example, if you have listed production rates in your report, don't repeat the same information in a table. Not only have you duplicated your data for no good purpose, but you have also wasted the reader's time.

When deciding whether to use an illustration ask yourself, if the reader really needs to see the data in the form of an illustration? If so, what form would present the data most clearly: a table, chart, or graph? What conclusions do you want the reader to draw when viewing the illustration?

You may use several kinds of illustrations; each will have advantages and disadvantages, as described below. Look them over carefully. Examine other reports with illustrations to determine how the authors used each type of chart, table, or graph. Experiment with each type, putting your data into several forms and noting the different effects each form has on the information presented.

1. Graphs. Graphs are visually more interesting than tables but often less accurate because you must draw the data along a continuum. The main advantage of graphs is that the reader can spot trends, cycles, or other movements more easily. Graphs can condense a large amount of data into a small space. Reports commonly use four kinds of graphs.

(a) *Line graphs* indicate the relationship of a series of data along a continuum. For example, you can chart sales of a number of products over a period of time.

Figure 10.15 Line Graph

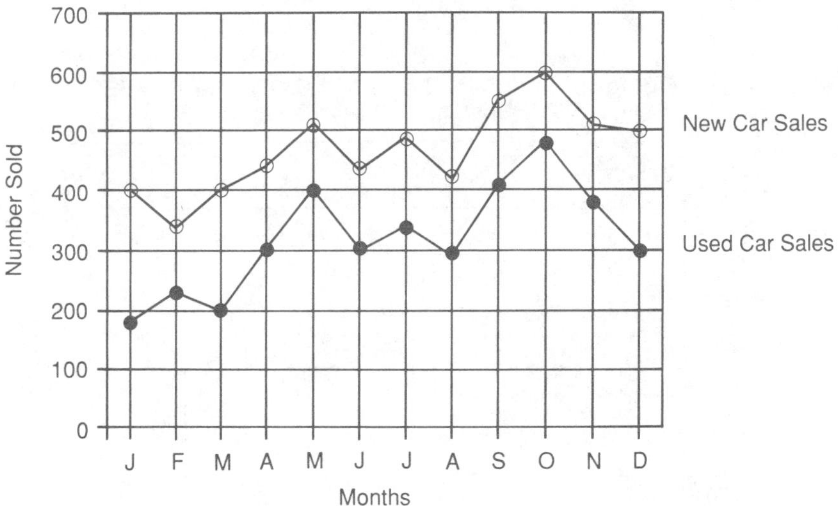

(b) *Bar graphs* are horizontal bars crossing the page from left to right. You may find planning a bar graph easier than planning a line graph. Horizontal bar graphs are useful for comparing data (see Figure 10.16 below).

Figure 10.16 Bar Graph

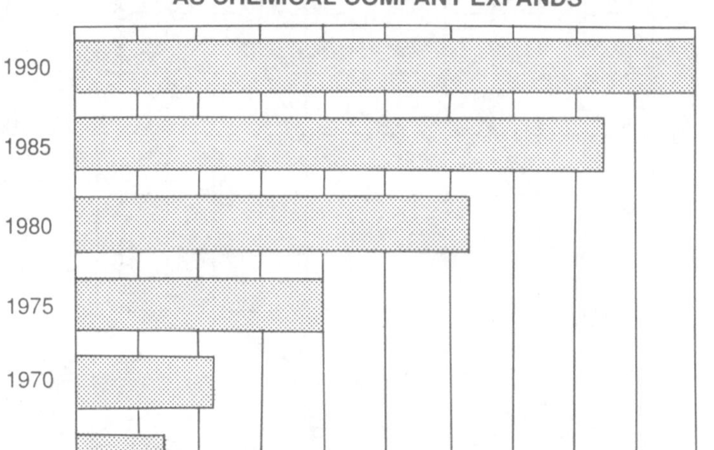

(c) *Column bar graphs* are made up of vertical bars. They are useful to show a comparison of groups of data over a period of time (see Figure 10.17 below).

Figure 10.17 Column Bar Graph

Figure 4.3 — EMPLOYEE DISTRIBUTION AT
SOUTHLAND ELECTRIC COMPANY

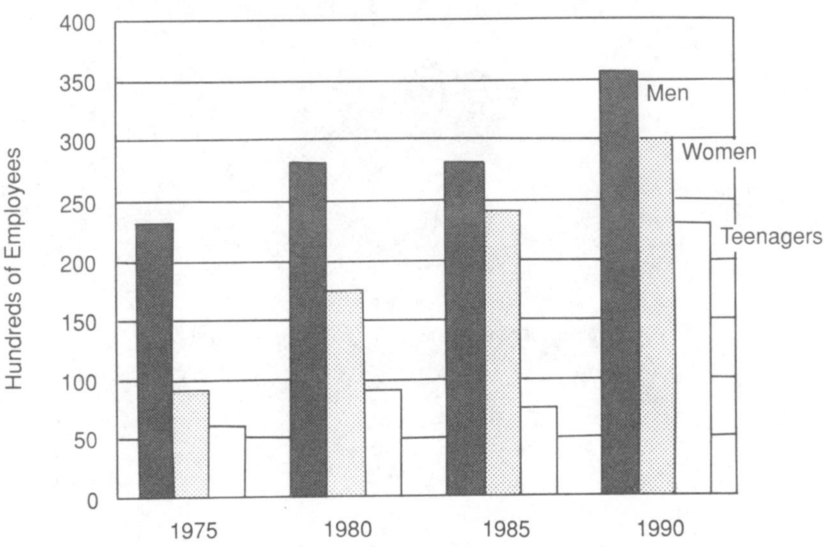

(d) *Pie graphs* are circles cut into sections like a pie. Each section represents a percentage of the total data being reviewed (see Figure 10.18 below)

Figure 10.18 Pie Graph

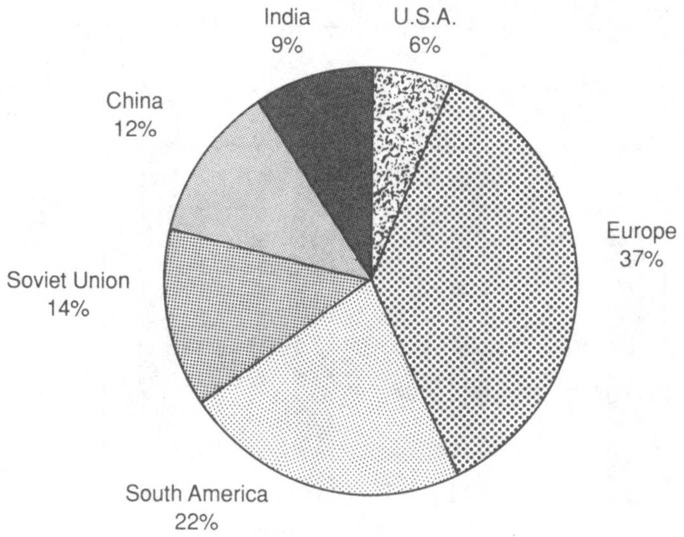

2. Tables. You may use tables to present data in columns, to summarize changes over time or to compare information, such as total sales among company divisions. Tables can include more detailed and complex information than either charts or graphs. They may even contain some narrative material explaining the various parts or data in the columns; however, trends or other movements over time are more difficult to spot in tables. See Figure 10.14 for a sample table.

3. Photographs. You can enhance reports that deal with organizational behaviour, as in the sample report, with photographs. You may also use pictures effectively in reports discussing site locations or new plant facilities. Keep in mind, however, that photographs are generally expensive to reproduce.

Number illustrations consecutively within a chapter or throughout the report if you do not have chapters. The designation 3.1 means Chapter 3, first illustration. Number tables by including the word *Table* followed by the chapter and table number and title. Here is an example:

Table 3.1 Company Performance by Yearly Income

Number figures in the same way with the word *Figure* preceding the chapter and figure number and title.

Figure 1.1 Production Trends from 1975-1985.

If you have no chapters in your report, number tables and figures consecutively.

Figure 1 Production Trends from 1980-1990
Figure 2 Absenteeism Rate from 1985-1990

Number illustrations in the Appendix according to the letter of each appendix; for example, illustrations in Appendix A would have the following notation:

Figure A.1 Historical Revenues for Automotive Firms

Each company usually has a particular style for labelling illustrations. Whichever style you use, follow it consistently throughout the report.

ACTIVITIES

1. Organize and re-write the following information into a memo report format:

19– 11 08

SAFETY WEEK – REPORT

OFFICE SAFETY

Attendance at this program was fair with approximately 25 people at Part I and 20 people at Part II. Marie Clarke was the instructor. The program was quite informative with an exceptionally good film which would be worth showing again sometime.

FIRE SAFETY

Unfortunately, attendance at the Fire Safety programs was poor. This was disturbing since we did have two guests from the Fire Department present to answer questions. Could the low attendance be the result of poor advertising or to lack of interest?

RESPONSIBILITY FOR SAFETY – NURSING SUPERVISORY STAFF

There was poor attendance for this program also. It appears that those people who did attend found it to be poorly organized and awkwardly presented. One person described it as a painful experience.

RESPONSIBILITY FOR SAFETY – SUPERVISORY STAFF

Although only 15 people attended this program, it was well received. The information was useful and interesting. The instructor, Della Hoy, offered some pertinent statistics and suggestions. She showed excellent film titled *The Trouble with Words*. The film is directed to Supervisory staff and would be worth booking for another time.

BACK TALKS – ALL STAFF

There was good attendance at almost all of the Back Talk programs. The success of the program and the quality of the information depended largely on the instructor. There were four different instructors over the five days for the general Back Talk programs. The amount of actual practice in lifting which the participants received varied from program to program.

An estimated 190 general staff members attended the Back Talk programs.

It is important to note that although our slide-tape program, *Your One and Only Back*, does not allow for practise, the quality of the program far surpasses most of the Back Talks held during Safety Week.

We will be showing *Your One and Only Back* during the week of December 4—December 8 in the Auditorium.

BACK TALKS – NURSING STAFF

These programs were held on the three floors in Extended Care. There was also one evening program held in the E.C.U. Gym. We had a total attendance of 85 staff members.

Aziz Shuel from the Workers' Compensation Board presented the programs with considerable assistance from two physiotherapists and several of the residents. They demonstrated different lifts using the proper techniques.

Lt. Kush Badh and Lt. Morley Deol from the Hamilton Fire Department attended the Fire Safety Programs. Although few people attended these programs, we wish to express our appreciation to those who did.

____

Rosemary Boyd
Inservice Education

RB:mt

2. Teresa Delaney has asked you to write a report on ONE of the following topics:

The Importance of Computer Literacy to Graduating College Students

or

The Importance of Good Communication Skills in the Computerized Office

Prepare a preliminary outline, conduct your research, prepare a final outline, and write your report.

CHAPTER 11 FINDING BUSINESS INFORMATION

The ability to locate the right reference and gather information that you can readily use is an invaluable skill in business writing and speaking. This section lists some of the basic research and information resources available to business people.

Libraries

Public and special libraries are among the greatest sources of information. A good reference librarian can act as a guide through these treasure houses. Most good libraries contain the following:

1. General Encyclopedias. *THE CANADIAN ENCYCLOPEDIA* includes articles on aspects of the Canadian economy, on specific industries, on statistical topics of interest to business, and on large corporations. *THE ENCYCLOPAEDIA BRITANNICA* is especially strong in business, science, and government.

2. Special Encyclopedias. The following publications are of particular interest to the Canadian business community. *THE FINANCIAL POST MONEYWISE MAGAZINE DIRECTORY OF PERSONAL FINANCE* by Andrew Weiner is a specialized reference guide to terms used in the Canadian financial marketplace. *THE CANADIAN EDGE*, an encyclopedia overview of the Canadian economy and business environment, offers a wealth of narrative and statistical information. *THE CANADIAN BUSINESS HANDBOOK* is an indexed guide to topics in business including stocks, banking, taxation, meetings, reports, office procedures, patents, and sources of business information.

3. Directories. There are a number of excellent Canadian business directories including the following:

BLUE BOOK OF CANADIAN BUSINESS — an annual publication that profiles over two thousand Canadian companies, and includes rankings of the top 500 in sales, the top 100 advertisers, and the top 100 stocks.

CANADIAN KEY BUSINESS DIRECTORY — a Dun and Bradstreet publication that lists Canadian companies by name, location, product classification code, and Dun and Bradstreet number. It includes yearly sales figures, number of employees, and chief personnel.

CANADIAN TRADE INDEX — an annual listing of member firms of the Canadian Manufacturers' Association. Each company description includes information on products, brand names, plants, parent firms, subsidiaries, executives, and number of employees.

FINANCIAL POST DIRECTORY OF DIRECTORS — an annual publication including professional information on Canadian company directors and an alphabetical listing of over 2 000 companies with addresses and principal executives.

FRASER'S CANADIAN TRADE DIRECTORY — an annual list of Canadian manufacturers with access by type of product, company name, and trade name.

4. Indices. There are three principal indices which are useful to business researchers. *THE CANADIAN BUSINESS INDEX* lists by subject, corporate name, and personal name, articles from over 200 Canadian business periodicals. *THE CANADIAN PERIODICAL INDEX* gives an alphabetical listing of authors, subjects, and corporate names for access to articles published in some 300 Canadian periodicals. *THE CANADIAN MAGAZINE INDEX* allows readers to look up subjects, company names, or personal names to find articles published in about 250 Canadian and American periodicals.

5. Government Publications. There are a number of government publications offering current statistical information.

CANADA HANDBOOK — a handbook, prepared annually by Statistics Canada, which includes extensive statistical and narrative information on the Canadian economy.

CANADA YEARBOOK — the basic source for statistics on every aspect of Canadian life, including the economy, trade, and finance.

FINANCIAL POST CANADIAN MARKETS — an annual handbook, published privately, based heavily on federal census data. It is a key resource for statistics on communities across Canada.

MARKET RESEARCH HANDBOOK — a useful resource for analyzing various aspects of Canadian markets. Statistics Canada publishes this handbook regularly.

In addition to those publications offering statistical information, the federal government also prints catalogues of publications. These include:

CANADIANA — a monthly bibliography which lists all materials published in Canada including publications of the federal and provincial governments.

GOVERNMENT OF CANADA PUBLICATIONS CATALOGUE — a quarterly list of federal government publications available from Supply and Services Canada.

STATISTICS CANADA CATALOGUE — an annual bibliography of publications available from Statistics Canada.

6. Other Reference Sources. Libraries have other useful references such as out-of-province telephone directories and street address directories. In addition, you may find the following almanacs useful to you:

CANADIAN ALMANAC AND DIRECTORY — a comprehensive, annual directory listing municipal, provincial, and federal government agencies, associations, television and radio stations, newspapers, financial institutions, lawyers, and other information.

CANADIAN WORLD ALMANAC AND BOOK OF FACTS — a typical almanac which is a treasury of facts and statistics covering all aspects of the Canadian economy.

Computer-Assisted Research

You may search for Canadian topics on all major U.S. online information retrieval systems. Major database services include Dialogue Information Services (DIS), System Development Corporation (SDC), Bibliographic Retrieval Services (BRS), Dow Jones and Company, The New York Times Information Service, Info Globe, Legi-Slate, Inc., and Mead Data Central. These databases also offer commercial contracts, a type of subscription service, to individual companies or business people. Fees may run from $50 to $100 per month. If you use the services only a few times a year, such a subscription is not cost effective.

As a result, most companies work through reference centres like those in public libraries.

Most databases are computerized versions of abstracting and indexing publications that list articles, documents, theses, books, journals, etc. Computer searches provide a display and printout of references on any topic you choose. Each reference includes the author, title, publication date, and, in many cases, a synopsis of the content.

There are some online information retrieval systems that offer specifically Canadian databases. A few of these are:

1. CAN/OLE (CANADIAN ONLINE ENQUIRY). Operated by the Canadian Institute for Scientific and Technical Information (CISTI), CAN/OLE makes over 40 Canadian and international databases available to researchers. The *Canadian Business and Current Affairs* database is of particular use in your search of business related topics.

2. INFOMART ONLINE. This system gives access to newspaper and business media across Canada and the U.S. Twenty-five of its databases correspond to American newspapers while eight correspond to Canadian news services. Five other specifically Canadian databases give information on such topics as the Canadian stock market and free trade.

3. FP ONLINE. This system offers access to *The Financial Post Electronic Edition* and to the full text of *Maclean's* magazine. Through simple but sophisticated searching techniques, subscribers can obtain national, U.S., and international business news as well as feature reports from the *Financial Times* of London.

4. INFO GLOBE. Produced by *The Globe and Mail*, INFO GLOBE gives full text online access to *The Globe and Mail* newspaper.

Another database of interest to business researchers is *The Canadian Periodical Index* online.

Conducting Computer-Assisted Research

Computer-assisted research can save you considerable time and money; for example, if you were searching for references on the foundation of The Canadian Labour Congress, you would set up a search using the organization's name and a key word or phrase like *Canadian Labour Congress, History of.* The computer would then search all relevant databases for material published on that topic. A reference librarian can help you focus your topic and select the proper key words or phrases to initiate the search. Computers can even combine two or more subjects in a single search, organize the printout alphabetically by author or publication, abstract or synopsis the references, and perform other specialized functions.

The printout may run from a few to several hundred pages, depending on how extensive a search you requested. You can then select the best references for your work, locate the publications in the reference section of the library, and photocopy the articles from each publication.

Using Business Databases

Computer searching can help you gather information for market research, grant proposals, and current developments in your field; locate experts in various specialties; obtain information on companies; and keep abreast of government actions and legislation affecting your industry.

The items listed and the years covered vary with each database. Most databases index material published after 1970. The reference librarian can help you find the right information source or additional sources not available through the computer.

The reference librarian can also provide a complete list of all databases that may be useful in your business writing. Fees for computer searches vary from database to database. The convenience and time saved in gathering information through computer-assisted research can be well worth the investment.

Resources for Practical Business Problems

At times you will need to know the best way to ship goods, where to look for travel information, and how to find the latest postal rates for business mail. The references listed below should answer those and many similar questions.

Mail and Transportation

1. *CANADA POSTAL GUIDE* — a regularly updated looseleaf handbook which comes in two sections. Part I is a guide to postal law and regulations. Part II is a guide to international mails, rates, and conditions.

2. *BULLINGER'S POSTAL AND SHIPPERS GUIDE FOR THE U.S. AND CANADA* — provides information on post offices, railroad stations, boat landings, schedules, freight shipping lines, and receiving stations.

Travel — Domestic and Foreign

1. *FODOR'S CANADA* — a source of both background information and practical details concerning hotels, transportation, and restaurants in Canada.

2. *BUSINESS TRAVELLER'S HANDBOOK: A GUIDE TO THE UNITED STATES AND CANADA* — one of a series of books designed to give the business traveller information about hotels, airflights, and so on.

3. *HOTEL RED BOOK* — American Hotel Association Directory Corporation, 221 West 57th Street, New York, NY 10019 — provides a current geographical classification of principal hotels in each state and Canada, with a further breakdown by cities.

4. *LEAHY'S HOTEL-MOTEL GUIDE AND TRAVEL ATLAS* — published by American Hotel Register Company, contains hotel, motel, and travel information with maps for The United States, Mexico, and Canada.

5. *OWEN'S COMMERCE & TRAVEL AND INTERNATIONAL REGISTER,* Owen's Commerce and Travel, Ltd., 886 High Road, Finchley, London, N12 9SB, England — provides detailed information concerning travel and trade in approximately 50 countries primarily in Africa, the Near and Middle East, Southeast Asia, and Far East. Entries include travel agents, airline offices, hotels, automobile hires, importers, exporters, and manufacturers.

ACTIVITIES

1. Research the databases available in your area. Write a memorandum report on your findings.

2. Research five databases not mentioned in the book and not covered in question 1. Write a memorandum to four of your colleagues giving basic information on these databases.

CHAPTER 12 PROPOSALS AND PRESS RELEASES

Proposals and press releases represent two other forms of business communication often used by companies in their daily operations. Proposals function as sales pieces and press releases inform the public about an event, discovery, or change associated with your firm. You will broaden your writing skills by learning to create these types of business communication.

Functions of Proposals

The writer will usually base proposals on studies conducted by an individual or group within a company and often use them to solicit business for the firm. Architectural companies, management consultants, independent contractors, and special service companies frequently submit proposals to potential clients.

You can also use proposals within a company; for example, the researcher might call upon personnel to prepare a proposal for implementing employee involvement programs. Often the writer will make an oral presentation to support the proposal.

Although proposals contain some elements of a formal report, their structure conforms more to the **AIDA** formula of a sales piece (see Chapter 4, page 41). Your primary goal is persuasion — either to convince management to accept your recommendations or to sell a client on your firm.

Since a written proposal must sell an idea, you need to support your argument in a compelling and convincing manner. You must show readers what you have to offer, how they will benefit, and why they should accept your proposal.

Step One: Prewriting

As in all business writing, the prewriting stage for proposals involves posing key questions that your finished work must answer. Asking these questions can help you plan your writing.

1. What is the purpose of your proposal—beyond selling your idea? Why are you writing it? What does the client need to know? If the client asked for a proposal on implementing an affirmative action program, for example, you would tailor your purpose toward that end. In a sentence or two, state the purpose of the proposal.

2. Who is the audience and what are their needs and motivations? Effective persuasion depends on your ability to identify and appeal to the recipients' needs and motivations. Who are the readers — upper management? the board of directors? your immediate supervisor? Research your audience so that you know how to appeal to their self-interest. The client or other readers should understand clearly how they will benefit from your efforts.

3. How do you catch the readers' attention? Once you have identified their needs, capture the readers' attention by addressing their primary concern first. Do readers want to save time and money? increase profits? change procedures? Are they motivated by prestige or convenience?

4. What results or outcomes would the reader like to have? A proposal asks for some change, perhaps a new policy or procedure, or the solution to a problem. Your job is to identify what outcomes the reader would like and then consider other outcomes the reader may have overlooked; for example, if you want to implement an affirmative action program, how might it affect the company's clients and competitors? how would the company's advertising change? where would they recruit new employees? Anticipating other outcomes and providing suggestions or possible solutions can help you gain the client's confidence. Be prepared, however, for objections to your proposal and be sure you can counter them.

5. What information or background research will you need in writing the proposal? Once you have determined the purpose, audience, and scope, you are ready to gather data.

Researching

For a client proposal, you will need to research the client's needs and problems thoroughly. You will gain your information from the company's management and personnel, its publications, information about the industry in which it operates, its markets and suppliers, and other historical documents that will give you an accurate picture of the company's current situation. If you are writing a proposal on implementing affirmative action programs, you would gather data on such programs in similar companies. What success or failure rates are available? How have these companies handled the impact on personnel, management, clients, competitors, market image, and daily operations? What methods of implementation have worked best for companies similar to the client's?

Estimate the time and cost of the project. Can you measure costs against specific gains or benefits? In the affirmative action proposal, for example, what advantages would the company gain once the program was operating smoothly? Explain time and cost estimates in terms of benefits to the client. These same preparation steps hold true if the proposal is for an individual or a group within your own company. Any change will cost a company time and money. Your proposal should persuade readers that the time and money will be well spent.

Step Two: Writing

Many companies have a standard format for proposals which simplifies the job of organizing and outlining your document. A standard proposal format might look like the following:

I. Background of the situation

II. Description of the current problem

III. Our approach to the problem

IV. Methodology and research

- A. Methods of gathering data
- B. How research would be conducted

V. Expected results

- A. Proposed outcomes
- B. Specific action steps

VI. Time and cost requirements

- A. Budget for proposed work
- B. Estimated time for completion

Writing the First Draft

A standard format provides headings and subheadings for your proposal. Keep in mind that you are not simply presenting facts or information but that you are seeking to persuade the reader to accept your ideas and approach; as a result, all information should support your position. You will want to put your ideas in their best light, tailored to the specific needs and purposes of the readers. Do not offer detailed explanation or technical facts unless the clients asks for them.

In every paragraph and sentence you should convey the impression that your ideas and approach are logical and appropriate. Where graphs, charts, or other illustrations will present the material more persuasively, use them; otherwise, keep them to a minimum to avoid distracting your readers.

Remember, your goal is to sell your ideas. Look over the material in Chapter 6, "Sales Letters," for additional guidelines on writing persuasive messages.

Step Three: Revising

Review, edit, and revise every part of the proposal. In many instances, thousands, even millions of dollars may hinge on a proposal's being accepted or rejected. Check and recheck all your facts. Pay particular attention to the choice of words and tone of the proposal. Is your tone positive without being too optimistic? The readers must believe you have appraised their problems realistically. Have you stated the situation clearly and tactfully, suggesting how the problem can be approached rather than focusing on how the client created the situation? Are your suggestions for the proposed work tailored to the client's specific needs?

If your proposal convinces your readers that you have done your research carefully and clearly understood their problems, you will probably sell your ideas. Ultimately, the acceptance of a persuasive message depends on the sender's credibility and the receiver's perception of direct benefits.

After you have keyboarded the proposal, proofread it carefully. Check for errors in grammar and spelling, for careless mistakes that may have previously escaped your eye, and for any inconsistencies in format.

SAMPLE PROPOSAL LETTER

19– 02 25

Mr. Bernard R. Wright
Wright Heating Systems, Inc.
94 Westmore Drive
Rexdale, Ontario
M9V 3Y6

Dear Mr. Wright:

Last week, you spoke with Mr. Stephen Chutus, our senior consultant, about some of the organizational problems your firm is experiencing. At that time, you asked our firm to submit a proposal outlining our approach to those problems and including an estimate of time and expenses. This letter is in response to your request.

OUR UNDERSTANDING OF THE CURRENT SITUATION

Charles Wright founded Wright Heating Systems, Inc. in 1935. The company grew modestly through the 1930s and 1940s and confined its business to the sale of heating equipment to small companies and private homes.

In 1958, Bernard Wright assumed leadership of the company and began diversifying into office appliances, service contracts, and some international sales. By 1965, the company had sales of $25 million, a workforce of over 120, and two new branch offices in Winnipeg and Quebec City. Over the next 20 years, the company continued to enjoy steady growth, with only two periods of decline during the 1970s oil embargo and severe recession of the early 1980s.

The company, however, has been experiencing organizational problems along with its growth. Communications among management levels and with support staff are often poor. Goals and objectives are not communicated clearly throughout the

Mr. Bernard Wright
Page 2
19– 02 25

organization. Sales and service areas overlap in some cases, and there is considerable confusion about who services which customers. Quality control is spotty at best, and faulty equipment and appliances have been turning up in customers' orders at an alarming rate. Worker morale is poor, and union organizers have approached the company within the past month to recruit union members from among employees in the firm.

In short, the company is experiencing growing pains in making the transition from a small, family-owned concern to a medium-sized firm with multinational connections.

OUR APPROACH TO THE PROBLEM

Wright Heating Systems is on the verge of entering a new phase in its development. We have assisted many firms in making the change from a small company to a larger concern. We can offer consulting services on reorganizing your management structure without losing key individuals or disrupting the flow of business. These services include setting up new office systems, accounting procedures, and distribution networks to help you manage your business more effectively. We will also provide training for support staff to involve them in the changes that need to be made.

We can help you devise forcasting and planning strategies to define your goals and develop plans to achieve them. You will be able to see where you are headed and what the greatest growth areas are likely to be. With these structures you can ensure that company goals are communicated clearly to all management and support staff levels.

Mr. Bernard Wright
Page 3
19– 02 25

ESTIMATED TIME AND EXPENSES

On the bases of our past experiences with companies similar to yours, we estimate that the transition period will be six months. At the end of that time, you and your management staff will have an organizational structure with clearly defined functional areas and responsibilities and well-designed channels of communication.

We will assign Mr. Stephen Chutus as senior consultant in charge of this project and form a team of consultants from our corporate staff. Mr. Chutus has worked with many large companies. He recently oversaw the complete reorganization of Western Industries, a multi-million dollar corporation. We are including the résumés of other proposed team members with this proposal.

We estimate the cost for the project will range from $135 000 to $150 000. This will include implementation of the recommended changes and follow-up visits three months and six months after completion of the project.

Wright Heating Systems, Inc. has an excellent record in the industry. We would be glad to assist your firm in its continued growth, and we appreciate the opportunity to work with you.

Sincerely yours,

FABER & THOLIN ASSOCIATES

Barbara Tholin

BT:wa
Enclosures: (5)

Functions of Press Releases

Press releases are the most journalistic of all business communications. Their purpose is to inform the public of events sponsored by, or occurring within, a company or industry. As such, they are a public relations message, promotional piece, and fact-finder all in one. Press releases announce promotions within a company, changes in product lines, creation of new departments or divisions, expansion into diversified products, mergers, and divestitures. They publicize grand openings, research findings, unusual events, humanitarian projects, and any other newsworthy items.

Nearly every major corporation and many smaller firms produce press releases for the public. They publish them in newspapers and periodicals and wire services, radio and television may even pick them up if the news is sufficiently interesting; for example, a company may achieve a breakthrough in an artificial sweetener or new diet medication. Since public interest in weight control is high, press releases announcing the new products would receive wide distribution and may even appear on the nightly television news.

Occasionally, reporters from newspapers or magazines have regularly assigned industry beats and will write the press releases. More often, writing a release will be the task of someone within the company. If that someone is you, your job will be to keep the public informed through the media about company events and activities. Press releases may be among the most creative and enjoyable writing assignments you do. They stress not only basic information but also human interest.

Since press releases may receive widespread attention, you must be sure that every statement is accurate and clear. A misquote, an ambiguous statement, or a wrong fact could damage your company's reputation and your own. If an outside reporter is writing the story and asks to interview you, make sure you have clearance from your superiors for the interview and that you discuss with them the subject of the release. A careless or off-hand remark can be distorted or misunderstood. Whether you are the writer or the interviewee, watch your language. You should also ensure that you do not release any news before its scheduled release date. Such an action would be disastrous in a take-over or merger situation.

Step One: Prewriting

The first step in preparing your press release is to identify the newsworthy story in each topic assigned to you and research the matter thoroughly. Suppose your company has discovered a way to double the life of AA batteries. In itself, this advance would be news; however, suppose the person who discovered the process is a 17-year old high school intern hired by the company as part of a field education project with the local school? The story now has a strong human interest element and might attract the national media. The company enhances its reputation on two accounts: as an innovator in youth job training and a technical leader in its field.

Once you have identified your story follow these steps:

1. Establish the facts. Remember the five *Ws* of journalism — *who, what, where, when, and why*. If you cannot answer all of them, go back for additional information.

2. Verify the facts. Remember the three rules of journalism — *accuracy, accuracy,* and *accuracy*. Check your facts by consulting at least two sources until you are confident your information is correct.

3. Secure releases or permissions. You must secure permission from a responsible source in the company to make all the information in your press release public. Never assume that the data you have are free for the taking. If you have secured permission from a superior or if your superior has requested the release, give the person a preview of what you intend to write. Make sure you have approval for the use of specific information.

4. Choose the media you will use. Generally the press release will be for general distribution and will go to all media and appropriate associations and individuals. In some cases, however, you may want to select a specific publication or media outlet for specialized press releases. If the material is urgent and needs immediate release, radio and television outlets are best. If the release has considerable detail, such as a list of names or scheduled events, the print media are better. Choose the media before you begin writing, since your choice will influence the presentation.

Step Two: Writing

Most companies have a standard format for press releases (see Figure 12.1).

Figure 12.1 Press Release

Name and Title	QUALITY CO. PRESS RELEASE
Recipients Date Contact	TO: All news media FOR: Immediate Release CONTACT: Wendell Simms Corporate Communications Quality Co. 2208 King Street Toronto, Ontario M6S 1E1 (416) 638-7459
Topic	QUALITY CO. APPOINTS FIRST WOMAN PRESIDENT
Body	Quality Co. announced today its appointment of Virginia Weston as the company's first woman president and chief executive officer. Ms. Weston, 42, first joined the firm in 1974 as the company's chief financial officer. She was responsible for saving several company stores from bankruptcy and urging corporate expansion into consumer electronics. Over the past ten years, Ms. Weston has been known for her outspoken views about the direction to be taken by Quality Co.
Margins	"No retail chain can afford to remain lost in the past," she stated in a speech before the Chamber of Commerce Thursday. "By shifting our product emphasis from clothing and hardware to electronics and career-oriented products, we maintain our market share. The Quality Co.catalogue should be a look at the future, not a reminder of the past."
Continuation	Ms. Weston will assume her office September 30 at the annual stockholders' meeting. Shareholders appear pleased with her choice as president. They sent her a congratulatory telegram when the company announced her appointment last week in the company newsletter.
End	X X X

Name and title:	Insert the name of the company issuing the press release. Provide a title: either *Press Release* or *News Release.*
Recipients:	List all recipients of the press release.
Date:	Provide a date when the media can print the release, e.g. 19— 06 01 or *Immediate Release.*
Contact:	Name the person within the issuing corporation the media should call for further information.
Topic:	Insert the topic of the release here.
Body:	Double space the body of a press release.
Margins:	Leave 3.75 cm (1 ½") margins.
Continuation:	If the release is over one page in length, keyboard *Continued* at the end of each page, except the last.
End:	Keyboard*XXX* or *END* at the bottom of the last page to indicate the end of the release.

Write press releases in the inverted pyramid style with the most important facts appearing first. Answer the five *Ws* in the first paragraph. Provide supporting details and further explanations in the succeeding paragraphs. Avoid stylistic tricks such as surprise endings or posing questions that you do not answer until the final paragraph. Your readers should be able to scan your story quickly for the main points. Remember, other stories and events are competing with yours.

Writing the First Draft

As you write the press release, ask yourself the following questions:

1. What is special or different about this person or product?
2. Who is my audience?
3. Which media should receive the release?
4. What does the product or this person's story mean for the readers?
5. What costs or savings are involved?
6. Are the facts verified?

Keep your paragraphs short so that you move the story along quickly while holding the reader's interest. Keep the press release to one or two pages unless the story is particularly newsworthy, such as the latest innovation in computer memory. A concise release is more likely to be read and distributed.

Aim for a conversational, journalistic style. Make your language lively and fresh. Avoid superlatives like *brilliant company executive* or *outstanding corporate achievement*. Most editors will simply delete them. Use well-chosen quotes and details to bring your press release to life and add to its impact. Always verify the accuracy of your quotes.

You may want to include a title with your press release but avoid clever or catchy headlines. Editors and newscasters usually rewrite or discard them. Let the editors decide on matters of style. Avoid underlining statements for emphasis. Use quotation marks only for actual dialogue or when you quote a passage from another source. Do not use quotation marks for titles of books, songs, documents, and films. Do not capitalize the names of departments, products, inventions, and the like even if your company tends to follow this style. The editor receiving your press release will adapt it to the style of the publication.

At times it is appropriate to include pictures or other illustrative material with your press release. Camera-ready photos reproduce well in print media. Contact the editor to find out what photos or visual aids are preferred. Mail photographs and other illustrations in well-protected envelopes. To avoid damage, do not staple or paper clip photos to your release.

Step Three: Revising

In revising the press release ask yourself:

1. Have I answered the five *Ws* of journalism?
2. Is the language lively and concrete?
3. Have I put the most important facts first and supporting facts and explanations after?
4. Are paragraphs concise?
5. Have I checked all my facts and obtained permission to use quotes, sensitive information, and proprietary data?
6. Do readers understand the story's implications for their own lives?
7. Have I checked for errors in grammar and spelling?

Proofread your final copy carefully and make sure you have addressed the press release to the proper media contacts. A well-written and carefully prepared release will help keep your company's name in the public eye.

ACTIVITIES

1. Read the following press release. Make improvements to increase its effectiveness.

```
             Triton Electronics Press Release


TO: All news media  FOR:         Immediate Release

                    CONTACT:     Cynthia Fostle
                                 Public Relations
                                 Triton Electronics
                                 41 Rideau Street
                                 Ottawa, Ontario
                                 (413) 591-4946

     Triton president Barry Dietz was on hand today
for ground-breaking ceremonies for the new cultural
arts building to be erected in Confederation Park.
The building will house art collections from three
nations and feature a special Native Canadian wing.
```

Mr. Dietz first proposed the idea of a cultural arts building ten years ago. Since then he has worked to raise funds and foster public support for the building. This year, donations from Triton Electronics and a matching grant from the Canadian Historical Society have made Barry Dietz's dream a reality.

"I believe that art belongs to the people," Dietz said. "For too long we have viewed culture as something only the elite can enjoy. Beauty shows us we are capable of more in this life than simply surviving."

The cultural arts building has been designed by Robert VanDeroue, whose architectural innovations have won him an international reputation. The building will feature three fountains in the central courtyard and an open-air cafe for visitors.

The building, which will take a year to complete, will cost an estimated $3.5 million. There will be a small admission charge for adult visitors but all children under 12 will be admitted free.

2. Contact a business in your community and ask for a copy of a proposal and/or a press release prepared by the company. Using the guidelines we have discussed in this chapter, analyze the material.

SECTION

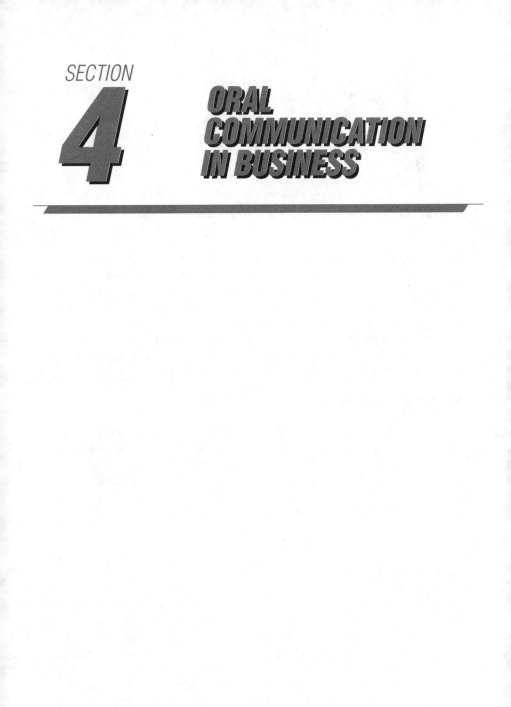

ORAL COMMUNICATION IN BUSINESS

CHAPTER

13 PUBLIC SPEAKING

During your career, there will be occasions when you will make oral presentations. Developing your skill as a speaker is important and will require both opportunity and practise. It is a generally accepted fact that speaking in public causes more fear to North Americans than any other activity. Overcoming this fear and mastering the techniques of good delivery are important to the success of any public speaker. In this chapter, we will look at non-verbal factors affecting public speaking, different styles of speaking, types of speeches, and how to prepare them.

Non-Verbal Factors

In the public speaking situation, non-verbal communication becomes vitally important. No matter how well prepared the talk, the sight of a speaker gripping the podium with white knuckles can do much to undermine the confidence of the listening audience. Similarly, the speaker who appears indifferent to the audience through a lack of eye contact or indifferent to the material by a lack of enthusiasm will have trouble generating interest in or reaction to the message being delivered.

Eye Contact

All of us can probably remember a teacher who spoke to only one side of the classroom. If you happened to be sitting on the other side you felt that your presence in the class was largely unimportant. When you are speaking in public, it is extremely important to develop a rapport or interaction with your audience. This interaction is dependent on the use of good eye contact. No matter how large or small the audience, you want to give each person the feeling that you are speaking to him or her.

You may begin by seeking out the friendly faces, those audience members who are nodding their heads in agreement with you or who are smiling at you. Pick several different parts of the room, and you will find yourself involving the entire audience rather than just a portion of it.

By maintaining good eye contact, you will be aware of how the audience is reacting to what you are saying. If you see a mass of puzzled faces, you can adjust your presentation to include further clarification, explanation, illustrations, or examples. By ignoring the audience and its feedback, your presentation will be less successful.

Posture and Movement

The posture you assume when you are speaking before a group can reveal much about your attitude and reflect directly on how your group receives your presentation. You will want to stand comfortably and with a confident bearing. Don't be afraid to move. Movement can help relieve your natural nervousness. Moving from one side of the podium to the other may indicate a transition in your presentation. You may be letting your audience know, non-verbally, that you are moving on to your next point.

You can use hand movements to emphasize a point. Some of us tend to talk with our hands in the course of normal conversation. When you are giving a formal oral presentation, be aware of any excessive hand movements which may distract your audience and try to limit them.

Voice

Your voice can certainly affect the success of your speech. The non-verbal message given by your voice can quickly weaken or strengthen the spoken messages.

1. The non-verbal message sent by a *moderately strong* voice is confidence and competence. If your voice is too weak, your audience will become frustrated and lose interest in what you are saying. It is important to pay attention to any non-verbal messages the audience may send to you such as, leaning forward. If you ignore the message, you may get another, stronger one from someone at the back of the room who will say, "Do you mind speaking up?"

2. Vary the *pitch and inflection* of your voice. The non-verbal message sent by a monotone speaker is indifference or boredom.

3. Your voice should be *clear* and your *delivery rate moderate*. The non-verbal message of a slow, stumbling speech is incompetence or

lack of confidence. A speaker who slurs or garbles his or her words is difficult to follow and irritates.

4. Reflect *enthusiasm* in your voice. One cannot say enough about the importance of enthusiasm in the public speaker. Your audience will catch your enthusiasm about your subject. Your voice reveals your attitude, and if you find your subject dull and uninteresting, your audience will too.

5. *Smile* when you speak. Your voice will sound more natural and you will look as if you are happy and relaxed. Smiling is infectious.

Later in this chapter, we will discuss the importance of rehearsing any oral presentation. Through practise, you will develop those non-verbal qualities in your speaking voice which will encourage maximum audience involvement.

Stage Fright

Most public speakers, like most athletes and performers, experience a certain amount of stage fright. Such nervousness or fear is not necessarily a bad thing. It can be somewhat invigorating and help get you ready for an oral presentation. Psychologists say that stage fright is greatest just prior to the actual delivery of the speech. Once you begin and the talk is underway, your nervousness will decrease and likely disappear.

It is interesting to consider why public speakers experience fear. Because most are not in any kind of physical danger, what could be the problem? None of us likes rejection. When you are preparing to speak before an audience of your classmates, co-workers, or strangers, you may worry that your material or your presentation may be unacceptable. Perhaps you think that your preparation has been inadequate. You may even worry that you will forget what you were going to say or that your ideas may be confusing.

There are ways in which you can minimize your nervousness. You can do physical exercises to help relieve the tension in your body. A yawn or two prior to walking to the podium will relax your voice. The key to minimizing nervousness and fear, however, is to follow the three basic steps for effective speaking:

Step One: Researching
Step Two: Organizing and Preparing
Step Three: Rehearsing and Delivering

Step One: Researching

The first step in preparing any oral presentation is to consider carefully your *purpose* in speaking. Before you can decide *what* you will say, you must be clear about *why* you are saying it. Will your speech inform? persuade? entertain?

Identifying the Purpose

1. The Speech to Inform. The purpose of any informative speech is always to give the audience information which it may not have had previously. You will build the central idea of the speech around the purpose of educating, informing, reporting, or instructing. In this type of speech, it is very important that you make each point clearly and that you are sensitive to audience feedback. You must also be careful to define any terminology which the audience may not know and to illustrate carefully your information within the frame of reference of your audience.

2. The Speech to Persuade. The purpose of any persuasive speech is to influence your audience to agree with you about a specific plan of action or belief. Many of the principles discussed in Chapter 6, "Sales Letters," apply here. It is important that you consider your audience in advance. How much opposition will there be to what you are proposing? Will your audience be receptive to your suggestions? The manner in which you develop your persuasive speech will depend on the answers to these questions.

3. The Speech to Entertain. Any speech can be entertaining. Specifically planned for that purpose are the after-dinner speech or the tribute speech. If your purpose is entertainment, you will want to consider the use of anecdotes, wit, and humour as an integral part of what you plan to say.

Considering the Audience

Once you have decided on your purpose in speaking, you must look carefully at the common characteristics of the people who will listen to you. You must attempt to assess their backgrounds, attitudes, and the knowledge which they may or may not have about your topic. In addition, you will want to anticipate their reactions to you. Will they see you as a credible speaker? If not, how will you establish your credibility?

Factors such as age, sex, educational background, and occupation will determine the level at which you speak and help you in conducting your research. Where possible, you will want to find examples and illustrations particularly relevant to your audience.

Considering the Time Limit

In business, when you give an oral presentation, you will have a time limit. It is important to remember that the people listening to you are not reading you. If they miss something you say, they can't go back to re-read or pick it up. You must, therefore, not try to do too much in any oral presentation. An audience will remember very little from a mass of information poorly presented. They will likely remember two or three ideas which you clearly present with good supporting evidence.

Before you begin to research any speech, decide what it is that you would like your listeners to take away with them. You may then undertake the research, planning, and delivery of your speech with this central idea in mind.

Considering Yourself

When you are developing the material for an oral presentation, you should consider your own background and interests. We have talked about the importance of enthusiasm to any speech. Speaking from your own experience with personal anecdotes can accomplish two things: (1) it can establish your credibility as a person who knows about the subject you are presenting; and (2) it can contribute to your enthusiasm for the topic. Never underestimate your own background as a resource for any oral presentation.

Finding Information

Many of the sources of business information which Chapter 11, "Finding Business Information," includes will be useful to you in preparing oral presentations. As with report writing, you will want to begin with a rough outline of the main points you want to make and conduct your research from it. The techniques discussed earlier for notetaking and documenting sources also apply here. You must attribute any quotation or statistics used in a speech to a specific source.

In compiling information for an oral presentation, you will want to have facts, statistics, definitions, opinions, and examples as supporting materials. Your rough outline, combined with your specific purpose in speaking, the needs of the audience, and the time limit will determine the extent of your research. While you are gathering your information, you will also want to consider using visual aids as part of your presentation. Chapter 14 discusses visual aids.

Step Two: Organizing and Preparing

When you are organizing and preparing an oral presentation, you should resist the temptation to write it out like a report. Unless you plan specifically to deliver a manuscript speech (see "Styles of Delivery," page 209) it is better to prepare your speech in an outline format. By using an outline, which you will later transfer to cue cards, you will be more spontaneous when you speak and avoid the pitfall of many speakers who try to either memorize what they are to say or read directly from their notes, often with disastrous results.

The speech outline includes three components: *the introduction, the body*, and *the conclusion*. As you plan and develop the outline, remember your time limit and be careful to allot an appropriate amount to each section.

The Introduction

The introduction of any speech has several important functions. It must gain the listeners' attention. The audience must immediately understand the relevance of what you are saying.

The introduction should also establish your credibility as a person qualified to present the topic. You may achieve this credibility by letting the audience know a bit about your background and your credentials for speaking. An effective delivery and good rapport with the audience will also increase your credibility.

The introduction should also serve as a road map to the speech. It should clearly limit the topic and let the audience know how you will organize and develop the speech.

In addressing students at her old alma mater, writer Alice Walker introduced her speech this way:

> "It may surprise you that I do not intend (until the question and answer period perhaps) to speak of war and peace, the economy, racism or sexism or the triumphs and tribulations of black people or of women. Or even about movies. Though the discerning ear may hear my concern for some of these things in what I am about to say. I am going to talk about an issue even closer to home. I am going to talk to you about hair. Don't be at all alarmed. This is not an

> appraisal, I simply want to share with you some of my own experiences with our friend hair and at the most hope to entertain and amuse you." (From a speech by Alice Walker at Spelman College, Atlanta, Georgia)

The introduction may also use anecdotes to gain audience attention and interest:

> "My background was historical. The ghosts of the gold rush walked the wooden sidewalks of the little town of Dawson City, and we lived with the memories of old men who had been young men and had gone over the trails and down the rivers.
>
> I remember hearing about Diamond Tooth Gertie. My mother knew her. She literally had a diamond in place of a tooth and it served her in good stead many times I think. And there was Cad Wilson, who wore a belt of matched nuggets. There was always one missing and whoever was dancing with her would say "You have a missing nugget, let me replace it"; and the next day a nugget would be missing again for the next dance." (Source: *The Empire Club of Canada Addresses, 1973-1974*, p. 46. Speaker: Pierre Berton. Topic: The Future of the North.)

Another technique often used by public speakers is to begin with a relevant quotation:

> "The most striking mark of man's genius as a species, as the most adaptable of animals, has been his ability to live in cities." So writes John Pfeiffer, author of *The Emergence of Man.* (Source: *The Empire Club of Canada Addresses 1973-1974*, p. 163. Speaker: Robert L. Armstrong (introducing David Crombie) Topic: The Mayor Reports)

Whatever approach you choose, remember that the introduction must give your audience a clear idea of what they can expect to hear and the direction the presentation will take.

The Body

The body of the speech includes the main points and the evidence which supports them. In your outline, you should determine the logical order of these main points and the manner in which you will develop your material. Because of the difficulties involved in listening to a speech, you should endeavour to make the organization of your talk as straightforward and easy to follow as possible.

The most common ways of organizing material for oral presentation are:

1. **Topical.** This arrangement is based on a logical division of your material. You should begin by outlining the major points you wish to make and then ensuring that you cover those points in an easy to follow manner.

2. **Chronological.** This arrangement may be particularly useful if you are asked to make a speech about a sequence of events or a particular process. You should base the order of your material on what happens first, what happens next, and what happens last.

3. **Geographical.** In this arrangement you divide your material according to physical location; for example, in preparing a speech about a new facility you could present your material in divisions similar to the physical divisions of the facility.

4. **General to Specific/Specific to General.** These arrangements are particularly effective in opinion speeches where you wish to argue a particular point of view. You may begin with a general statement and then provide specific examples and illustrations or, conversely, you may present a number of specific examples and then draw a general conclusion.

5. **Cause-Effect.** This arrangement is useful when you are asked to give a speech dealing with a particular problem and its consequences. The speech has two main divisions: the first describes the cause of the problem: the second deals with the effects of the problem.

6. **Problem-Solution.** This arrangement is similar to the cause-effect arrangement in that the speech has two main parts. In the first, you outline the problem: in the second, you propose the solutions. The arrangement is particularly useful in persuasive speaking.

Supporting Materials

Once you have decided on the organizational pattern and have outlined your topic, you must choose appropriate supporting materials. Because an audience can only hear and remember a limited amount of information within a given time frame, the supporting materials must be interesting, relevant, accurate, and appealing.

1. Examples and Illustrations. While an example may refer to a specific instance, the illustration is more of a narrative. Both may be useful to you in clarifying points and helping your audience to better remember what you are saying. In a speech entitled *Three Precepts for Living*, the speaker used examples and illustrations to offer advice to graduating students from the University of Alberta:

> "I want to put before you three simple, almost simplistic, propositions that I have gleaned from a long experience of our contemporary society. The first is, 'never be afraid of something just because it is new.' Mankind has always been afraid of the untried and the unknown. It is much more comfortable to follow the beaten paths and to accept the conventional wisdom. Yet all history demonstrates that the human race has advanced on the shoulders of those who 'have seen beyond the lean horizon of their years.' We think in this connection of Pasteur and Lister in medicine, of Wilberforce fighting for a quarter of a century to abolish slavery, of Watt with his steam engine, and Edison who gave us the incandescent lamp. These and thousands of others dared to 'dream dreams and see visions' which in due course have become realities that have enhanced and enriched life on our planet. (Source: *Tommy Douglas Speaks*. Ed. L.D. Lovick, Lantzville, B.C.: Oolichan Books, 1979)

2. Statistics. You may use statistics to help you substantiate your information and to show the development of trends or patterns. You must use them with caution. They must be accurate, up to date, and clearly spoken. Often it is useful to write statistics on the chalkboard or to represent them visually on a chart or overhead transparency.

> "Hourly wages rose at a 5% annual rate in the past three months, compared with 2.5% in all of 19—. While the nation's jobless rate was 5.9% in March, many regions are experiencing even lower unemployment. During the past year jobless rates have dipped below 4% in two Eastern provinces."

3. Comparison. When you use a comparison, you show your audience how one thing is like another. You may compare a concept you would like them to understand with something which if familiar to them.

In a radio broadcast Christmas Message, the speaker compared current events with those thousands of years earlier:

"I can hear some cynic saying, 'How can you talk about Peace on Earth in a world where wars, revolution and terrorism are everywhere and at a time when violence and a total disregard for human life is all to prevalent?' That is true; and it was even more true on the first Christmas. Two thousand years ago the world of that day lay under the military might of the Roman Empire. A large segment of the population were slaves, and many more were subject people who lived under Roman tyranny without any of the basic human rights for which mankind has always yearned." (Source: *Tommy Douglas Speaks*. Ed. L.D. Lovick. Lantzville, B.C.: Oolichan Books, 1979, p. 257)

4. Repetition. When you are delivering a speech, you may repeat a phrase or idea to emphasize its importance to your audience.

"I have a dream that one day on the red hills of Georgia the sons of slaves and the sons of former slaveowners will be able to sit down together at the table of brotherhood.

I have a dream that one day even the state of Mississippi, sweltering with the heat of injustice, sweltering with the heat of oppression, will be transformed into an oasis of freedom and justice.

I have a dream that my four little children will one day live in a Nation where they will not be judged by the color of their skin, but by the conduct of their character...." (Source: Rev. Martin Luther King's *I Have a Dream* speech, 1963, *A Treasury of the World's Great Speeches*. Ed. Houston Peterson. New York: Simon and Schuster, 1965, p. 839)

5. Quotations. A very effective method of supporting your ideas in a speech is by using quotations. Obviously, you will want to use sources that are dramatic or memorable and ones that will lend credibility to what you are saying.

"It has always seemed to me, and I was raised with them, that the native peoples realized long before we did what the true value of this country is. I always like to tell the story of the Dog Rib Indian and the Oblate Priest. The Dog Rib Indian said to the Priest, 'Tell me Father, what is the white man's Heaven?' And the Priest replied, 'It is the most beautiful place in the world.' Here is what the Indian said. He said. 'Tell me Father, is it like the land of the little trees when the ice has left the lakes? Are there great musk oxen there? Are the hills covered with flowers? There will I see caribou everywhere I look? Are the lakes blue with the sky of summer? Is

> every net filled with great, fat whitefish? Is there room for me in this land, like our land, the Barrens? Can I camp anywhere and not find that someone else has camped? Can I feel the wind and be like the wind? Father, if your Heaven is not like all these, then leave me alone in my land, the land of little sticks.'
>
> And if you set that to music it might make a pretty good National Anthem." (Source: *The Empire Club of Canada Addresses, 1973-1974*, p. 56. Speaker: Pierre Berton. Topic: The Future of the North.)

Making Use of Transitions

Because your audience will hear your speech only once, it is important that you use transitions and summaries to remind listeners of what you have said and to indicate the next point you will be discussing. Use transitions between each of the main divisions of the speech. Some common transitional expressions include:

> first of all ... secondly ...
> in addition to
> furthermore
> on the other hand
> another point ...

Transitions act as guideposts. They let listeners know that even if they have missed some of what you have said, they can still tune in for what is coming next.

The Conclusion

The conclusion of an oral presentation is very important and deserves the same care and planning as the introduction. Usually, the conclusion offers a summary of what has been said, but it may include recommendations or, in the case of a persuasive talk, an urge to action. A well-planned conclusion gives the audience a sense of completion. It should leave your listeners with the single impression or idea you have been trying to get across to them.

In his inaugeration speech President John F. Kennedy summarized this way:

> "Finally, whether you are citizens of America or citizens of the world, ask of us here the same high standards of strength and sacrifice which we ask of you. With a good conscience our only sure

reward, with history the final judge of our deeds, let us go forth to lead the land we love, asking His blessing and His help, but knowing that here on earth God's work must truly be our own." (Source: *A Treasury of the World's Great Speeches.* Ed. Houston Peterson. New York: Simon and Schuster, 1965, p. 835)

Styles of Delivery

There are four styles of speech delivery. Each is different and may be used with varying effectiveness.

1. The impromptu style of speaking occurs when you have no advance warning and little time, if any, to prepare. You need to organize your thoughts quickly and decide on the main points you will make.

2. The extemporaneous style of speaking involves advance preparation. Although you will have organized your material with a proper introduction and conclusion, the delivery will still have a quality of spontaneity and informality. You will speak from notes rather than a prepared text.

3. The manuscript style of speaking occurs when the speaker takes a full manuscript or text to the podium. It is common for politicians to use this type of delivery. Speakers whose speech depends on absolute accuracy use manuscript delivery. The main drawback of this style of speaking is that not every speaker can master the techniques required. The speaker may inadvertently become so attached to the manuscript that all contact and rapport with the audience is lost.

4. The memorized style of speaking is highly undesirable. The lack of spontaneity and stilted delivery which often characterize the memorized speech will put an audience off.

Step Three: Rehearsing and Delivering

1. After you have researched and organized your speech, make notecards (see Figure 13.1 below) indicating the main points you wish to make. Carefully transcribe statistics and quotations for accuracy.

Figure 13.1 Note Cards

1.

INTRODUCTION

1. Introduce myself
   Outline my background - use background sheet

2. Disclaimer - My views not necessarily those of your law firm and vice versa

3. State seminar objectives - to review legal support staff's role in a law firm

2.

4. What is the primary role of legal support staff? Elicit participation.

   Maintaining law firm image.

MAINTAINING LAW FIRM IMAGE

1. Neatness of documents and correspondence.

2. Accuracy of documents and correspondence.

3. Good communication - use overhead

2. Organize your notecards in logical order.

3. Rehearse your speech with the visual aids which you will use with your presentation. Time yourself to make sure you are within the required limit.

4. Familiarize yourself with, but don't memorize, the logic and order of the ideas and material you will present.

5. Check the room where you are to speak. Make sure everything you require is available.

6. Stand in a comfortable position. Pause before you begin to give your audience a chance to give you their undivided attention.

7. At the time of your actual presentation, don't ever apologize for yourself or what you are about to say.

8. Check the tone of your voice and the volume and rate of delivery.

9. Establish and maintain good eye contact with your audience.

10. Be sensitive to the non-verbal feedback which the audience gives you and make adjustments where you can.

The Question and Answer Period

You may enhance the effectiveness of any oral presentation by the inclusion of a question and answer period. The audience will have a chance to ask about areas of your presentation which particularly interested them and you will have a chance to receive some valuable feedback. You will want to let the audience know at the outset that a question and answer period will follow your speech. People are likely to listen more closely if they know there will be an opportunity to ask questions later.

The following guidelines will help you in handling an effective question and answer period.

1. Ask for questions in a positive way. Sound as if you *want* questions. Begin with, "Who has the first question?"

2. If you get no questions, pose a question and answer it. Say, "A question I'm often asked is ..." State the question and then answer it. If you get no other questions, you can say "Are there any other questions?" Another version of the same technique is to ask your audience a question. "Are there any of you who have...?"

3. Look at the person asking the question, and then repeat it. By repeating the question you have time to think, you ensure that you understand what the person has asked, and you give the entire audience a chance to hear the question.

4. Look at the whole audience when you are answering the question. Because you are in a public speaking situation, the whole audience should hear your answer. As you finish your answer, look at the person who asked the question.

5. Keep the answer concise. The audience will get bored if you take forever to answer a question. If you can answer with a "yes" or "no," then do so.

6. Maintain control. When you open up your presentation for audience participation, there are risks of losing control. Minimize these risks by planning ahead and anticipating questions. Don't be afraid to say, "I don't know." Don't hesitate to label a question as irrelevant and always keep calm when handling a particularly irritating question asker.

Meetings and Small Group Conferences

In addition to speaking formally before groups, you will use your oral communication skills in other settings. Meetings and small group conferences are common in business and will require your participation either as a group member or chairperson. Good communication skills are essential in either of these roles.

Chances are you will find yourself participating in discussions more often than you will be making formal oral presentations. Because of the informal atmosphere which often surrounds an office meeting or conference, people sometimes don't pay enough attention to good listening and speaking skills. Because you know everyone in the room, it is easy to become casual. Often you waste a great deal of time because participants in meetings and conferences come ill prepared and not committed to the seriousness of the tasks before them.

The success of any meeting or conference will depend on the participants' clear understanding of its objectives and their achievement goals. If you find yourself chairing a meeting or leading a small group discussion, it will be up to you to announce these objectives and goals to the assembled group and to keep the discussion moving forward towards them. At the outset, it will be your job to advise everyone present of the format you will follow. Will you allow each person to speak initially? Will there be a time limit on each aspect of discussion?

Prior to the actual meeting or small group conference, you will want to circulate an agenda outlining the main items to be covered by the meeting. By giving group members a chance in advance to consider the topics under discussion, they may be better able to participate. (See Chapter 9, "Organizing the Plan"; "Outlining the Report.")

During the meeting, you may appear to be friendly and informal but there should be no doubt about your control of the agenda and the ultimate goals.

As the chairperson, participants perceive you as having authority and considerable influence. It will be up to you to conduct the proceedings in a democratic atmosphere, not allowing your own beliefs or opinions to interfere with those of the participants. As the chairperson, it is also your job to protect the group from its more troublesome members. If you are dealing with an individual who is monopolizing the discussion, you must make a concerted effort to ask for comments from others in the group. If you find there are one or two group members saying nothing, it is up to you to seek their participation. If you find out-right hostility and disagreement among group members, you have to act as a mediator and attempt to resolve the dispute.

As a member or participant in such a meeting or conference, your responsibilities are somewhat different. Where possible, you should prepare in advance by reading any materials for discussion, by becoming familiar with the agenda, and by briefly noting comments you may wish to make. Once the meeting is underway, you should respect the wishes of the chairperson and limit your participation to the format outlined. Don't monopolize the discussion. Democracy is slow and everyone, theoretically, has the right to participate. You must listen and consider the views of those with whom you do not necessarily agree. Attempt to keep an open mind and be willing to change your position if it is in the best collective interests of the group. Ask questions and say what you think. Avoid making long winded speeches that have everyone squirming in their chairs, wishing you would be quiet.

As a group member or participant, you may be asked to keep minutes of the meeting or conference. Accurate minutes come from careful listening and good notetaking skills (see Chapter 9, "Notetaking"). Many good listeners can take notes in outline form with memory-jogging words which will allow them to fill in the details later. It is important to accurately record any specific figures and names during the meeting or conference. Minutes should have a tone of objectivity and impartiality and be of future use to the group. They must be complete.

Usually, a meeting or small group conference ends with a

commitment management will expect a report. A problem may have developed which will need further research and analysis. A smaller sub-committee of the group may even look more specifically at some of the issues raised. Whether you are the chairperson or a participant, there should be no doubt in your mind when you leave the meeting room what is to happen next. The result of a successful meeting or small group conference is that each member has a feeling of accomplishment and a sense of the group's direction.

Videoconferencing

Some companies use the latest technological advances in telecommunications to set up electronic conferences. Instead of participants gathering at one central location for a meeting, the meeting can come to them. Video pictures are relayed to several locations and telephone links transmit the sound to each smaller conference. The participants can discuss a project as if they were present in the same room even though they are actually hundreds, even thousands of miles apart. Videoconferencing offers a way to close the distance between locations and provide instant, effective business communications.

Videoconferencing systems are simple to operate and allow face-to-face communication with sound, graphics, and simultaneous transmission of data and facsimiles. See also Chapter 15, "Teleconferencing."

ACTIVITIES

1. The following speech by Chief Dan George of the Burrard Indian Reserve in North Vancouver, British Columbia, was first read at a public ceremony in Vancouver's Empire Stadium on July 1, 1967. In reporting the event, the Vancouver Sun noted that "the jubilant crowd of 32 000 was silenced by the moving—and bitter—soliloquy." Based on our discussion of the criteria for organizing and planning the oral presentation, consider the effectiveness of Chief Dan George's speech.

Lament for Confederation

"How long have I known you, Oh Canada? A hundred years? Yes, a hundred years. And many many seelanum[1] more. And today, when you celebrate your hundred years, oh Canada, I am sad for all the Indian people throughout the land.

[1]A Squamish Indian word meaning "lunar months."

For I have known you when your forests were mine; when they gave me my meat and my clothing. I have known you in your streams and rivers where your fish flashed and danced in the sun, where the waters said come, come and eat my abundance. I have known you in the freedom of your winds. And my spirit, like the winds, once roamed your good lands.

But in the long hundred years since the white man came, I have seen my freedom disappear like the salmon going mysteriously out to sea. The white man's strange customs which I could not understand, pressed down upon me until I could no longer breathe.

When I fought to protect my land and my home, I was called a savage. When I neither understood nor welcomed this way of life, I was called lazy. When I tried to rule my people, I was stripped of my authority.

My nation was ignored in your history textbooks—they were little more important in the history of Canada than the buffalo that ranged the plains. I was ridiculed in your plays and motion pictures, and when I drank your fire-water, I got drunk – very, very drunk. And I forgot.

Oh Canada, how can I celebrate with you this Centenary, this hundred years? Shall I thank you for the reserves that are left me of my beautiful forests? For the canned fish of my rivers? For the loss of my pride and authority, even among my own people? For the lack of my will to fight back? No! I must forget what's past and gone.

Oh God in Heaven! Give me back the courage of the olden Chiefs. Let me wrestle with my surroundings. Let me again, as in the days of old, dominate my environment. Let me humbly accept this new culture and through it rise up and go on.

Oh God! Like the Thunderbird of old I shall rise again out of the sea; I shall grab the instruments of the white man's success – his education, his skills, and with these new tools I shall build my race into the proudest segment of your society. Before I follow the great Chiefs who have gone before us, oh Canada, I shall see these things come to pass.

I shall see our young braves and our chiefs sitting in the houses of law and government, ruling and being ruled by the knowledge and freedoms of our great land. So shall we shatter the barriers of our isolation. So shall the *next* hundred years be the greatest in the proud history of our tribes and nations." (Source: Dawe, Alan. *Profile of a Nation*. Toronto: Macmillan of Canada, 1969.)

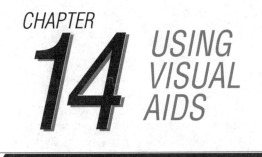

CHAPTER 14 USING VISUAL AIDS

For maximum effectiveness of any oral presentation, you will want to make use of visual aids. Your choice will depend on a number of factors including the length of your presentation, the type of room where you present it, the available equipment, the size of your audience, and the needs of your topic. A good visual aid appeals to the senses and attracts and holds attention. Visual aids can emphasize and clarify aspects of your presentation and make what you say more interesting.

Whatever visual aid you choose, you must prepare and rehearse. In this chapter, we will look at some of the visual aids available to you and consider the advantages and disadvantages of each.

Handouts

The use of handouts as a visual aid is commonplace. A handout, an effective way for you to give your audience accurate information which they may keep as reference material, can include diagrams, charts, tables, and illustrations. The following suggestions may help you in the use and design of handouts:

1. Always distribute the handout at a time when you can afford to lose the undivided attention of your audience. The end of the presentation is often a good time for handouts unless you need them for an aid to your presentation.
2. Present the handout in an attractive and easy-to-follow format.
3. Make handouts concise, readable, and to the point.
4. Give your audience clear instructions about what they are to do with the handout. Are they to read it now or later?

If you can find out in advance how many people will be listening to your presentation, you can prepare enough handouts for everyone plus a few extras.

The Chalkboard

Often referred to as the *old faithful* of visual aids and, because it is so readily available, unfortunately speakers often take the chalkboard for granted and spend little time mastering its use. The chalkboard allows you considerable flexibility since you may leave on, erase, or replace material. The following are ways in which you can use the chalkboard for maximum effectiveness:

1. Don't talk to the chalkboard. The importance of maintaining good eye contact with your audience cannot be overemphasized. Turn and face the audience so that everyone will hear what you are saying.
2. Keep the boardwork neat. A chalkboard that becomes messier and messier as you speak negatively reflects on what you are saying.
3. Consider how you will use the chalkboard prior to your presentation and plan your boardwork.
4. Draw any large or complicated diagrams on the board in advance of your presentation, and reveal them only when you are going to use them.
5. Organize your chalkboard well. It should be easy for the audience to refer to the board at any time.
6. Make certain everyone can see the board without straining. Yellow chalk is easier to see on either a black or green board.
7. If you are speaking in a room with windows, be aware of how light reflects off the chalkboard. Adjust blinds as required.
8. Print legibly with letter size about 5 cm (2") high.
9. Use the chalkboard to list key points during the presentation.
10. Learn to write on the chalkboard without squeaking the chalk.

You may want to use a *flip chart* in addition to or instead of the chalkboard. Prepare the flip chart illustrations in advance and move the equipment when required. Use a variety of colours in your illustrations to provide maximum effectiveness.

Many of the suggestions given for use of the chalkboard apply to flip charts.

The Overhead Projector

The overhead projector has many advantages which may make it your main choice of visual aid. You may prepare materials ahead of time and you can control how much time the audience spends looking at any given image. You may easily project charts, diagrams, and tables for the audience to view. You can also face the audience and maintain eye contact.

You may use prepared transparencies with the cover-up technique where part of the image remains unrevealed until it becomes relevant. You may develop a series of transparencies into an overlay sequence, superimposing one transparency upon another to build up the details of a complex diagram. Whether you decide to use prepared transparencies or to write directly on the acetate sheets or acetate roll attached to the machine, there are a number of ways to use the overhead well.

1. Always set the overhead up before your presentation and check out its operation carefully.
2. Learn how to load the roll cartridges and change the bulb.
3. Place the overhead 2 m (6' - 7') from the screen for best results.
4. Avoid direct light from windows.
5. Focus images to get a sharp picture.
6. Be sure your writing is large, clear, and legible. Use a large typeface when preparing printed overhead transparencies because regular typeface is difficult for some people to read.
7. Use a pen or pointer to identify particular points of the transparencies.
8. Don't leave the projector turned on any longer than is necessary.
9. Avoid making transparencies of pages from books that have cramped, hard to read parts.
10. Mount prepared transparencies in cardboard transparency frames for easy handling.
11. Number your transparencies to avoid confusion.
12. Check the placement of your transparencies by a quick look at the screen.

Projection of Microcomputer Images

The *electronic transparency* combines the technology of the personal computer with that of the conventional overhead projector. You can create screen images in advance on your personal computer, save the digitized screen images on diskette, and later project them on a large screen.

To project microcomputer images you need an ordinary transmissive overhead projector, an intermediate system made up of a liquid crystal display (LCD) and a projection pad, and a compatible personal computer. Other components include a hand-held wireless remote control device for specialized functions and operating software.

The advantages of such a visual aid are numerous. You can present selected images in a predetermined order or you can quickly access and project other images. Split screen capability enables you to show images side-by-side making it easy for the audience to compare information. You can also modify images while the presentation is in progress by using the computer keyboard; for example, you can add to or delete from text, update a spreadsheet, revise a chart, or alter a diagram.

Slides

With the use and availability of the 35 mm camera, the projected slide has become a very effective and valuable visual aid. By using a single slide projector, you can bring to your audience a multitude of images to enrich your presentation. It is important that the slides be in the correct sequence and that you have keyed your notes to that sequence. It is also important that you begin and end your presentation with the lights on in order to develop audience rapport before and after introducing the slides. You may communicate a great deal of detail and emphasis through a slide presentation. You have control because you may advance the slides at will. You must plan carefully for this visual aid:

1. Project the slides right side up and in the correct order. Nothing disrupts a presentation any more than badly projected slides.
2. Number your slides ahead of time.
3. If you are using printed material on a slide, be certain that the print on the slide is legible.
4. Don't attempt to include too much print on any one slide.
5. Develop a good projection time. Pacing is extremely important to the effective use of slides as a visual aid.

A combination of slides and audiotape made into a slide-tape presentation can also be a powerful and versatile visual aid. Pictures for the slides are accessible from books, magazines, and other printed material. You can easily record narration, sound effects, music, and your own voice and use them on the sound track. A slide-tape presentation is particularly useful to open or conclude a talk.

Video and Film

The availability of video equipment and video cassette has helped make video and film popular visual aids. You will want to choose your video tapes carefully, selecting only those portions most relevant to your presentation. It is important to remember that video does not display well before large groups because of the limited size of the monitor screen. Assuming that the room size is suitable to your audience's viewing needs, you should keep the following things in mind when using video and film as visual aids:

1. Always preview any video tape or film before showing it to an audience. There are many sad tales of public speakers who have chosen video tape or film by its title, shown it before an audience, and had a catastrophe. A careful preview will allow you to choose and time the portions you wish to use in your presentation.
2. Prepare the audience for what they will see. The audience should have a clear understanding of your reasons for showing the videotape or film.
3. Make sure you are familiar with the equipment. Set up properly before you begin.
4. Know the location of the light switches and at the appropriate time, ask someone to turn off the lights. It is important that the room be suitable for viewing and that the audience can easily see the projected image.

Other Visual Aids

Speakers often use *objects* as visuals. They have an advantage in that members of the audience can examine and handle the objects, allowing them to relate to shapes and sizes better than any other visual aid.

The *cutaway model* is useful for showing internal parts and their locations. *Actual working models* allow the audience to see the movement of parts in a system. If you are going to use an object, be sure that it is large enough for your entire audience to see; otherwise, you might be better off with an enlarged photograph.

Speakers may also effectively use *graphs, enlarged photographs, charts, maps*, and *diagrams* as visual aids. They must be large enough for all those present to understand easily.

Hints on Preparing and Using Visual Aids

1. A visual aid should be **large enough for the audience to see** clearly.
2. A visual aid should be **easy to interpret and understand.** Your audience should quickly understand the point you are attempting to illustrate.
3. A visual aid should be **professional in appearance.** It should be colourful and neat.
4. Display your visual aid only when it is **relevant**. A sheet or diagram can distract your audience and divert attention away from you.
5. Always **rehearse** with your visual aid prior to your presentation. Familiarize yourself with any equipment you intend to use.
6. Work at **maintaining eye contact** with the audience as you use your visual aid. Face the audience and be sure not to obscure your face or voice with a visual aid.

ACTIVITIES

1. Prepare and deliver a ten-minute speech on a topic of your choice. You must prepare note-cards and appropriate visual aids.

CHAPTER 15 USING THE TELEPHONE

No matter what your position in a company, you will be required to use the telephone. Businesses depend on the telephone to expedite decision-making, to save time, and to increase efficiency in company operations. It is important to remember that the manner in which you receive and make calls will reflect not only on you, but on the entire company. The tone and inflection of your voice, the promptness with which you return or answer messages, and the listening skills you exhibit all do much to encourage or discourage business.

Telephone communication does have its drawbacks. Although you can respond to the verbal and non-verbal messages of the voice you hear, you are denied face-to-face contact. Remember that just as you are forming impressions of the person on the other end of the line, that person is forming impressions of you based on your voice. It is sometimes amusing to compare your image of a telephone caller, based on voice, with the physical reality of the same person.

Because the telephone is so vital, you must develop excellent skills in its use. In this chapter, we will look at a three-step approach to handling telephone calls as well as at some telephone procedures and techniques which will help you.

Just as you have used three steps in business writing and speaking, so you may use three steps in dealing with telephone communication.

Step One: **Making a Call**
Step Two: **During the Call**
Step Three: **Following Up**

Step One: Making a Call

Before making a telephone call, you should think carefully about the need for the call and what you hope to achieve by it. Gather any information you may require: files, area codes, and telephone numbers. If the call is likely to be complicated, outline the points you intend to make or ask about. Ensure that you have a pen and paper handy before you make your call.

Step Two: During the Call

When placing your telephone call, be patient; let the telephone ring six to ten times. You will begin your conversation by politely asking for the person you wish to speak to, e.g. "Good morning, Mrs. Galbraith please." If the person you are calling is unavailable, don't sound annoyed, leave a clear message and a time when you will be available to receive the return call. If the person you are calling is available, identify yourself when the person answers the phone, e.g. "Good morning, this is Mr. X of ABC Company calling."

You may continue your conversation by asking if this is a convenient time for your call, particularly if you will need more than a few minutes. You should then state the purpose of your call and get to the heart of the conversation. It is important that you take notes throughout. Do not rely on your memory.

If you have to leave the telephone to obtain information, explain this to the other party and ask if he or she wishes to wait or have you call back. If the party decides to wait, excuse yourself and get the information as quickly as possible.

Since you have made the call, it will be up to you to end it. You will not want to stay on the telephone any longer than is necessary after your business is complete. End your conversation politely, e.g. "Thank you for your assistance/help." Wait for the other party to finish speaking, then hang up *gently*.

Step Three: Following up

When you have completed your call, re-read your notes and add any missing information. If you need to write a letter confirming the conversation and the decisions made, undertake this task immediately. Similarly, if you need to do any follow-up work, begin it at once.

If you made a telephone call on behalf of someone else in your office, you must report back to that person, *especially if you were unable to complete the call.*

Telephone Procedures

Many businesses have standard procedures for making or receiving calls. There are some general rules of thumb concerning telephone etiquette which will be useful to you in any business situation.

1. **ANSWER YOUR PHONE PROMPTLY.** People do not like to be kept waiting. Answer your phone on the first or second ring. If you have to put a call on hold, make an effort to speak briefly with the caller before doing so, e.g. "Good morning, XYZ Company, just one moment please" or "Good morning, XYZ Company, would you hold please? Never sound rushed or impatient. If you are answering the telephone frequently, avoid developing a mechanical or sing-song voice.

2. **IDENTIFY YOURSELF IMMEDIATELY.** If you are answering the switchboard, you will state the name of the company, e.g. "Good morning, XYZ Company, may I help you?" Most companies have very clear guidelines regarding the way in which you should answer their switchboard. If a call has come through the switchboard, however, you should answer with your name, e.g. "Good morning, Ms. A. speaking" or "Computer Centre, Ms. A. speaking." Never say "hello" or remain silent. If you are answering another person's telephone, identify yourself and the person whose telephone you are answering, e.g. "Good morning, Ms. B's line, Mr. C. Speaking."

3. **BE POLITE.** Use the words *Please* and *Thank You.* However annoying or obnoxious a caller is, you must always be calm and polite. Refrain from interrupting the caller.

4. **SPEAK CLEARLY.** Speak distinctly and directly into the telephone receiver with your lips about 1.25 cm (1") from the mouthpiece. If you hold the receiver under your chin or too far away from your mouth, your voice will be indistinct. Ensure that the volume of your voice is moderate and that the pitch is low. Pronounce your words clearly.

5. **MAINTAIN A POSITIVE ATTITUDE.** Smile as you speak on the telephone. Sound lively, alert, and interested in the caller. If your voice is monotone, harsh or frantic, the listener will gain the impression you are indifferent or incompetent. Make your caller feel comfortable throughout the conversation by using cues such as "I see," and "Yes."

6. **HANDLE CALLS QUICKLY AND EFFICIENTLY.** It is important to listen closely and to assess the purpose of the call. Endeavour to act as quickly as you can in order to satisfy the request of the caller.

Here are some suggested procedures, when the called person is unavailable:

Situation	Answer
Does not wish to be disturbed	Mrs. A. is not available this morning. May she call you this afternoon?
At a meeting until 11:00 a.m.	Ms. A. is at a meeting until approximately 11:00 a.m. May I take a message?
On another line	Mr. A. is on another line at the moment. Would you care to wait or may I have him call you back?
With a client	Mrs. A. has someone with her just now. May she return your call later?
Away from desk (washroom)	Miss A. is not available just now. May I take a message?
Having coffee	Ms. A. is out for 15 minutes. May I take a message?
Out at lunch	Mr. A. is out of the office until 2:00 p.m. May I take a message?
Out of town	Mrs. A. is away from the office until May 3. Could someone else help you or do you wish to leave a message?
Sick	Mr. A. is away from the office today. Could someone else help you or would you like him to call you when he returns?

7. TAKE ACCURATE MESSAGES. You must be a competent message taker. Most businesses have a standard message form such as the one below which will help you to record the appropriate information.

Figure 15.1 Telephone Message Form
(Reprinted by permission of and copyright by 3M Canada Inc.)

Scotch 7660 "Post-it" Telephone Message Pad

To DA

Date 19-- 08/02 Time 9 30 am

WHILE YOU WERE OUT

MR YVAN LINDT

of LINDT, SIGGIA + CO.

Phone No. (819) 291-4484

TELEPHONED	✓	PLEASE CALL	✓
WAS IN TO SEE YOU		WILL CALL BACK	
WANTS TO SEE YOU		URGENT	✓
RETURNED YOUR CALL			

Message Wants to discuss German acquisition

Operator SM

You should repeat the message to the caller to ensure that you have noted all the details correctly. Leave message forms in a predetermined place for pick-up by office personnel. Do not leave message forms on desktops where they may get lost.

8. TRANSFER CALLS EFFICIENTLY. You will sometimes have to transfer calls. There are many different switchboard systems and the transfer procedures vary; therefore, you must learn how the transferring system works in your office. There is nothing more frustrating to a caller than to be cut off or to hear loud transfer beeps. When transferring a call, tell the caller what you are doing, e.g. "Just one moment, Mr. X, I will transfer your call to Mr. A. who will help you." If you place a caller on hold, go back to the caller frequently and give him or her the option of continuing to hold, e.g. "Mr. A's line is still busy, would you care to continue to hold or would you like me to take a message?" Do not place long distance callers on hold for any extended period of time.

9. SCREEN CALLS POLITELY. Sometimes you will have to screen incomings calls for your supervisor. You must know what your company's procedures are and follow them. A standard procedure is to say, "I'll see if Ms. A. is available. May I have your name please?

10. END CALLS POSITIVELY. Let the caller know what you intend to do about the call and thank him or her for dealing with your company. End the conversation on a positive note, e.g. "I'll courier the Swiss contract to you today. Thank you for calling, Mr. J. Goodbye." Let the caller hang up first.

Voice Messaging Systems

Voice messaging systems are very common today, both in and out of the workplace. Sometimes it is difficult to talk to a machine, particularly if you don't say exactly what you mean and have to re-phrase your message. It is important to be succinct and to make sure that you have left a message that can be returned or acted upon. Always indicate the *date* and the *time* of your call as well as your *name, phone number*, and *message*.

Teleconferencing

Teleconferencing is a method of conducting a meeting using the telephone. Instead of business people gathering at one central location, the meeting can come to them via the telephone. At a predesignated time each meeting participant telephones into a *bridge* and is linked into the conference call. The meeting progresses in the normal manner, with a chairperson in control and the proceedings being tape recorded. Participants discuss problems and policies as if they were in the same room. If you are participating in such a conference, remember to identify yourself *each* time you speak because there is no visual contact.

CHAPTER 16 MASTERING DICTATION

Dictation is a valuable skill to have in today's business world. Technological improvements in recorders and tape machines now make it possible for busy managers and executives to dictate letters, reports, memos, and other data practically anywhere outside the office. Whether you work for yourself, a small company, or a large multinational firm, mastering the art of dictation can increase your productivity and save you time.

You can adapt the three steps for effective business writing to help you dictate your messages. Your first step is to plan your message and gather any data you may need. The second step involves the actual dictation. Finally, you will need to revise, edit, and proofread the finished copy of your material.

Step One: Preparing

1. Know how to use your equipment. Although this step may seem obvious, too many people overlook it. Learn the features and conveniences of your dictating machinery.

2. Arrange a comfortable and quiet work area. If you are dictating while you are travelling, you should try to find a room or area where there is a minimum of background noise. You want your recorded voice to be clear and distinct. If you dictate at home, you should do it away from distractions such as television, stereos, cassette players, video games, and the like. The transcriber must be able to hear every word.

3. Collect reference materials before you dictate your message. References could include notes from meetings, previous correspondence, price lists, or sales figures. Arrange them in the order you will need them. You don't want to spend valuable time searching for information once you have started to dictate your message.

4. **Develop an outline** before you start. The outline, as in the case of written work, gives you a structure to help you develop your letter, report, or memo. It will help you keep your *purpose, audience*, and *subject* in focus.

5. **Practise dictating** before you begin to dictate the messages for transcription. Beginners often collect their material, write their outline, turn on the machine, and freeze. Microphone fright is common when people first use dictating machines. Practise by reading material into the microphone. After you write out a short message and dictate it, either have someone transcribe the message or transcribe it yourself. Don't worry about doing the job perfectly. You will soon be able to relax and focus on what you are saying rather than how you are saying it.

Step Two: Dictating

The art of dictating is the ability to state verbally what you want to appear as final keyboarded copy. You will need to verbalize paragraph breaks, punctuation, underlining, capital letters, spacing, reference lines, and the spelling of all proper names, products, and any unfamiliar terms.

Your instructions to the transcriber at the beginning of the dictation should begin with the person's name, if you know it, or with the title "operator." By using the person's name or title, you are warning him or her not to keyboard your instructions. Other guidelines for effective dictation include:

1. **Identify yourself** by stating your name, department, and any other information to let the transcriptionist know who is dictating the message. Leave a phone number where you can be reached should the transcriber have any questions.

2. **Describe the material** you are dictating, whether is it a letter, memo, or report. Estimate its approximate length and whether it is to be a rough draft or final copy. Include any special instructions such as the format, number of copies, distribution, mailing instructions, stationery, and priority of each message.

3. **Speak distinctly and slowly.** Enunciate each word, especially its ending. Keep the volume of your voice even, maintaining a uniform distance from the microphone. It is frustrating for the transcriber to hear your voice rise and fall, obscuring the message.

4. Avoid distracting personal mannerisms. As you dictate do not drum your fingers on the desk, jingle keys or loose change in your pockets, or tap objects with a pencil or pen. The microphone will pick up these sounds which may distort or cover your words.

5. Give adequate instructions as you dictate the message.

- Indicate any special formatting such as use of bullets, underlining, spacing, indentations, and the like.
- Spell words that are likely to be a problem — foreign words and names, cities, technical terms, words that sound alike (cite, sight, site), and all proper names. Distinguish sound-alike letters by such phrases as "B as in boy" or "F as in Frank," and so on.
- Indicate capital letters before you say the word you want capitalized (Example, "...send the invoice to the capital S sales capital D department...").
- State how you want numbers keyboarded ("...the sales totalled dollar sign one zero, zero, zero..." or "...we have about one thousand orders for January. Operator, spell out figure...").
- Signal paragraph breaks by saying "Paragraph" before dictating the text.
- Dictate all punctuation. Indicate opening and closing dashes, brackets, quotation marks, and parentheses.
- Indicate how you want measures, weights, and other technical or scientific notations keyboarded ("...two five centimetres..." or "...two five space cm...").
- Indicate which complimentary close you will use, unless your company has a standard closing for letters.
- Dictate any enclosures, copies, and other material that may follow the signature.
- Indicate when you have finished a message and when you have dictated the last message of the tape. A typical conclusion would be "End of letter, end of tape."

6. Stop when you have said what you have to say. While this step might seem self-evident, one of the hazards of dictation is that you always have one more thing to add. Before you realize it, you have wandered far from your outline. Warning signs of this tendency are repeating points you have already made, including less important points or using clichés and empty phrases that pad your message. With practise, you will know when you have finished the message.

Step Three: Revising

When you see the transcribed message, you will be able to correct any errors or make any needed changes. You may find that three sentences in a row start with the word *I*; that you should place information from the first paragraph in the second; or that you must revise paragraph breaks.

Often discovering how carelessly they speak surprises people who are beginners at dictation. We cannot transcribe our conversational English directly into written English — spoken words usually contain too many sentence fragments, half-finished thoughts, and grammatical errors. Dictation, in fact, frequently has the effect of forcing people to pay more attention to the quality of their verbal communication.

As you become more skilled in dictation, you will begin to correct your errors as you speak. Study the sample dictation and keyboarded version below. Notice that the speaker indicates how the operator should transcribe every item in the letter:

> "Operator, keyboard this letter in semi-block style on letterhead stationery.
>
> The letter is one page long. Date it 19— 01 06. Send it by certified mail. The inside address is:
>
> First line. Mr. Francis (F as in Frank r-a-n-c-i-s) Inglewood (that's I-n-g-l-e-w-o-o-d). Next line. Four six seven Crain (C-r-a-i-n) Street. Next line. Chicago comma Illinois six oh six one one hyphen two one four eight. Next line. U period S Period A Period. Salutation. Dear Mr. Inglewood. Colon. Paragraph. I am enclosing a copy of the survey maps you requested in your October three-oh letter. Period. You will find that the maps numbered one through twenty-two (Operator, keyboard the numbers one and twenty-two as figures.) cover Markham (M-a-r-k-h-a-m) and Don Mills (D-o-n space M-i-l-l-s). Period. Paragraph. I am also including a copy of the government pamphlet quote marks initial capitals Choosing the Best Site for Your Small Business. Period. End quote marks. I believe comma as you will see in the pamphlet comma that this publication offers valuable tips on selecting a prime location for your firm. Period. Paragraph. I hope you will find this information helpful. Period. Call me if you need further assistance. Period. Sincerely

yours comma Frank Ritter. Place the word Enclosures after the reference initials. End of letter."

Do not assume that the transcriptionist will automatically understand how you want an item spelled or keyboarded. Take the time to give clear, explicit instructions. Again, this process will become more automatic as you acquire skill in dictation.

Here is the transcribed version of the dictated letter.

SLOVAK, SYMES & DELOITTE

800 Denison Street, Unit 2 — Telephone: (416) 657-7654
Markham, Ontario L3R 5M9 — Fax No. (416) 657-7655

19-- 01 06

CERTIFIED MAIL

Mr. Francis Inglewood
467 Crain Street
Chicago, Illinois 60611-2148
U.S.A.

Dear Mr. Inglewood:

I am enclosing a copy of the survey maps you requested in your October 30 letter. You will find that the maps numbered 1 through 22 cover Markham and Don Mills.

The government pamphlet "Choosing the Best Site for your Small Business," also enclosed, offers valuable tips in selecting a prime location for your firm.

I hope you will find this information helpful. Call me if you need further assistance.

Sincerely yours,

Frank Ritter

FR/--
Enclosures

After you have edited your message, proofread the final copy for errors that may have slipped through.

Voice-Activated Computer Dictation Systems

It is now possible for individuals, such as doctors, to dictate material directly into a computer.

The system is based on advanced voice recognition technology which receives spoken words through a microphone and displays them on a computer screen. The dictator can correct and edit material by using the computer keyboard and can obtain a printed copy with a verbal command.

ACTIVITIES

1. Dictate a letter from this book to a classmate. Have your classmate dictate a letter to you. Prepare the finished copy. Compare your results with the original.

SECTION

5

THE JOB SEARCH

CHAPTER 17 RÉSUMÉS, APPLICATIONS, AND EMPLOYMENT LETTERS

Your first job search usually follows completion of your formal education. By that time you have identified some of your interests, skills and abilities, and you are looking for a position to match these qualities. The time has past when the job search simply involved visiting employer's offices, completing an application, and interviewing for the position. Today, you must be much more resourceful and develop a personal job search strategy which will maximize your opportunities for employment. Searching for work can be a full-time job in itself. To ensure your success, you should approach and treat it as an important task.

As you gain experience in the working world, the nature of your job search is likely to change. You may decided to switch career fields or to look for a position that offers greater opportunities for growth and advancement. You may want a job that has less security and more risk. Your company may move to another location, and you decide to remain where you are. There are many reasons you may find yourself job hunting several times during your working life.

As a result, you should know how to write employment-related letters; put together a résumé summarizing your work history, experience, and skills; and complete a variety of job applications. Since the purpose of any letter of application and résumé is to obtain an interview, it is up to you to sell yourself. You can use a similar three-step approach as you did for your business writing and speaking:

Step One: Prewriting — Identifying your abilities, interests, and skills; researching job sources

Step Two: Writing — Preparing résumés and application letters

Step Three: Revising — Editing, proofreading, final keyboarding and printing of résumés and application letters.

Step One: Prewriting

Identifying Your Abilities, Interests, and Skills

The job search process has its preparation and research stages. At the outset, you must have a sound understanding of your qualifications as well as a good sense of your employment needs. It is worthwhile to consider such important factors as the kind of work you want to do, where you want to live, and how much money you would like to make. It is useful to determine which of these factors is most important to you. To find out about a particular job, you might want to spend some time with a person who has that job. A clear understanding of your own goals and abilities will help you as you enter the employment market.

How do you identify your skills and abilities? Some will be obvious, such as skills in electronics, computers, mathematics, writing, and professional skills gained through education in medical, legal, business, and other fields.

You will acquire other skills as you work. Some abilities, however, are not easy to recognize. A woman, for example, who has spent most of her working years raising a family may feel she has no marketable skills. Through the years of child-rearing, however, she has had to be an organizer, manager, budget-keeper, and volunteer worker. With additional training, these skills translate well into the contemporary employment market.

On the other hand, you may need to think back to your childhood to recall what gave you the most pleasure. Perhaps you liked sports, crafts, exploration, solving problems or puzzles, building with your hands, working with machines, raising animals. All these activities contain clues to skills you have developed and may not recognize. In one instance, a man who had organized neighbourhood clubs as a child found a satisfying career directing fundraising efforts for national charities.

Various vocational assessment and skills tests are available to help you identify your skills and abilities. Local colleges and universities or Canada Employment centres can help you find where you may take such tests and their costs. The investment could net you a new career and more satisfying work life. In addition, many books on the market describe how to organize your skills and abilities and to discover those still unknown to you. Take the time to know yourself better. It can be one of the most valuable steps you take in your career.

Researching Job Sources

Once you have assessed your qualifications and determined which jobs you would like to have, you need to locate the right position. Don't ever under-estimate the importance of your friends and associates in giving you leads. In this regard, it is a very good idea to develop a job search system in which you record the names and phone numbers of any contacts suggested to you or that you uncover in researching the job market. There are a number of employment sources that can help you find job openings that match your qualifications. Some will be more appropriate than others at different times in your life, but you should be aware of all the sources available.

1. Personal Referrals and Recommendations. Of all the ways that people find new jobs, personal referrals or recommendations are by far the most common and effective. One employment expert estimated that over 80 per cent of the jobs people hold they obtained through someone else's personal recommendation. When you let people know you are job hunting, you activate your network. Others will pass on information about job openings.

2. Your Own Research. Because you will be actively looking for work, you should make a list of all the companies, businesses, agencies, and so on that you think might have the job you want. Make an effort to obtain the name of the individual who could hire you and include an approach to these individuals in your job search.

3. School Placement Offices. If you are still in school or have recently graduated, the school placement office is a good place to start your search. If your school has a good reputation for providing occupational training and support for graduates, you may have a choice of a wide range of job opportunities. Your teachers may also be able to supply additional leads or have direct contacts with companies looking for qualified graduates.

4. Employment Agencies. Canada Employment and private employment agencies also help to match job applicants with job openings. You may register free of charge at any Canada Employment office where a counsellor will likely interview you. Private employment agencies place only about 4% of new job seekers and thus are not particularly effective.

5. Professional Groups and Associations. Some of the other sources of employment mentioned here are part of the numbers game in which applicants simply comb through job listings and eliminate the unsuitable ones. As you build experience and get to know others in your field, you will build a network of contacts you can use to locate new positions. Professional groups and associations are excellent sources of job leads since you share in the same profession and know the field, the employers, and job opportunities well. Joining professional groups at the outset of your career can help you move up in your profession.

6. Civil Service and Institutional Offices. Job openings in the civil service at the federal, provincial, and municipal levels are also excellent employment opportunities. Various levels of government regularly publish notices of positions available. If such a career interests you, contact your local government employment offices for information and applications.

In addition, hospitals, school districts, colleges, universities, and other institutions have business offices that employ clerks, keyboard operators, office assistants, secretaries, managers, administrators, and data analysts. If you would like to work outside the traditional business fields, you might like to consider one of these institutions.

7. Individual Companies. Many companies do not actively recruit candidates through the usual channels of classified ads or employment agencies. Applicants apply directly to the personnel office of the company and inquire about job openings. Even if there is no immediate job opportunity the company will place your résumé on file for future reference.

A better way to deal with the company which has no immediate openings is to talk with someone who might be hiring at a later date. Not only will you make a contact which may prove valuable, but you will also have a chance to find out a bit more about the company and its operations. If you do decide to leave a résumé, follow up with a phone call after a reasonable time lapse. Do not let your résumé be simply filed away never again to be looked at.

In larger companies, the turnover rate is sometimes high, and the personnel office is constantly recruiting and hiring new employees. If you contact these firms directly, you may find your call coinciding with an opening in the company. At the least, you have contacted the firm and made your qualifications and interests known.

Step Two: Writing

Preparing Résumés

When you have completed your preparation and background research steps, you are ready to write your résumé. You have identified your qualifications and the jobs best suited to them. A résumé, your covering letter, and your interview can help sell employers on your skills and abilities.

A résumé is a written summary of your qualifications, experience, and education. It usually includes your career objective, employment record, and a summary of your formal education. It can also include references, special interests and activities in which you may participate, and information such as professional memberships, awards, publications, and other items that will highlight your abilities. The key to the successful résumé is careful selection of the information you plan to include.

Because your résumé is a sales piece, you must prepare it as carefully as any sales letter. It must represent you to an employer in the best possible light. Like a sales letter, you may tailor a résumé to the needs of various employers; for example, you may have two or three résumés on hand, each one emphasizing a different aspect of your abilities. You may have one that highlights your writing skills, another that summarizes your management abilities and experience, and still another that emphasizes your work as an information analyst. Research the companies which interest you and tailor your résumé to their job openings. The more exactly you fit the requirements of the job, the more likely you are to secure it.

The physical appearance of your résumé is important. As a sales piece, it should attract the eye of a busy employer. Keyboard the résumé, using desktop publishing software if possible or, if you have the time and money, have a professional printer typeset it. As a rule, try to keep all information to one or two pages. As you gather experience and further your education, you may wish to use two or three pages: one or two for the basic information summarizing your qualifications and work history, and another to list publications, achievements, awards, and other such information.

You should print or photocopy your résumé on good bond paper. If you are applying for a job in a bank, insurance company, or other conservative institution, use a white or off-white bond and a conservative format. If a more creative organization interests you, such as an advertising agency or graphic arts company, you may want to be more innovative and use tinted paper and a more experimental format. Only use such an approach if you are confident that the company will receive it positively.

In preparing your résumé, here are the important things to remember:

1. Avoid any mention of membership in a specific religious or political organization. Since your résumé may go before you to an employer, you must not include information which might bias an employer before you have secured an interview.

2. Don't include a photograph, unless a company asks you to do so.

3. Attempt to stress your accomplishments in terms which will show the employer that you are responsible, dependable, and able to work independently or cooperatively with others.

4. Don't mention money. The discussion of your salary can wait until the job interview.

5. Ensure your résumé is accurate and concise. Since many résumé readers base their judgments on a quick look, be sure that the résumé is easy to read and to the point. Make sure there are no spelling, punctuation, or language errors.

Your résumé will act for you in your absence. It is imperative, therefore, that you take great pains to create the very best impression. Spare no effort in making sure that the résumé not only looks professional but also conveys both your personality and background in the best possible way.

Formatting Résumés

There are no fixed rules for résumé format and layout, but you must plan your résumé in such a way that it will be clear, concise, and readable. There are two basic types of résumés: the *chronological* and the *functional*. The following pages include examples of each. Where the chronological résumé lists the jobs and responsibilities you have held, usually following a sequence of dates, the functional résumé focuses on your accomplishments and the skills you have acquired in your work life. The functional résumé is particularly useful when you wish to change career fields because you can show how your skills and qualifications can be transferred from one field to another.

In both résumés, your name, address, and telephone number appear at the top of the page and may be centered or flush left or right. It is unnecessary to list your age, marital status, state of health, birthdate, height, or weight.

The *chronological* résumé usually contains the following headings:

1. Position Sought or Career Objective. At a glance the employer can see the position you would like and the job opportunities for which you are looking. If possible, use the specific title or competition number of the job for which you are applying.

2. Experience. This section is more than simply a list of places you have worked. It can serve as a summary of your responsibilities and indicate to a prospective employer the skills and experience you have gained through your work life. Be sure to use strong action verbs such as implemented, initiated, organized.

For each job you have held, list your title, the name and address of the company, dates of employment, and a brief summary of your work responsibilities and skills. List your last job first and work back to your first job. If you have held many jobs, group them together and highlight your main duties.

Be sure you account for any obvious gaps in your work history; for example, you may have returned to school, stayed home to care for small children, travelled overseas, or undergone medical treatment.

3. Education. For recent graduates from high school, college, or university who have limited or no job experience, the education section of the résumé will be the most important and should appear before experience. Here you can include specific details about your education and training that qualify you for the job.

List special interests and skills, making sure you include awards, honours, scholarships, and other recognition you have received. Membership or offices held in campus groups, team sports, and outside activities can demonstrate leadership, imagination, and management potential. Even though your outside activities may not relate directly to the position, they will interest employers. Use this information to show the range and depth of your abilities.

4. References. In some cases you will list the names of people your prospective employer can contact for more detailed information about you. Make sure you obtain permission from references before listing them on your résumé. In general, you need only three or four names, but you should have backup references who can attest to your experience, work record, education, and character.

If possible, tailor your references to the job for which you are applying. If an assistant editor's job interests you, a reference from a writing or journalism instructor would be more appropriate than one from your minister. Tell your references the position you are seeking so they will know which of your capabilities to emphasize when an employer calls. The reference list should include the following information:

(a) The full name and appropriate title of each person.
(b) The name and address of the company or institution.
(c) A work or home telephone number.

A final word about references: obviously, it is in your best interests to ask only those individuals for references who will speak glowingly of you and your abilities. If you are in any doubt about what the person might say of you, be sure you ask. If you have lost a job or have left it under less than desirable circumstances, it is worth your while to find out exactly what this employer will say about you if asked. If you know in advance of the job interview that you may receive an unfavourable reference, you can deal with it on your own terms at the time of the interview.

CAMERON W. HERYET

2976 Chicory Place
Burnaby, B.C. V5A 3X5
Tel: (604) 420-1941

CAREER OBJECTIVE:

To enter the field of multi-image production, with a keen focus on photography and production.

EXPERIENCE:

Presently involved as a freelance photographer, with an emphasis on sports and audio-visual photography.

Date:	May 19— to August 19—
Location:	Founders Centre, 1701 Hollis Street, Halifax, Nova Scotia. B3J 2N7. Telephone: (902) 418-4309 Executive Director: Clodagh Canavan
Position:	A/V Producer
Project:	Produced a single tray slide/tape show that described the many functions of the Centre; presently being used for fund raising and public relations campaigns.
Duties	Scripting, interviewing, photography, audio recording and mixing, programming, staging, packaging.
Reasons for Leaving:	Returned to second year of the Media Resources Program at Capilano College.

2.

Date:	May 19– to July 19–
Location:	Welland Glass, 11 Helen Avenue, Kitchener, Ontario. N2G 3W6. Telephone: (519) 850-1138 Manager: Nigel Vener
Position:	Journeyman glazier and auto glass mechanic
Duties:	Installations, counter representative, estimates.
Reasons for Leaving:	Accepted a position in Media Resources Program at Capilano College to pursue interest in media production.

EDUCATION:

September 19– to April 19–
Capilano College, 2055 Purcell Way, North Vancouver, B.C. V7J 3H5.
Telephone: (604) 986-1911

Graduated from the two-year Media Resources Program.

Courses: Photography, multi-image/slide-tape production, film, animation, computer programming/graphics, scripting, storyboards, and interviewing. Acquired experience in the operation of related A/V equipment.

September 19– to May 19–
University of Victoria, Victoria, B.C.
Fine Arts Program – Music

September 19– to June 19–
Graduated from Oak Bay High School, Victoria, B.C.

3.

ADDITIONAL COURSES:

September 19– to June 19–
Camosun College, Victoria, B.C.

Completed the following non-credit courses: Photojournalism, Nature Photography, Darkroom Photography, Professional Film Making, BASIC Computer Programming, Introduction to Micro Computers, and Drafting.

ADDITIONAL SKILLS:

April 19–
St. John Ambulance, Victoria, B.C.

Industrial First Aid Ticket

AWARDS

Capilano College

Fall 19–, Spring 19–, and Fall 19–: Dean's List (awarded for maintaining a G.P.A. of over 3.50.

19–/19–: Tuition Fee Waiver Scholarship (awarded for achieving the highest G.P.A. in the Media Resources Program).

Fall, 19– and Spring 19–: Government of B.C. Scholarship.

The *functional* résumé may contain the following headings:

1. Position Sought or Career Objective. The career objective should be concise, specific, and unpretentious.

2. Experience. You may write this section in a short paragraph or two. Condense your employment history and summarize your qualifications.

3. Achievements or Areas of Accomplishments. List several accomplishments about which you are particularly confident. You may wish to include accomplishments which will illustrate your abilities in supervision, management, or public relations. You might express your ability to communicate well or to work productively with others. It is important to recognize your own strengths and make sure that the list of accomplishments reflects them.

4. Education. A summary paragraph or two will suffice. You must be sure to include highlights from your education or training that will underline your accomplishments.

5. Other Data. You may include any other relevant information here which has not appeared in the other categories.

CAMERON HERYET

2976 Chicory Place
Burnaby, B.C.
V5A 3X5
Tel: (604) 420-1941

CAREER OBJECTIVE:

To enter the field of multi-image production, with a keen focus on photography and production.

EXPERIENCE:

Actively involved as a **freelance photographer,** with an emphasis on sports and audio-visual photography.

Was employed as an **A/V Producer** for a non-profit organization. Responsible for producing all aspects of photography, scripting, audio, interviewing, and staging of a single projector slide/tape show presently being used for fund-raising and public relations campaigns.

Was previously employed as a journeyman glazier and auto glass mechanic. Duties included counter representative, estimates, and installations.

EDUCATION:

Graduated from the two-year Media Resources Program offered at Capilano College, and specialized in **photography and multi-image production** (please see attached production credits).

2.

In addition, completed the first year of a Bachelor of Music degree at the University of Victoria and the following non-credit courses at Camosun College:

Photojournalism
Nature Photography
Darkroom Photography
Professional Film Making
BASIC Computer Programming
Introduction to Micro Computers.

INTERESTS:

Photography, tennis, skiing, fitness.

REFERENCES:

Mrs. Clodagh Canavan, Executive Director, Founders Centre. Tel: (902) 418-4309.*

Mr. Nigel Vener, Manager, Welland Glass. Tel: (519) 850-1138.*

Ms. Jackie Koo, Program Director, Media Resources Program, Capilano College. Tel: (604) 986-1911, local 2134.

Mr. Klaus Friesen, Photographer/Instructor, Capilano College. Tel: (604) 986-1911, local 2131.

*Please see attached copy.

PRODUCTION CREDITS

HIGH ENERGY	A six projector multi-image production on professional athletes.
20/20 VISION	A three projector multi-image production highlighting Capilano College.
RIP CORD	A two projector slide/tape production about sky diving.
T.V. IN THE MAKING	A single tray slide/tape production about television production.
FOUNDERS CENTRE	A single tray slide/tape show describing the many services of this non-profit organization.
SUNSET GRILL	A thirty minute television variety show.
RAILWAYS	A short film depicting trains and railways.
BROOKS WETSUITS	A seven minute video describing the manufacturing process of wetsuits and drysuits.
A GENERIC FILM	A short film using a variety of animation techniques.
KEN KENNEDY	A photographic essay.
ALZHEIMER'S DISEASE	A fifteen minute audio documentary.

Preparing Employment Letters

You will use employment letters to apply for a job, request a reference or letter of recommendation, accept or refuse a position, acknowledge the help of others in your job search, and resign from a position you currently hold. Throughout your career you will need to write one or more of these letters. Knowing how to compose effective employment letters can help you compete successfully in the job search.

Employment letters include the following:

1. **Application/Covering Letters.** You have seen a position advertised, had a friend pass on a recommendation, or located a possible job opportunity yourself. A letter of application introduces you to the prospective employer and a résumé usually accompanies it.

2. **Reference/Recommendation Letters.** You are asking people who know you well and have knowledge of your skills and experience to act as a reference or write a letter of recommendation to a prospective employer.

3. **Thank-you Letters.** You are writing an interviewer a letter of thanks for the time given you. You can emphasize your qualifications for the job in this letter.

4. **Acceptance/Refusal Letters.** You are accepting or refusing a job offer.

5. **Appreciation Letters.** You are acknowledging the help each person gave you in your efforts to secure the job.

6. **Resignation Letters.** You want to leave your current position under the best circumstances possible.

This chapter covers the first two categories. Chapter 18 covers the last four categories of letters.

Preparing Application/Covering Letters

1. **Purpose.** The letter of application is likely the most important letter you will write in your business career. It is not meant to secure a job; rather, its main purpose is to catch the interest of a prospective employer and help you obtain an interview. Employers cull through

application letters to weed out candidates who are obviously unsuitable and to select the few they will pursue further. You will need to make your application, along with your résumé, stand out from the others.

Since your letter of application (covering letter) is the employer's first introduction to you, think carefully about how you would like to present yourself. What do you want the letter to say about your qualifications, work experience, and abilities? In addition to the content, the appearance of the letter is important and can do much to help create a favourable impression.

2. Appearance. The following guidelines can help you prepare an application or covering letter that will represent you in the best light.

- Use a good grade of 8½ x 11 inch paper (white or off-white bond). Do not use erasable bond paper. Even though it makes correcting mistakes easier, it also smudges easily and picks up ink from the platen of your typewriter. Make sure your paper is free from fingerprints and other marks.
- Balance your letters on the page.
- Make sure corrections are invisible. Use a ribbon that is new or relatively new so that letters appear sharp and clear. Avoid strikeovers, erasures, or squeezing words into too small a space. Though the steps may seem elementary, many applicants overlook them and prejudice their application at the outset.
- If you are using a word processor to prepare your letters, make sure you have a letter-quality printer or its equivalent. Dot matrix printers look too rough for high-quality letters. You want a polished, professional appearance for your application letter, not something that looks like a first draft.

3. Content. The application letter must capture the reader's attention and focus specifically on those qualifications which meet the needs of your prospective employer. The application letter is a sales letter, and you can judge its success by whether or not you get the interview. The *you* attitude is important: see the situation from the employer's point of view and write the letter with the attitude *I have this to offer you*. Often the application letter has three or four paragraphs which feature your most relevant qualifications. The letter must always be readable and free of any mistake that might suggest carelessness on your part.

Address the letter to a specific person. If you are answering a classified ad and have the name of the company, call to find out who will be receiving the letter. If you do not have the company name but only a box number, address the letter "Dear Sir or Madam:" It is always better to address a particular individual. It tells the reader that you took the time and initiative to research the job opening.

There are several ways of beginning. You may want to start your letter with a summary of your qualifications. This approach gives the reader an immediate appraisal of your abilities and training. If you have caught the reader's interest, you can be sure that they will read the rest of your letter.

> My four years as an editor with Copp Clark have given me well-rounded skills in editing, production, writing, and permissions. These skills should qualify me for the editor's position in your company.

> A ten-year record in sales as one of the top sellers in chemical products has given me the seasoning and skills to meet the challenge of Sales Director with your firm.

> My two years as a lab technician at the Regina General Hospital have provided me with the experience in medical and clinical pathology that your lab assistant position requires.

> Three years ago, I was fortunate enough to get introduced to video. I have just completed the Media Resources program at Red Deer College and feel that I now have the qualifications and interest to make me a productive employee at your television station.

If you learned of a vacancy through a friend, relative, employee of the organization, or other individual, it may be to your advantage to mention the person's name (after obtaining their permission) in the letter. You must remember, however, that there can be danger in this approach. You run the risk of mentioning the name of an individual the employer may not like and thus jeopardize your own chances.

> Mr. Nizar Villani, a former employee with your firm, told me that you needed an administrative assistant with excellent dictation and word processing skills. I have been an executive secretary for three years with Landrum, Kall and Watson, an advertising firm. I believe I have the qualifications you need.

> Ms. Lily Ng, the career counsellor at Hudson High School, told me that you are looking for a trainee to start in your shipping department. I have worked in a small manufacturing plant for three years,

and I am familiar with ordering and invoicing procedures.

You can use a creative approach to the opening, such as the following question and answer technique:

> Are you looking for someone who combines word processing skills with good telephone techniques? Can you use a person who is a self-starter and can organize routine office work? If your answer is yes, I can help you.
>
> Is there a place in your company for someone who enjoys a high-pressure working environment and can keep on top of client work? someone who can manage office staff and supervise the workload?
>
> Can you use a salesperson who has a knack not only for first time sales but also for capturing repeat business? someone who has been in sales since high school?

You must exercise extreme care when using these dramatic openings. Some companies do not like heavy sales pitches.

Once you have established the employer's needs and how your qualifications match them, you can support your case in the following paragraphs. Keep your letters brief and focused. Highlight aspects of your educational background and business experience that relate directly to the job you are seeking. If you have researched the company, you may want to mention why this particular firm interests you. Showing knowledge of the company's business and activities will generally impress the reader.

If you are applying for the information processing position mentioned above, for example, the second paragraph of your letter might look like this:

> I am experienced in several hardware systems and applications software programs, including Lotus 1-2-3, dBase III, PageMaker, QModem, WordStar, Microsoft Word, and WordPerfect. I have worked on IBM, TRS-80, and Apple systems.

If you were writing your letter in response to an advertisement for a telemarketing position, your second paragraph might state:

> My enclosed résumé presents my training and experience in telemarketing over the past six years. I have developed programs for firms whose budgets ranged from $50 000 to $3 million. I believe this experience has given me a solid background in telemarketing

techniques and will enable me to get results for your firm.

As in any sales letter, the concluding paragraph should tell the reader what action you want taken. In the application letter, you want the reader to give you a personal interview. Make your request easy to grant.

> I will be in Winnipeg June 9-12. May I talk with you about the job opening on one of those days? Please let me know a date and time convenient for you. My phone number is (208) 459-9244.
>
> I believe I can explain in just a few minutes why I am a likely candidate for your position. Can we arrange for an interview? You can reach me at 866-4311 after 6:00 p.m.

Remember that the purpose of the application letter *is not* to tell the whole story of your working career but to *convince* the employer to grant you an interview. The interview is the time to discuss your career skills and experience in more detail.

2976 Chicory Place
Burnaby, B.C.
V5A 3X5

May 1, 19--

Mrs. P.A. Lueck
Arctic Productions Ltd.
308 Main Street
Whitehorse, Yukon
Y1A 2B5

Dear Mrs. Lueck:

I have recently graduated from the Media Resources Program at Capilano College, and I feel that I have the skills and work habits necesssary to fulfill the position of Production Assistant.

My training at Capilano College has provided me with an excellent insight into multi-image production, and I have acquired skill in scripting, storyboarding, and sound. In addition, I have worked very hard expanding my knowledge of leisure-time programming, with particular attention to the AVL Genesis Language.

My work experience in media began last year when I produced a fifteen minute slide/tape show designed for use by public relations and fund raising campaigns. Since then I have been actively pursuing my interest in photography, shooting events varying from political rallies to professional sports.

Your reputation as an industry leader would provide me a great deal of opportunity and challenge. I feel I am well qualified for the position and enclose my résumé for your consideration. I would appreciate your granting me an interview. I can be reached by telephone at 420-1941.

Yours truly,

Cameron W. Heryet

CWH
Enc.

93 Morningside Avenue
Toronto
Ontario
M6S 1E4

19-- 03 04

Box 5320
The Globe and Mail
1250 Bay Street
Toronto, Ontario
T4W 3W3

Dear Sir

I believe my training and experience, as a driver of all types of heavy vehicles, including buses, qualify me for the position which you advertised in The Globe and Mail of February 15, 19--.

I have been driving buses and other types of heavy equipment for over twenty years and hold the Ontario Class 2 licence which you require. My experience includes the operation of my own trucking business in addition to working as a driver for other companies.

I also have an extensive background in the Canadian Armed Forces as a driver-mechanic, heavy equipment operator, and heavy equipment crew chief. During one posting in Europe I drove buses a great deal and supervised other personnel and their equipment. I have had considerable experience in supervisory positions and in dealing with the public.

I have included more specific details about my qualifications on the enclosed résumé.

In all my employment experience, I have worked with other people and have been expected to make decisions under pressure. I feel I could do your job well and would like to talk to you about it. May I have an interview? I can be reached at 856-8953 anytime after 5 p.m.

Sincerely

A. Glen Joe

AGJ
Enc.

Preparing Reference/Recommendation Letters

During your career, you will probably write two types of reference letters: letters requesting references from others and letters of recommendation for someone else.

1. Reference Request Letters. Employers need to have information regarding the character, work habits, training, and experience of their candidates. You can ask others to act as references for you and supply their names, addresses, and phone numbers to the prospective employer; or you can ask your references to write a letter of recommendation directly to the employer. You must always ask permission before listing anyone as a reference. A letter requesting such permission might look like the following:

> Dear Professor Martyniuk:
>
> I am applying for a position as a management trainee with A. M. Electric in Yellowknife.
>
> Since I received my training in both marketing and merchandising in your classes and completed my practicum at Daleys under your supervision, I would very much like to use your name as a reference.
>
> I look forward to hearing from you and I have enclosed a stamped, self-addressed envelope for your reply.
>
> Sincerely,

Notice that the writer:

1. Stated the position being applied for;
2. Gave reasons for wishing to use the professor as a reference; and
3. Enclosed a stamped self-addressed envelope for the professor's reply.

By telling your reference the position you are seeking and why you would like to use them as a reference, you help them know in advance what questions a prospective employer is likely to ask them.

At times, you may need to have a letter of recommendation sent directly to the employer.

```
Dear Professor Martyniuk:

I am applying for a position as a management trainee
with A. M. Electric in Yellowknife.

Since I received my training in marketing and mer-
chandising in your classes and completed my prac-
ticum at Daleys under your supervision, I feel you
are a good judge of my work habits and abilities.

Would you be willing to write a letter of recommen-
dation on my behalf to Ms. Agnes Louie, the
Personnel Supervisor at A. M. Electric? I've
enclosed a stamped envelope addressed to A. M.
Electric for your convenience.

Sincerely,
```

2. Recommendation Letters. At times you may be asked to write a letter of recommendation for a friend, former employee, or colleague. Your letter should include the following information:

1. How long you have known the person.
2. The nature of your relationship or acquaintance (boss, friend, colleague, teacher).
3. Your assessment of the person's qualifications, character, and work.

As you write the letter, keep in mind that the person who requested it may read it. This fact may tone down your frankness but may also increase your sensitivity about the information you are revealing.

You will reflect your enthusiasm about the candidate in the amount of detail you provide. You would give a few, generalized statements about someone you know slightly or about the work record of a person you observed but did not directly supervise. On the other hand, explicit detail in several paragraphs indicates that you believe the candidate has superior abilities, work habits, and skills. Employers appreciate knowing as much about candidates as possible, even about some of their weaknesses. An employer can then take steps to play up the strengths of the candidates and compensate for weaknesses.

The following letters are samples of an open recommendation, i.e. addressed "To Whom It May Concern," and a closed recommendation, addressed to a specific person or company.

February 28, 19--

TO WHOM IT MAY CONCERN:

<u>Mrs. Clara Baigent (nee Schmidt)</u>

Mrs. Baigent has been employed by us as an executive assistant (the last two and a half years for two Directors of our Investment Management Company) since July 29, 19--. She has submitted her notice to leave on June 30, 19--, because of a proposed move to Saskatchewan in a few months' time. This action on her part is an indication of her considerate and loyal attitude since she felt it fair to give us more time to seek a satisfactory replacement.

The quality of Mrs. Baigent's work has proved consistently excellent in every respect and we shall certainly miss her cheerful and efficient services.

Mrs. Baigent takes with her our sincere appreciation for her assistance and our good wishes for the future.

Sincerely,

BLUE CHIP INVESTMENT CO. LTD.

Marcella Wong
Personnel Officer

514/RB/W

February 28, 19--

PERSONAL AND CONFIDENTIAL

D. C. Kellough, Esq.
Messrs. Swinton, Davis & Kellough
Barristers and Solicitors
400 - 1975 Scarth Street
Regina, Saskatchewan
S4P 2H3

Dear Sir

<u>Mrs. Clara Baigent (nee Schmidt)</u>

Mrs. Baigent has been employed by us as an executive assistant to two Directors of our Investment Management Company since July 29, 19--.

The quality of Mrs. Baigent's work has been consistently excellent in every respect. Her organizational and time management techniques are top quality. She is hardworking, willing to try new equipment and procedures, and does not hesitate to help others in achieving deadlines.

Mrs. Baigent's educational background is solid as demonstrated by above-average written and oral communication skills. Her cheerful personality has earned us a reputation with our clients.

We have no hesitation in recommending Mrs. Baigent to fill your securities position as she has extensive knowledge in this area.

Yours truly

BLUE CHIP INVESTMENT CO. LTD.

Per:

Marcella Wong
Personnel Officer

514/RB/MW

Step Three: Revising

Because of the importance of résumés and employment letters, you should ensure that you:

1. **Edit and rewrite your drafts** for clarity, tone, accuracy, and brevity.

2. **Proofread your work carefully.** Concentrate on correct grammar and spelling. Ask a colleague to do a final proofreading of your work to make sure that you have not missed any errors. Remember that errors in either your résumé or application letter will result in your not being offered an interview.

3. **Produce a neat final copy** which is easy to read, consistently formatted, and free of erasures, strikeovers, and smudges.

The guidelines in this chapter for an effective job search strategy should help you seek and find employment.

ACTIVITIES

1. **In a small notebook, begin to compile a list of all possible employment contacts. Include the names and phone numbers of those individuals suggested to you by your instructors, family, and friends and the names and phone numbers of any companies, institutions, or businesses you may wish to investigate further.**

2. **Write a complete self-inventory. Include all your employment experiences, education, volunteer and club activities, awards, certificates (first aid, driver's licence, and so on), and other achievements.**

3. **Based on the self-inventory above, organize and write two résumés: one chronological, the other functional.**

4. **Prepare a covering letter to accompany one of the above résumés. Focus it on a job that you'd like an employer to offer you — one that you have seen advertised in the local newspaper. Attach the advertisement to your assignment.**

CHAPTER 18 THE JOB INTERVIEW

If all goes well, your letter and résumé have secured you an interview with a prospective employer. You are now one of a select group being considered for the job. It is, therefore, vital that you thoroughly prepare for the interview to give yourself the best possible chance of success. The three step approach will work well for you here:

Step One: **Researching and Preparing**
Step Two: **Interviewing**
Step Three: **Following Up**

Step One: Researching and Preparing

There are a number of important things you can do to prepare for the job interview. Once the date and time have been set, it is well worth your while to know exactly where you will go on the day of the interview. Take a drive or bus ride to the place of the interview. Note how long it takes. It goes without saying that you must be on time for your interview.

Another important advance step is to consider carefully what you will wear for the job interview. A general rule of thumb is that men wear a jacket and tie, women a skirt and blouse, a dress, or a suit. If you are applying for a job where you know that dress is casual, you should adapt your appearance. When in doubt, you should lean towards conservative dress.

Equally important is the research you do into the background of the employer interviewing you. One question that invariably comes up in every job interview is "Why do you want to work for us?" You must have a clear understanding of the work the company performs as well as a good grasp of the duties which it will require of you. Your answer to this question will keenly interest the interviewer. Evidence that you have done your homework will be very much to your advantage.

One very important area which you can expect to discuss in the interview is salary. You owe it to yourself to find out in advance what other individuals performing the same duties are receiving as salary. The interviewer may deal with the salary question in several ways. If the company places employees on a scale, the interviewer will likely produce the scale and show you what your qualifications and experience would entitle you to. Sometimes the interviewer will ask you what you want in the way of salary. Rather than answering the question with a specific figure, you are better off to reply that you would expect to receive the same amount as others with your qualifications. Let the interviewer put the figure forward. In your mind should be three figures: the one which you know is fair; the one which is far too low; and the one which is higher than you expected. If the offer is low, you must let the interviewer know that based on your research, you expect more money. The whole issue of salary is often difficult to discuss, but you must make your position clear. If you accept a job at a salary which is too low, it may be some time before you can negotiate a more satisfactory wage. Don't ever let an interviewer ask you what you need. *Need* is irrelevant. The salary you receive should be based on your worth and have nothing whatever to do with need.

To complete your research in advance of the interview, you may wish to talk to other people doing the same job for which you have applied. Such conversations will give you a clear idea of what to expect in terms of salary, hours, variety, and lines of authority.

There are a number of commonly asked questions in the job interview. By thinking about them in advance, you will be better ready for them.

1. Tell me about yourself. Both your answer to the question and how you react to it will interest the interviewer. You should make an effort to include only those things about you that directly relate to the job at hand. Be brief and to the point.

2. What do you see yourself doing in five years? The interviewer wants to know two things: do you have some career goals? do you intend to stay with this company?

3. What are your major strengths? You must be confident and tell the interviewer your strengths. Attempt to relate them to the job at hand.

4. What do you know about us? The interviewer wants to see evidence of your research into the company and its operations.

5. How did you happen to choose this field? The interviewer is hoping to uncover your sense of direction and your ability to achieve your goals.

6. Do you have any questions? You most certainly will have questions. The job interview is a two way process: you are interviewing the employer as much as you are being interviewed. You will have to make a decision as to whether or not you wish to work for this particular company. The questions you ask in the interview will help you make the decision. Your questions should be appropriate. You may want to know if the company will require you to relocate, work shift, or supervise other employees. Your research should give you some valid points to raise in this section of the interview.

By preparing in advance for these questions, you will have less difficulty dealing with them when the interviewer asks them. By your replies, you will also be letting the interviewer know that you have taken the interview seriously and have thought carefully about it.

Step Two: Interviewing

The culmination of all your efforts at the job search arrives with the interview. You will look and feel your best, although you may experience the normal nervousness common to all job applicants. Remember that the reason the employer is interviewing you is that he or she wants to explore further your qualifications. You must be confident in your ability to present yourself well and to answer the interviewer's questions clearly.

In most job interviews, the employer is looking primarily to see how you will fit in with those individuals already hired. In order to create the best possible impression you should keep the following tips in mind:

1. Don't smoke, chew gum, or play with a pencil or anything else.
2. Follow the interviewer's lead. Make sure that you answer the questions with complete replies rather than a simple yes or no.
3. Pay attention to what is being said. Don't ever rush or interrupt the interviewer.
4. Avoid an argument at any cost. Be wary of any question which may lead you into a discussion of controversial subjects, such as politics, race, or religion.
5. Be sensitive to the interviewer's non-verbal messages. A smile or nod of the head may indicate that the interviewer agrees with or

likes what you are saying. A quick glance at a watch may tell you to hurry up or that the interview is winding down.

6. Don't take anything other than a notebook, briefcase, or portfolio to the interview. Certainly, don't take a friend.
7. Always attempt to maintain eye contact with the interviewer. This shows that you are honest and have nothing to hide. Be careful, however, not to stare at the interviewer.
8. Ask for clarification of any question you don't understand.
9. Be enthusiastic. Project a positive attitude and the desire to do a good job.
10. Thank the interviewer. Mention the fact that you have enjoyed the interview.
11. Always ask when you can expect to hear about the results of the interview. Don't ever leave the interview without this information.
12. If the employer offers you the job on the spot, accept only if you are absolutely certain. You may ask for a day or two to think over your decision. Most employers appreciate the fact that you will want to have some time to reflect on the interview and to make you choice carefully.
13. Make a good *last* impression. People are hired on the basis of how they end the interview, just as much as on how they begin it.
14. Don't ever apologize for your age, your lack of experience, or your education. Take pains to maximize the positive qualities you have to offer.
15. Don't be discouraged if your interview is unsuccessful. The more job interviews you do, the more accomplished you become. Regard each interview as a positive experience which will prepare you for the next one.

Completing Employment Applications

Nearly all business firms have application forms that candidates fill out when they apply for work. Generally, you will fill out an application before the interview and hiring, although in some instances, you will fill out the application after you have been hired. Applications are part of a company's personnel record for each employee.

Figure 18.1 Application Form

The Corporation of the
Township of
RICHMOND

PERSONNEL DEPARTMENT
6911 No.3 ROAD, RICHMOND, B.C. V6Y 2C1

Application for Employment

TYPE OF WORK OR POSITION APPLIED FOR | TODAY'S DATE

LAST NAME | FIRST NAME | MIDDLE INITIAL | SOCIAL INSURANCE NUMBER | HOME PHONE NUMBER

BUSINESS PHONE NUMBER

PRESENT ADDRESS Street City Province Postal Code

MESSAGE PHONE NUMBER

MAILING ADDRESS (If different than above) Street City Province Postal Code

PERSON TO CONTACT AT MESSAGE NUMBER

PREVIOUS ADDRESS Street City Province Postal Code

LENGTH OF TIME AT PRESENT ADDRESS YEARS/MONTHS | LENGTH OF TIME AT PREVIOUS ADDRESS YEARS/MONTHS | Do you have a valid B.C. Driver's Licence? ☐ YES ☐ NO | ARE YOU LEGALLY ENTITLED TO WORK IN CANADA? ☐ YES ☐ NO

MINIMUM SALARY EXPECTED $ | OR OPEN TO DISCUSSION

IF PRESENTLY EMPLOYED, HOW MUCH NOTICE IS REQUIRED? | DATE AVAILABLE FOR WORK | WORK PERIOD DESIRED ☐ FULL TIME ☐ PART TIME ☐ SUMMER ☐ TEMPORARY (Until)

PRESENT OR LAST EMPLOYER		CITY	PROVINCE	FROM mo /yr	TO mo /yr.	FINAL SALARY $
SUPERVISOR'S NAME	SUPERVISOR'S TITLE	PHONE NUMBER	YOUR POSITION TITLE			
YOUR DUTIES			REASON FOR LEAVING OR DESIRING CHANGE			

2nd TO LAST EMPLOYER		CITY	PROVINCE	FROM mo /yr	TO mo /yr.	FINAL SALARY $
SUPERVISOR'S NAME	SUPERVISOR'S TITLE	PHONE NUMBER	YOUR POSITION TITLE			
YOUR DUTIES			REASON FOR LEAVING			

3rd TO LAST EMPLOYER		CITY	PROVINCE	FROM mo /yr	TO mo /yr.	FINAL SALARY $
SUPERVISOR'S NAME	SUPERVISOR'S TITLE	PHONE NUMBER	YOUR POSITION TITLE			
YOUR DUTIES			REASON FOR LEAVING			

4th TO LAST EMPLOYER		CITY	PROVINCE	FROM mo /yr	TO mo /yr.	FINAL SALARY $
SUPERVISOR'S NAME	SUPERVISOR'S TITLE	PHONE NUMBER	YOUR POSITION TITLE			
YOUR DUTIES			REASON FOR LEAVING			

PLEASE TURN OVER

NAME OF SCHOOL ATTENDED LOCATION (City and Province)	COURSE, PROGRAMME OR MAJOR FIELD	HIGHEST GRADE COMPLETED OR CREDITS, DIPLOMA OR DEGREE ATTAINED	DATES ATTENDED FROM MONTH YEAR	TO MONTH YEAR
SECONDARY				
COMMUNITY COLLEGE				
UNIVERSITY				
TRADE OR TECHNICAL				

NIGHT CLASS / OTHER COURSES NAME OF COURSES	DURATION	NAME OF SCHOOL	LOCATION (City and Province)	DATES ATTENDED FROM mo. yr.	TO mo. yr.

LIST ADDITIONAL QUALIFICATIONS, SKILLS OR EXPERIENCES OF VALUE

LIST LEISURE ACTIVITIES AND INTERESTS (exclude names of political, ethnic or religious organizations)

TYPING SPEED W.P.M. SHORTHAND W.P.M.

TO BE FILLED IN BY LABOURER, TRUCK DRIVER, EQUIPMENT OPERATOR, TRADES, AND SIMILAR APPLICANTS

DRIVERS LICENCE CLASS? ☐ 1 ☐ 2 ☐ 3 ☐ 4 ☐ 5 ☐ 6 AIR BRAKE ENDORSEMENT? ☐ YES ☐ NO DRIVERS LICENCE NUMBER

LIST CONSTRUCTION AND MAINTENANCE EQUIPMENT OPERATED BELOW Type and size of truck or equipment	Length of experience Years Months

MAY WE CONTACT YOUR PRESENT EMPLOYER IF CURRENTLY WORKING? ☐ YES ☐ NO

APPLICANT'S DECLARATION — 1. That all statements made in this application are true and I understand that any mis-statements of material facts herein may cause forfeiture of my rights to employment with The Corporation of the Township of Richmond. 2. That I understand appointment to any position is dependent upon: a) My ability to pass a medical examination. b) Successful completion of applicable probationary period. 3. That I will take an Oath of Allegiance. 4. That The Corporation of the Township of Richmond may contact my former employers to obtain references.

____________________ RICHMOND - Application for Employment

The information you supply on the application form helps the interviewer know what questions to ask about your education, training, and experience. Interviewers can also tell a great deal about you from the way you complete the form; for example, how accurately and completely did you answer each question? Can you follow directions? Is your handwriting legible? This point may be important if your job involves taking handwritten orders or messages over the phone. How neatly did you complete the form? Although this concern might seem trivial, neatness, or the lack of it, says something about your ability to organize your surroundings and thoughts. If the job calls for precision and orderliness, the appearance of your application can provide important clues regarding your work habits.

When you fill out an application form, keep the following suggestions in mind:

1. **Make sure you have reliable pens.** A small detail, but it shows that you think ahead. You don't want to interrupt your session to ask for a pen or mar the appearance of your application by using a pen that smudges the page.

2. **Have additional copies of your résumé.** You can leave one with the interviewer or others in the company who may interview you. Keep a copy on hand as a reference in filling out the application form.

3. **Take your driver's licence, social security number, and any other special identification or information that you will need to complete the form.** You may want to memorize your social security number for your job search.

4. **Take the time to write legibly.** Make sure that you clearly write figures, particularly for addresses and phone numbers. Illegible handwriting can bias the interviewer against you. Interviewers who have difficulty reading your handwriting may decide not to make the effort and pass you over for another candidate, especially if they must sort through several hundred applications. Whether it is fair or not, most people equate legible handwriting with intelligence and aptitude for learning.

5. **Double-check all information you have supplied.** Have you given the proper year for your birth if the question is asked? Many people, under the stress of the moment, put the current year. Make sure you have provided the correct address and telephone number for

yourself, previous employers, and references.

6. Don't leave blanks in the application. If the questions do not apply to you, draw a line through the section or write *Does not apply, Not applicable*, or *N/A* in the space provided.

7. Read the directions for each section carefully and follow them exactly. Companies have reasons for requesting the information. Read through the directions until you understand what they are asking you to do. If you still have doubts, ask for assistance.

Be sure to follow directions carefully. If the instructions ask you to print, do not handwrite your answers. Check to see if the application calls for your last name first, your last place of employment first, and the like. If you show that you can follow written instructions accurately, the interviewer will have greater faith in your ability to follow more complex written and spoken instructions on the job.

Step Three: Following Up

After the interview, you will probably write one or more of the following employment letters: thank-you letter for granting the interview; acceptance or refusal letter if there is a job offer; and appreciation letter to acknowledge the assistance of others in your job search.

Thank-You Letter

This letter, written after your interview, gives you the chance to:

1. Thank the interviewer for the time and courtesy shown you.
2. Let the interviewer know of your continued interest in the job.
3. Remind the interviewer of your qualifications for the position and how the company would benefit from your experience.
4. Provide any additional data requested by the interviewer that you may have needed time to collect.
5. Turn in an application form or other standard company forms you may have received to complete at home.

Sample Thank-You Letter

Dear Ms. Chow:

Thank you for discussing with me the position of assistant buyer in your firm. You were very helpful in explaining the specific job requirements.

Since our talk, the job interests me even more. I believe that my three years as a buyer for Winnipeg Inland Clothing has given me the experience I need to step into the position with a minimum of training.

As you requested, I am enclosing my job description, and have asked my references to send letters of recommendation to you directly.

I hope that my qualifications meet your criteria for the assistant buyer's position. Please call me if there is any additional information you would like to have.

Sincerely,

Acceptance Letter

When you decide to take a job, write a letter of acceptance. The letter should include:

1. A statement accepting the position.
2. A brief paragraph restating why you believe your new employer made the right choice.
3. A date when you can report for work.

Your letter of acceptance might look like the following:

Sample Acceptance Letter

```
Dear Mrs. Rhodes:

It is with pleasure that I accept your offer of a
sales representative position at Field Enterprises.
You can be assured that I will bring all my
experience and enthusiasm to bear on this job and
justify your confidence in me.

I will be able to start Monday, April 14, as we
discussed on the phone. I will report to the
personnel office at 8:30 a.m. and to your office at
9:00 a.m.

Thank you for this job opportunity. I look forward
to working with you and others in the Sales Office.

Sincerely,
```

Refusal Letter

You might refuse a job offer for several reasons: perhaps you have received another offer that you like better or you have realized you are not really suited for the particular company or position. Whatever the reason, you should respond to any offer with a tactful, friendly letter of refusal. You want to keep the lines of communication open because at some time you may wish to reapply to the company.

Use the standard rejection format for your refusal letter: Express appreciation for the offer and give your reasons for refusing before you state your decision.

Sample Refusal Letter

Dear Mr. Shuel:

Thank you for your kind offer of a position as security officer at the Bank of Montreal. I would have enjoyed working with the other security personnel at the bank.

Three days before receiving your letter, however, I was offered a position at the Mt. Pleasant Credit Union. Because this job is closer to my home and would require significantly less travel time, I have decided to accept their offer.

I appreciate the time and effort you spent on my application. I know you have many fine candidates who can fill your job opening.

Sincerely,

Appreciation Letter

When you accept a job offer, you may want to write letters thanking all the people whose support, encouragement, and suggestions helped you get there. An appreciation letter is a brief note to your supporters mentioning their specific contribution and letting them know which position you accepted.

Sample Appreciation Letter

Dear Ms. Kassam:

I would like to thank you for all the support you have given me during the past six months while I was job hunting. You will be pleased to know that I accepted the position of accountant in the legal firm of Tonsoo, Letterby, and LaCroix.

Your advice on how to write letters of application and to conduct myself during the interview proved invaluable. I want you to know how much I appreciate your help.

Sincerely,

Resignation Letter

During your career you may need to write a letter of resignation. Your reasons for resigning may be as different as a decision to go back to school or a personality clash with your supervisor.

Regardless of the circumstances, write your letter of resignation in a courteous, positive tone. Barring any overt hostility between you and your supervisor, you may want your former employer to act as a reference or to write a letter of recommendation for you.

Letters of resignation generally follow the rejection/refusal format. The following example uses this letter plan.

Sample Resignation Letter

```
Dear Mrs. Archer:

I have enjoyed working with you and Mr. Conroy these
past four years at Energy Systems International. The
job has taught me a great deal, and I have made
several close friends here.

Recently, I have decided to return to College to
obtain an electronics degree. I would appreciate it,
therefore, if you would accept my resignation,
effective September 10.

Sincerely yours,
```

ACTIVITIES

1. Imagine that as a result of your résumé and application letter prepared in Chapter 17, you have an interview with the company next Wednesday.

(a) Prepare a list of questions that you will ask at the interview.

(b) Consider what clothes you would wear to be appropriately dressed for the interview.

2. You have attended the interview. Prepare a thank-you letter.

3. You have been offered the job. Prepare a refusal letter.

SECTION

6 APPENDIX

PART

A PARTS OF SPEECH

The parts of speech — nouns, pronouns, verbs, adverbs and adjectives, and prepositions, conjunctions, and interjections — each have their own forms, characteristics, and uses. Knowing how to use these parts will enable you to write with greater clarity, accuracy, and style. Good writing, like any skill, involves mastering basic guidelines and learning how to apply them.

Nouns

Nouns are words that name persons, places, or things (objects, events, or concepts).

Persons	**Places**	**Things**	**(objects, events, concepts)**	
worker	office	desk	picnic	freedom
woman	city	window	meeting	equality
child	beach	chair	skiing	liberty

Common, Proper, and Collective Nouns

Common nouns refer to a general category or class of persons, places, or things. Proper nouns, on the other hand, name a particular person, place, or thing. You must use a capital for each. Collective nouns name a group or unit and can be singular or plural.

Common Nouns	**Proper Nouns**	**Collective Nouns**
typist	Jack Bartell	staff
town	Saskatoon	management
meeting	Housewares Show	team

You do not have to use capitals for common nouns used with proper nouns: Xerox copiers, IBM computers.

Functions of Nouns

Nouns can serve as the subject, direct object, indirect object, or complement of a linking verb, and the object of a preposition. In some cases they can serve as adverbs or adjectives. Nouns can also show possession.

Subject:	The *employees* arrived early. (Tells *who or what* does or is something.)
Direct Object:	The employees celebrated the *anniversary*. (Tells *what* is celebrated.)
Indirect Object:	She gave *Jim* the book. (Tells to *whom* the book was given.)
Complement of Linking Verb:	John is the *chief executive officer* of our company. (Explains the subject and is identical to it. The linking verb is *is*.)
Object of Prep:	She keyboarded the name *under the signature*. (Completes the preposition by telling *what* was under.)
Adverb:	We'll be arriving *tomorrow*. (Tells *when*.)
Adjective:	She is an *executive* secretary. (Tells *which one, what kind*.)
Possession:	The *office's* air conditioning system shuts off automatically at night, except in *Howard's* section. (Shows possession.)

Plural Nouns

You can make nouns plural in various ways. Most nouns form the plural by adding *s* to the singular form. For other plural forms, such as *es* and *y* changing to *ies*, see the Appendix Part E, "Spelling."

Singular	**Plural**
hotel	hotels
chief	chiefs
association	associations
name	names

Collective nouns can be singular or plural depending on the context in which you use them. If collective nouns act as a unit, they are singular. If they act as individuals in that unit, they are plural.

Singular	**Plural**
The staff is adequate.	The staff *vote* on every issue.
The board *meets* tonight.	The board *are* still divided on the merger.

Plurals of compound and hyphenated nouns can be troublesome. For a fuller treatment of these plural nouns, see the Appendix, Part E, "Spelling."

Possessive Nouns

A possessive noun shows ownership or possession. The possessive is formed by adding *'s* or *'* to the end of the noun.

To form the singular possessive, add *'s* to all nouns.

Singular	**Singular Possessive**
The *profits* of the company	The *company's* profits
The *rules* of the manager	The *manager's* rules

To form the plural possessive of nouns that end in *s* or *es*, add an apostrophe to the end of the word.

Plural	**Plural Possessive**
Papers *of the lawyers*	The *lawyers'* papers
The *wages of the secretaries*	The *secretaries'* wages

For nouns that form the plural in any other way, add *'s* to the end of the word, except when the final *s* is a *z* sound (*houses*), then add only the apostrophe (*houses'*).

Plural	**Plural Possessive**
men	the *men's* jobs
children	the *children's* department
notaries	the *notaries'* seals

When you are uncertain whether to place the apostrophe before or after the *s*, follow this simple rule. Rephrase the sentence by substituting an *of phrase* for the possessive noun to help you decide if the noun is meant to be singular or plural.

The (employee's, employees') decision was made on the spot.

Of Phrase	**Possessive Form**
the decision of the employee (Singular)	The employee's decision
the decision of the employees (plural)	The employees' decision

To show joint ownership, make the final noun possessive. To show individual ownership, make both nouns possessive.

Joint Ownership: Greg and Carla's assignment is to survey the west end of the city. (Greg and Carla share the same assignment.)

Individual Ownership: Greg's and Carla's assignments are due on Friday or Monday. (Each person has a separate assignment.)

Generally, in individual ownership, the noun following the possessives is plural. Look for this clue when deciding whether to use joint or individual possession (*Brenda and Larry's car, Brenda's and Larry's cars*).

Pronouns

Use pronouns to take the place of one or more nouns. Like nouns, they can refer to persons, places, events, objects, or concepts.

Examples: The managers approved the report. *They* felt it gave *them* a clear picture of the problem. (The pronouns *they* and *them* take the place of the noun *managers*. The pronoun *it* replaces the noun *report*.)

The director and supervisor argued about equal employment. They couldn't agree on a definition of it. (The pronoun *they* replaces the two nouns *director* and *supervisor*. The pronoun *it* takes the place of *equal employment*.)

Personal Pronouns

Use a personal pronoun as the subject of a sentence, as the object of a verb or preposition, to show possession, for emphasis (called *intensive pronoun*), or to refer action back to the subject (called a *reflexive pronoun*).

Subject: *I* am not going to the conference next month.

Object: Ruth told *him* to come Wednesday. Give the letter to *her*.

Possessive: *Their* talk was enlightening. I hope *your* job improves.

Intensive: The manager *herself* approved the change. (Pronoun *herself* emphasizes the subject *manager*.)

Reflexive: I taught *myself* to type. They criticized *themselves*. (The pronouns refer the action back to the subjects.)

The following chart shows the personal pronouns in all their forms for the first person (*I, we*), second person (*you*), and third person (*he/she/it/they*).

Person		**Singular**	**Plural**
First:	subject	I	we
	object	me	us
	possessive	my/mine	our/ours
	intensive/reflexive	myself	ourselves
Second:	subject	you	you
	object	you	you
	possessive	your/yours	your/yours
	intensive/reflexive	yourself	yourselves
Third:	subject	he/she/it	they
	object	him/her/it	them
	possessive	his/her/hers/its	their/theirs
	intensive/reflexive	himself/herself/itself	themselves

Possessive Pronouns

Unlike possessive nouns, possessive pronouns never take an apostrophe. As you can see from the chart, personal pronouns have a possessive form (*my, mine, our, ours, your, yours, his, her, hers, its, their, theirs*). The pronouns *who* also has a possessive form, *whose*.

Examples: Is this desk *mine*?
They have accepted *my* application.
Will you look at *her* report or *his*?
This file is *hers*.
The department has prepared *its* final statement.
We looked over *their* specifications.
I think the best bid is *theirs*.
Our office is closed on Saturdays.
Are these letters *ours*?
Whose messages were left on my desk?

Some possessive pronouns sound exactly like other pronoun or noun forms (*its/it's, whose/who's, your/you're, their/they're/there*). One easy way to keep the possessive forms straight is to remember that possessive pronouns never take an apostrophe. When pronouns have an apostrophe, they are contractions, a combined form of the pronoun plus a verb; for example, *it's* equals *it is*; *they're* equals *they are*.

its The company reported *its* earnings.
it's *It's* (it is) easy to work with Jim.

whose *Whose* car should we take?
who's Who's (who is) coming to the conference?

your Is this *your* proposal?
you're Let me know if *you're* (you are) available.

their They sold *their* last shipment yesterday.
they're Mark said *they're* (they are) low on this item.
there Put the box over *there* by the cabinet.

Gerunds

A gerund is a verbal noun, made by adding *ing* to a verb form; for example, in the sentence "*Keyboarding* is a valuable skill," keyboarding is a gerund used as the subject. If a pronoun precedes the gerund, the pronoun is in the possesive form.

Examples: Did you hear about *his calling* sixteen clients in one morning?

I would appreciate *your providing* me with more work forms.

Because a gerund is a noun, nouns are also in the possessive form before it.

Example: We heard about *Julia's winning* the top employee award last month.

Pronoun-Antecedent Agreement

A pronoun must always refer to a word called its antecedent. You must make sure that a pronoun refers to a specific antecedent. Many writers misuse the pronouns *this, that, which, it*, and *they* to refer to entire phrases or sentences.

Vague: The fax machine and electronic mail make businesses more efficient; they are a good investment.
(What is a good investment, the fax machine and electronic mail or businesses?)

Better: The fax machine and electronic mail make businesses more efficient and profitable.

Vague: Cliff Lendl, the sales manager, and Henri Leconte, the vice president, prepared the year end report together but he did the bulk of the work.
(Who did the bulk of the work, Cliff or Henri?)

Better: Cliff Lendl, the sales manager, and Henri Leconte, the vice president, prepared the year end report together, but Cliff Lendl did the bulk of the work.

Pronouns must agree with their antecedents in person, form, and number. Review the personal pronoun chart on page 281 for the appropriate pronoun forms.

Incorrect: When the operator exits the program, *you* must use the proper sequence.

Correct: When the operator exits the program, *he or she* must use the proper sequence. (Operator as the antecedent requires the *third-person* singular pronoun, not the second-person pronoun.)

Incorrect: Each December the company publishes *their* report.

Correct: Each December the company publishes *its* report. (*Company* is a third-person singular noun and requires a third-person singular pronoun, in this case the possessive form.)

Incorrect: The caller asked, "Is this Carol?" Carol replied, "Yes, this is *her*."

Correct: The caller asked, "Is this Carol?" Carol replied, "Yes, this is *she*." (The pronoun *she* refers to the subject. When in doubt about which pronoun form to use, reverse the pronoun and noun. "*Her* is (Carol)" makes no sense. "*She* is (Carol)" is the proper form. *Is* is the linking verb.

When you join two antecedents with *and*, use a plural pronoun. If you join the antecedents with *nor* or *or*, or form a unit (*research and development*), use a singular pronoun.

Examples: *Jason and Arlene* gave *their* boss the questionnaire.
Either *Robert or John* will take his car tomorrow.
The *secretary and treasurer* takes *her* duties seriously.
The *secretary and the treasurer* take *their* duties seriously.

Who or Whom?

Even experienced writers sometimes confuse *who* or *whom*. In modern usage, the tendency is to drop the more formal *whom* and use *who* in all cases. Yet you can master the rules for using these pronouns very easily. Once you have learned them, you should have no trouble choosing the correct pronoun.

Always use *who* as the subject of a sentence or of a phrase or clause within a sentence. Never use as an object.

Examples: *Who* talked to the director? (*Who* is the subject of the sentence.)
I can tell *who* is coming. (*Who* is the subject of *is coming*.)
Give the package to *whoever* can pick it up. (*Whoever* is the subject of *can pick* and not the object of the

preposition *to*.)

Always use *whom* as the object of a verb or preposition. Never use *whom* as the subject of a sentence or of a phrase or clause within a sentence.

Examples: To *whom* did you give your time sheets? (*Whom* is the object of the preposition *to*.)
Whom did you see yesterday? (*Whom* is the object of the verb *see*.)
Is that the manager *whom* you met last week? (*You* is the subject of the verb *met*. *Whom* is the object of that verb.)
Give the package to *whomever* you call to pick it up. (*Whomever* is the object of the verb *call*. Compare this sentence with the one using *whoever*.)

Verbs

Verbs express action or states of being. Verbs provide the power or drive for your sentences.

Examples: He *changed* the title of the report. (action)
The company *merged* with Cascade Industries. (action)
She *appears* calm in front of a group. (state of being)
The office *looks* more attractive. (state of being)
My father *is* an honest man. (state of being; linking verb)

Active and Passive Voice

You may use verbs either in the active or passive voice. If the subject of the sentence performs the action, the verb is in the active voice; if the subject receives the action, the verb is in the passive voice.

Active Voice	**Passive Voice**
We *delivered* the package. (The subject *we* performs the action *delivered*. *Package* is the object of the verb.)	The package *was delivered* by us. (The subject *package* receives the action *was delivered*. It no longer serves as the object.
He *has checked* the message.	The message *has been checked*.

In general, use the active voice in your writing. It adds interest and liveliness to your message. You may however, use the passive voice for variety and in cases where you want to minimize the source of the action or in cases when you do not know the source of action; for example, compare *Your credit rating has been reviewed* (passive voice) to *We have reviewed your credit rating* (active voice). The passive voice establishes a more neutral, objective tone and places the emphasis on the reviewing of the customer's credit rating, not on the persons who evaluated it.

Verb Tenses

Verb tenses enable you to place an action or state of being in the past, present, or future. They give you a way of talking about time. You form the various tenses in English by using the basic elements of the verb: base form (*promote*), past tense (*promoted*), past and present participles (*promoted, promoting*), and auxiliary verbs (*was* promoted.)

To be a verb, the past and present participles require a helping auxiliary verb; for example, *I have promoted* and *I am promoting*. You cannot use *promoted* or *promoting* alone as verbs. Participles are only parts of verb phrases.

English has both regular and irregular verbs. You will need to know the basic verb forms of these words in order to form the tenses and to avoid mixing tenses in your writing. This section gives examples of regular and irregular verbs, the basic tenses, and how to use each tense.

Basic Verb Forms

From a few verb forms you build all verb tenses and phrases. These include the base form (verb), the infinitive (*to* + verb), the past tense, the past and present participles, and the gerund (verb + *ing*, used as a noun).

Base Form:	I *invest* my money.
Infinitive:	It is wise *to invest* your money. (The infinitive here is used as an adverb modifying *wise*.)
Past Tense:	I *invested* $500 last month.
Present Participle:	He has *invested* $500 as well. (Perfect tense)
Present Participle:	I am *investing* another $500 this month. (On-going tense)

Gerund (noun form): *Investing* is a good way to ensure your future. (*Investing* is the noun.)

Avoid splitting the infinitive in your sentences.

Correct: We need to *pursue* this client *aggressively.*
Incorrect: We need to aggressively pursue this client.

In a series, repeat the preposition *to* before each infinitive verb form.

Example: We can change the program *to provide* more flexibility, *to store* additional data, and *to save* on file space.

Auxiliary Verbs

Use auxiliary verbs with main verbs to signal a change in tense (*he used, he had used*) or a change in voice (*she gave, she was given*). The most commonly used auxiliary verbs follow:

Auxiliary	Auxiliary plus Main Verb
has/have	He *has sent* the cable. I *have received* it.
is/are	She is *going* tonight. They *are going* tomorrow.
can/could	I *can do* it. They *could* help.
should/would	The company *should pay* more. He *would like* it.
will/shall	It *will happen. Shall* we *decide* later?
must/ought	We *must remain* here. They *ought to* call.

Regular Verbs

Form the past tense and past participle of regular verbs by adding *d* or *ed* to their base form. Form the present participle by adding *ing* to the base form. Most verbs fall into this category.

Base Form	Past Tense	Past Participle	Present Participle
call	called	called	calling
watch	watched	watched	watching
create	created	created	creating
delay	delayed	delayed	delaying

Irregular Verbs

There are no fixed rules for forming the past tense and past and present participles of irregular verbs. As a result, you will need to memorize most of the forms or consult a good dictionary, which will tell you the correct verb forms. Some of the most commonly used irregular verbs follow:

Base Form	**Past Tense**	**Past Participle**	**Present Participle**
be	was	been	being
begin	began	begun	beginning
bite	bit	bitten	biting
blow	blew	blown	blowing
break	broke	broken	breaking
bring	brought	brought	bringing
burst	burst	burst	bursting
buy	bought	bought	buying
catch	caught	caught	catching
come	came	come	coming
do	did	done	doing
draw	drew	drawn	drawing
drink	drank	drunk	drinking
drive	drove	driven	driving
eat	ate	eaten	eating
fall	fell	fallen	falling
fight	fought	fought	fighting
flee	fled	fled	fleeing
fly	flew	flown	flying
forget	forgot	forgotten	forgetting
get	got	got/given	getting
give	gave	given	giving
go	went	gone	going
grow	grew	grown	growing
hang	hung	hung	hanging
hide	hid	hidden	hiding
know	knew	known	knowing
lay	laid	laid	laying
leave	left	left	leaving
lend	lent	lent	lending
lie	lay	lain	lying
lose	lost	lost	losing

Base Form	Past Tense	Past Participle	Present Participle
pay	paid	paid	paying
ride	rode	ridden	riding
ring	rang	rung	ringing
rise	rose	risen	rising
run	ran	run	running
see	saw	seen	seeing
set	set	set	setting
shake	shook	shaken	shaking
shine	shone	shone	shining
shrink	shrank	shrunk	shrinking
sit	sat	sat	sitting
speak	spoke	spoken	speaking
steal	stole	stolen	stealing
strike	struck	struck	striking
take	took	taken	taking
tear	tore	torn	tearing
throw	threw	thrown	throwing
wear	wore	worn	wearing
write	wrote	written	writing

Common Errors in Using Verb Tenses

People frequently use the wrong verb forms for various tenses. While your reader may overlook occasional errors in conversation, such mistakes are glaringly evident in written communication. They lower the tone of your message and may cause the reader to question the accuracy of other parts of your communication.

Incorrect: He *has went* to check on last week's record.

Correct: He *has gone* to check on last week's records. (Most tenses formed with auxiliary verbs use either the present or past participle of the main verb (see p.287). *Gone* is the past participle of *to go* and is the correct form. It must always have *has* or *have* with it. *Went* is the past tense of the verb and is incorrect.)

Correct: He *went* to check on last week's record. (*Went* is the past tense of the verb *to go* and is correct. Note: There is no auxiliary verb with past tenses.)

Incorrect: We *done* it yesterday and turned in the report.

Correct: We *did* it yesterday and turned in the report. (The action takes place in the past and requires the past tense. *Did* is the correct past tense form of *to do*. *Done*, the past participle, is incorrect. You must use a form of *have* with the word *done*.)

Incorrect: We *are studying* the effects of inflation and *use* the Friedman model.

Correct: We *are studying* the effects of inflation and *using* the Friedman model. (The action is ongoing in the present — the present progressive. *Are* is the auxiliary verb for both main verbs. Both verbs must be in the present participle form for the present progressive tense. This is referred to as parallel structure.)

Incorrect: We have *mailed* the questionnaire, *wrote* the personnel directors of the companies, and *gave* each firm a code.

Correct: We *have mailed* the questionnaire, *written* the personnel directors of the companies, and *given* each firm a code number. (The action was taken and completed in the present — the present perfect, formed by the auxiliary verb + the past participle. *Have* is the auxiliary verb for each main verb in the series; therefore, the past participles *mailed, written*, and *given* are correct. *Wrote* and *gave* are the past tense forms and are incorrect.)

Another common error in written communication is incorrect tense sequence (mixing verb tenses in the same sentence or paragraph). When the action or state of being takes place in the same time frame, the verb tenses must be consistent.

Incorrect: We *looked* up the information, *reported* to the manager, and *turn* in our findings.

Correct: We *looked* up the information, *reported* to the manager, and *turned* in our findings. (The actions all take place in the past. The present tense confuses the time frame.)

Incorrect: We *received* the customer's order on Friday. We *give* the order to the sales department, although I *was* sure that there *is* an error in the part number. I *have been filling* these orders for a long time, and the number *looks* strange to me.

Correct: We *received* the customer's order on Friday. We *gave* the order to the sales department, although I *was* sure that there was an error in the part number. *I have been filling* these orders for a long time, and the number *looked* strange to me. (The paragraph refers to a sequence of actions taken in the past. The verb tenses must be consistently in the past tense)

Incorrect: The report *is* ready for the committee to study. *It showed* that sales *were* increasing over the past six months.

Correct: The report *is* ready for the committee to study. It *shows* that sales *have been* increasing over the past six months. (References to the report are in the present tense. The present perfect tense refers to something occurring in the past and continuing into the present such as the increase in sales.)

Subject-Verb Agreement

In the previous section, you learned that pronouns must agree with their antecedents in person, form, and number. Verbs must also agree with their subjects in person and number.

The first person subject is the person or persons speaking in a sentence (*I, we*). The second person subject is the person or persons addressed (*you, you*). The third person subject refers to the person or thing spoken about and can be any noun or third-person pronoun (*he*/*she*/*it*). Verb forms change to agree with changes in person.

Agreement in Person

First:	I receive	We receive	Regular verb
	I am	we are	Irregular verb
Second:	you receive	you receive	Regular verb
	you are	you are	Irregular verb
Third:	He/she/it receives	they receive	Regular verb
	He/she/it is	they are	Irregular verb

Verbs must agree with their subjects in number. A singular subject takes a singular verb; a plural subject takes verb form that agrees with it.

Agreement in Number

Singular	**Plural**
The *calculator is* inexpensive. (The calculator is a single object, not male or female, so *it* applies here. (The third person singular.) The third person singular of the verb *to be* is *is*.)	The *calculators are* inexpensive. (The calculators means there are several of them. They are objects, so the third person plural applies. The third person plural of the verb *to be* is *are*.)
The *assistant writes* quickly.	The *assistants write* quickly.

And easy way to check your accuracy is to substitute a pronoun for the noun, eg. *She writes quickly* as opposed to *The assistant writes quickly. She* is third person singular, so the verb must be in the third person singular.

I am not ready to leave.	*We are* not ready to leave
Jay, *you get* two boxes of pens.	*All of you get* two boxes of pens.

Compound subjects joined by *and* generally take a verb that agrees with the plural subject, even if one of the subjects is singular. Compound subjects joined by *or* or *nor* are plural if the subject nearest the verb is plural or if both subjects are plural.

Examples: The president *and* vice president *are* available for interviews.

Three city workers *and* one company employee *were* injured at work.

There *are* one premium *and* two certificates for each customer.

I don't know if memo pads *or* time sheets *are* reordered first.

Neither the director *nor* the managers *were* invited to the reception.

Compound subjects joined by *and* take a singular form of a verb when (1) the subject is a unit; for example, *research and development*; and (2) when both parts of the subject have *each* or *every* preceding them.

Examples: *Shipping and receiving* is less efficient under the new system.

Each supervisor and every worker *fills* out the hourly sheet.

Compound subjects joined by *or* or *nor* take a singular form of a verb if (1) the subject next to the verb is considered singular; or (2) if both parts of the subject are singular.

Examples: The top files *or* the bottom drawer *is* the place to store records.
The shop steward *or* the employee representative *has* responsibility.
Neither the assistants *nor* the shipping clerk *knows* where he is.

Plural nouns used as the titles of courses or subject areas take a singular form of a verb. Nouns used as measurements or units of quantity (dollars, kilograms, metres, etc.) also take a singular form of a verb.

Examples: *Physics is* not a required course in most business schools.
Human relations is an important subject area for most managers.
I notice *mathematics has* been added to the list of requirements.
Forty-five dollars is a good price for the ribbon we need.
Is twelve kilograms over the limit?
Does three metres sound right to you?
Fourteen kilometres is too far to travel without a car.

A collective noun can take either the plural or singular form of a verb. If you wish to emphasize the group as a unit, use the singular form of a verb. If you are emphasizing the individuals within the group, use the plural form of a verb.

Examples: *Management is* as concerned about job security as the unions are.
Top management are never sure of their long-term successes.
We appreciate the efforts the *staff makes.*
The *staff are* used to taking their coffee breaks early.

Prepositional phrases following the subject or material set off from the subject by commas do not influence the form of the verb. If you are in doubt about which form to use, simply block out the prepositional phrase or additional material and look only at the noun or pronoun and the verb.

Examples: *Each* of the managers *is* due for a raise. (Each ~~of the managers~~ is)

All of the managers *are* due for a raise. (All ~~of the managers~~ are)

Our *plant*, along with other plants, *has* expanded production.

Many *plants*, particularly the one in Thunder Bay, *have* expanded production by thirty percent.

Adjectives

Adjectives modify nouns, pronouns, and other adjectives by describing some quality or characteristic about them. You may use adjectives to give your writing more varied shades of meaning and to add pertinent information about the main topic. Adjectives answer the questions Which one? What kind? How many?

Examples: Let me have the *blue* file. (Which one?)

The director wants a *tiny, two-colour* one. (What kind?)

We need *four* graphs tomorrow. (How many?)

Limiting Adjectives

Many adjectives are used to identify or number the nouns they modify. Some of these limiting adjectives follow. In nearly all cases, the limiting adjective comes before the noun it modifies.

Limiting Adjective	**Noun**
a/an	a dictaphone, an audit
the	the client, the clients
this/these	this account, these accounts
that/those	that carload, those carloads
few	few deliveries
many	many receivables
every	every worker
each	each rule

both	both workers
several	several orders
some	some letters
any	any paper
most	most employees
one	one day

Comparisons

Many adjectives show comparisons between or among persons, places, or things. The *positive, comparative*, and *superlative* forms represent different degrees of a quality or characteristic. The positive form is simply the base word (high). You form the comparative by adding the suffix *er* or using the word *more* (higher, more careful). For the superlative, you add the suffix *est* or use the word *most* (highest, most careful).

Positive	**Comparative (er/more)**	**Superlative (est/most)**
hard	harder	hardest
sound	sounder	soundest
fortunate	more fortunate	most fortunate
critical	more critical	most critical

There are several irregular comparison forms.

far	farther	farthest
good	better	best
bad	worse	worst

When you are comparing two items, use the comparative form. When you are comparing more than two items, use the superlative.

Examples: Today's shipment is *larger* than yesterday's. (comparative)
Today's shipment is the *largest* one of all our order. (superlative)
Greg's judgment is *better* than Jim's. (comparative)
Greg's judgment is the *best* in the company. (superlative)
This case is *bad*, and that one is *worse*, but the one

over here is the *worst* of all. (positive, comparative, superlative)
My opinion is *more* negative than yours. (comparative)
He has the *most* negative opinion of anyone. (superlative)

Compound Adjectives

You usually hyphenate compound adjectives when they precede the noun they modify. When they follow the noun, they are two words.

Examples: A *fast-thinking* executive
An executive who is *fast thinking*

The *decision-making* process
A process of *decision making*

A *two-metre* retaining wall
A retaining wall of *two metres*

A *part-time* job
A job which is *part time*

A *past-due* bill
A bill which is *past due*

Adverbs

Adverbs modify verbs, adjectives, and other adverbs. They answer such questions as *When? Where? How? How much* ? Adverbs give additional information and describe an action or state of being in greater detail.

Examples: She *never* leaves the office before I do. (when?)
I think they went *upstairs*. (where?)
Please keyboard this *quickly*. (how?)
I agree *somewhat* with your decision. (how much?)

Types of Adverbs

Most adverbs end in *ly*; some do not. Those indicating direction, place, time, or degree look the same as nouns, prepositions, or adjectives. Listed below are examples of the different types of adverbs.

Adverbs of Time/frequency (when)		**Adverbs of Place/direction (where)**	
now	once	in	over
before	never	upstairs	by
forever	immediately	under	down
seldom	Monday	through	sideways
occasionally	frequently	here	out
eventually	often	there	across

Adverbs of Degree (how much)		**Adverbs of Manner (how)**	
somewhat	completely	carefully	nicely
most	much	earnestly	arrogantly
more	less	resentfully	orderly
totally	thoroughly	painstakingly	carelessly
entirely	excessively	quickly	tirelessly
nearly	however	contentedly	equally

Comparisons

You will use many adverbs — like adjectives — in comparisons. You form the comparative by adding *er* or by using the word *more* and the superlative by adding *est* or by using the word *most*.

Examples: They work *fast*. (positive)
They work *faster* than the night crew. (comparative)
They work the *fastest* of any group. (superlative)
She keyboards as *well* as Frank. (equal comparison)
She keyboards *better* than the younger workers. (comparison)
She keyboards *best* when working alone. (superlative)
He speaks *softly*. (positive)
He speaks *more softly* than Lucille. (comparison)
He speaks the *most softly* of any trainer. (superlative)

Adverb Position and Meaning

The position of the adverb, particularly the word *only*, can affect the meaning of a sentence. Make sure that the adverb position reflects what you intend to say.

Only Jocelyn approves expenses.	(No-one else approves expenses.)
Jocelyn *only* approves expenses.	(She does not do anything else with them, e.g. pay them.)
Jocelyn approves *only* expenses.	(She does not approve anything else, e.g. purchases.)

Prepositions

Prepositions always appear in a phrase. Nouns or pronouns serve as the objects of the preposition. A preposition and its objects form a prepositional phrase. You can use prepositional phrases as either adjectives modifying nouns and pronouns or as adverbs modifying verbs, adjectives, or other adverbs.

Examples: on the board (the noun *board* is the object of *on*)
to them (the pronoun *them* is the object of *to*)
through the office (the noun *office* is the object of *through*)

Below is a list of some of the most commonly used prepositions.

about	beneath	in	to
above	beside	into	toward
across	besides	like	under
after	between	near	underneath
against	beyond	of	until
along	by	off	up
among	concerning	on	upon
around	down	over	with
at	during	past	within
before	except	through	without
behind	for	throughout	
below	from		

Phrasal Prepositions

Although most prepositions are one word, phrasal prepositions consist of phrases. They are familiar constructions in any type of communication.

Examples:	in place of	because of	in spite of
	in case of	by means of	on account of
	in lieu of	instead of	in front of

Examples: We had to work weekends *because of* the tight schedule.
We shipped the order *in spite of* the transit strike.
In case of bad weather, we will cancel our seminar.

Common Errors to Avoid

Do not put unnecessary prepositions at the end of the sentence.

Incorrect: Where are the envelopes *at*?
Correct: Where are the envelopes?
Incorrect: The meeting is now over *with*.
Correct: The meeting is now over.
Incorrect: Where did the Jensen document get *to* ?
Correct: Where is the Jensen document?

In formal writing and in most of your business communications, avoid putting a preposition at the end of the sentence.

Avoid: I'm not sure which data they are referring *to*.
Better: I'm not sure *to* which data they are referring.
Avoid: Whom did they ask *for* ?
Better: *For* whom did they ask?

Conjunctions

Coordinating Conjunctions

Coordinating conjunctions *and, but, or, nor, for, yet*, and *so* join two or more elements of equal rank. These elements can be single words such as nouns, adjectives, adverbs, pronouns, or verbs; or they can be phrases or clauses. (Clauses are groups of words with a subject-verb combination. For more about clauses see p. 308.)

Examples: The receptionist *and* switchboard operator are here. (joining nouns)
We have talked *and* argued for days. (joining verbs)
We have tired *but* happy work crew. (joining adjectives)
This file doesn't go on the desk *but* in the drawer. (joining phrases)
Did you keyboard this letter quickly *or* carefully? (joining adverbs)

Choose between him *or* her for the job. (joining pronouns)
The bank has never closed its doors, lost an account, *nor* refused a qualified borrower. (joining verb phrases in a series)
The lawyer did not sign the contract, *nor* did he approve it. (joining clauses)

You usually use the conjunctions *but, or, nor* with the adverbs *never* or *not.*

Correlative Conjunctions

Correlative conjunctions are coordinating conjunctions that you may use in pairs. Their function is to emphasize the elements you join. Some of the most frequently used correlative conjunctions follow:

Examples: both...and
not only...but also
neither...nor
either...or

Use correlative conjunctions to join words or groups of words of equal rank. Make sure that the elements following each part of the construction are truly equal.

Examples: *Either* the janitor *or* the security guard is on duty. (noun)
She is *both* intelligent *and* sensitive. (adjective)
Neither you *nor* we are taking a vacation this year. (pronoun)
You should *not only* tell the manager *but also* clear it with me. (verb phrase)

Linking Adverbs

Linking adverbs join two independent clauses. (Independent clauses are groups of words with a subject-verb combination that can stand alone (see page 308).) Linking adverbs indicate how two ideas expressed in clauses or sentences relate to one another. Generally, linking adverbs reflect results, contrast, or continuation.

Results	Contrast	Continuation	Examples
consequently	however	furthermore	for example
therefore	nonetheless	further	for instance
thus	nevertheless		namely
as a result			
accordingly			

Linking adverbs can occupy two positions in a sentence. They can come at the beginning of the second clause or sentence they are joining. In such cases, usually a semicolon precedes and a comma follows them. They can stand within the second clause or sentence set off by commas.

Examples:

The ledger entries seem correct; *however*, check them again.

The programmer made a mistake; *as a result*, everyone's cheque was four days' late.

She was appreciative of Angie's work; *furthermore*, she gave her a raise that following month.

She encouraged two-way communication; the employees, *accordingly*, felt free to discuss their concerns.

The production date was moved up; *therefore*, we had to make many changes.

We have increased prices; our sales, *therefore*, have decreased.

Subordinating Conjunctions

Subordinating conjunctions join unequal elements in a sentence, usually a subordinate clause (a group of words with a subject-verb combination that cannot stand alone) and an independent clause. Commonly used subordinating conjunctions follow. Notice that some of them also serve as prepositions and relative pronouns.

Examples:

after	in as much as	when
although	provided	where
as	since	which
as much as	than	while
because	that	who
before	though	whom
how	unless	whoever
if	until	whomever
in order that	what	

A subordinating conjunction can come at the beginning of a sentence as well as between the sentence parts it joins. When the subordinate clause comes at the beginning, a comma follows it.

Examples: *While I was in the bank*, I filled out an application for a loan.

I filled out an application for a loan *while I was in the bank.*

As soon as the position opened up, three employees applied.

Three employees applied *as soon as the position opened up.*

Restrictive and Nonrestrictive Subordinate Clauses

When a clause, joined to a sentence by a subordinating conjunction, is essential to the meaning of that sentence, the clause is restrictive. When the clause is not essential to that meaning of the sentence, it is nonrestrictive and is usually set off by commas.

Restrictive: The assistant *who reorganized the office* has been asked to speak at Working Women conventions. (The clause *who reorganized the office* distinguished this assistant from all others.)

Nonrestrictive: Her assistant, *who reorganized the office*, has been asked to speak at Working Women conventions. (The clause is incidental information. It could be eliminated without changing the meaning of the sentence.)

Interjections

Interjections are words or phrases used to express emotion or to capture the reader's attention. You should punctuate strong interjections (wow! call today! act now!) with an exclamation mark. Use milder interjections (indeed, yes, well,) with a comma.

You should rarely use interjections in formal business writing. They appear mainly in advertising and promotional materials.

Mild interjections: *Yes*, we can complete your order today. *Indeed*, we appreciate our customer's concern.

Strong interjections: *Outstanding*! That's the verdict from first-time users of Florentine Vinyl.

Your suppliers may be saying, "*Hey*! What's happened to the old-fashioned cardboard box?"

Words Used as Interjections

Here are some words that writers commonly use as interjections:

Examples:

ah	hurry	no way
alas	hey	oh
congratulations	hooray	ouch
good grief	my goodness	outstanding
great	never	ugh
help	no	wow

Punctuating Interjections

You may follow interjections by either an exclamation point or by a comma. Capitalize the word following the exclamation point because it is the first word in a new sentence. When you use a comma after an interjection, do not capitalize the next word because it does not begin a new sentence.

Examples: Yes, we are very pleased with the new modem.
You got an "A" on the test? Great!
Good grief, Fisby, a creature is emerging from the laboratory!

EXERCISES — PARTS OF SPEECH

1. Choose the correct pronoun for each of the following sentences:

(a) (who's, whose) expense report is this?
(b) I initiated the action but it was (they, them) who saw it completed.
(c) We assume that Boris or Martin will give (their, his) acceptance speech Friday night.
(d) The credit goes to (him, he) and (we, us) for a 10% increase in monthly sales.

- **(e)** I appreciate (him, his) coming forward with that information.
- **(f)** Promise me you will assign that task to (whoever, whomever) you feel is the most efficient.
- **(g)** (who, whom) left the message for me?
- **(h)** Just between you and (I, me) the new procedure is a disaster.
- **(i)** The person who suggested the new procedure is the same one (whose, who's) disks were stolen yesterday.
- **(j)** The company reported increased revenues in (it's, its) annual report.
- **(k)** They asked (who, whom) gave us our information.
- **(l)** We should send the results of the survey to (them, they).
- **(m)** The new chairperson will be (whoever, whomever) the group elects.
- **(n)** You and (I, me) must meet again soon.
- **(o)** I listened carefully but I couldn't understand to (who, whom) the office manager was referring.

2. Correct the verb errors in the following sentences.

- **(a)** Two accountants and three auditors has been fired.
- **(b)** He will contact the manager and told her about the missing data.
- **(c)** The union is filing their grievances.
- **(d)** I have wrote them about the expansion but they haven't replied.
- **(e)** Either Yvan or his two colleagues were in charge of the reunion.
- **(f)** The reactions of one individual often determines the outcome.
- **(g)** The disk drive in each of the computers were defective.
- **(h)** You should contact the wholesaler, explain your dilemma and be asking for prompt delivery.
- **(i)** Two new sales representatives and one systems analyst is needed.
- **(j)** I have asked them to take shorter coffee breaks, but they ignored my request.
- **(k)** Each one of the engineers report difficulties on the construction site.
- **(l)** The writer, the creative director, and the artist, deserves a prize for the new ad campaign.
- **(m)** Two thousand dollars is plenty to complete the project.
- **(n)** He left the office before I can start to object.
- **(o)** Research and development generate new strategies all the time.

3. Correct the following sentences:

(a) Where was the report mailed to?
(b) She has both the personality and she has the qualifications for the position.
(c) He wasn't sure whom those requisitions should be sent to.
(d) I only work with spreadsheets and not with word processing.
(e) These are the people which we did the proposal for.
(f) He neither plans for the future or cares about the past.
(g) What miracle was he counting on?
(h) The plan was to not only changing the mail room distribution but the inter-departmental requests.
(i) This should be sufficient for you to go on with.
(j) We either list our criteria or ignore them.

4. For each of the following sentences, provide an appropriate adverb or adjective.

(a) He keyboards reports _________.
(b) He completed his task _________.
(c) The promotion procedure is _______ for everybody.
(d) That is the _________ new software over there.
(e) This fax machine runs __________.
(f) She asks for meetings __________.
(g) Carole and Suki have __________ plans.
(h) Most employees are ________ when they are _______ treated.
(i) The purchasing department asks for the _______ bids.
(j) They were rejected because of a __________ attitude.
(k) Her manner on the telephone was __________.
(l) She was _________ angry when she returned to the store.
(m) Her job involved a __________ drive to the office.
(n) The director asked for _________ individuals as his assistants.
(o) His employees consider him to be a _________ man.

PART B SENTENCES AND SENTENCE PATTERNS

In Part A you studied the individual elements of the sentence — nouns, pronouns, verbs, adjectives and adverbs, prepositions, conjunctions, and interjections. In this section, you will look at the building blocks of sentences — phrases and clauses — and the various ways to construct sentences. These different constructions can add variety to your writing and communicate your messages more effectively.

Sentences, Fragments, and Run-Ons

A sentence is a group of words that expresses a complete thought. It begins with a capital letter and ends with a period, question mark, or exclamation point. Sentences can be declarative (a statement), interrogatory (a question), imperative (command or request), or exclamatory (for emphasis).

Declarative: Two-way communication is essential in an office.
Interrogative: Why is motivation so important to the productivity?
Imperative: Give him the key. Please return the file.
Exclamatory: We get three weeks' vacation this year!

Fragments

Not every group of words is a sentence. Fragments are groups of words that appear to be sentences but do not express a complete thought.

Examples: Received by the front office
Decisions made yesterday
When the client accepts

Fragments make no sense by themselves and leave important questions unanswered. What is received? What about the decisions made yesterday? When the client accepts, what happens? To form a complete thought, fragments must join other sentence parts.

Run-Ons

Run-ons are two or more complete thoughts — often unrelated — that run together without punctuation.

Example: We cannot fill your order because shipment has been delayed and we tried to call you earlier this week. (The run-on connects two unrelated thoughts together. The meaning is not clear.) The board voted on the measure and the stockholders approved the new management plan. (The run-on connects two related thoughts but without punctuation.)

Revised: We cannot fill your order because shipment has been delayed. We tried to call you earlier this week to discuss possible substitutes for the parts you wanted. (The reason for the attempted call is now clear.)
The board voted on the measure, and the stockholders approved the new management plan. (A comma before *and* separates the two complete thoughts and corrects the run-on sentence. You can also correct the run-on by making the two thoughts into separate sentences; for example: The board voted on the measure. The stockholders approved the new management plan.)

Reread your communications carefully to make sure you have no fragments or run-on sentences. They can be confusing to the reader and can distort your message.

Sentence Structure

Besides the various parts of speech, you can construct sentences out of phrases and clauses.

Phrases

Phrases are related groups of words that do not contain a subject-verb combination.

Prepositional Phrase	**Verb Phrase**	**Participial Phrase**	**Infinitive Phrase**
on the corner	has been told	writing the speech	to sell shares
among the files	was sent	connected to us	to return parts

Clauses

Clauses are related groups of words that do contain a subject-verb combination. Independent clauses can stand by themselves as complete thoughts or sentences. Dependent or subordinate clauses cannot stand by themselves but serve as part of a complete sentence. They are subordinate to an independent clause.

Independent Clauses	**Subordinate Clauses**
she was hired today	when she was hired
each one of us called	when each one of us called
I'm five minutes late	because I'm five minutes late
the routine is changing	why the routine is changing

Examples: She was hired today *when the manager approved her application.*
I'm five minutes late *because the train was delayed.*
When each one of us called, we asked the same survey questions.
Why the routine is changing, I haven't any idea.

Sentence Variety

There are four types of sentence constructions: simple, compound, complex, and compound-complex. Each of these constructions uses the same basic elements of the sentence — individual parts of speech, phrases, and clauses — as building blocks.

Simple Sentence

A simple sentence is an independent clause with no subordinate clauses. It is distinguished from an dependent clause by a capital letter and an end mark — period, question mark, or exclamation point. Simple sentences vary considerably in length.

Examples: The Praedo file is on the back shelf.
We gave the Praedo file to the consulting team from

Alberta.

We gave the Praedo file to the consulting team from a vocational school affiliated with the University of Alberta and connected with Petro Canada's field-study program.

Compound Sentence

A compound sentence contains two or more independent clauses but no subordinate clauses. The two independent clauses can be joined by coordinate or correlative conjunctions (*but, and, or, nor, either...or, neither...nor, both...and, not only...but also*), by a semicolon followed by a linking adverb and a comma (; however, ; therefore,) or by a semicolon alone.

Examples: We have two weeks to fill the order, or we lose the account.

The managers complained about the cold, but there was no way to regulate the heat.

I like the benefits at this company, especially the life insurance and the major medical; however, I think the pay raises are too small.

Complex Sentence

A complex sentence has an independent clause and one or more subordinate clauses. The subordinate clause can act as an adverb, adjective, or noun in the sentence.

Examples: After he read the letter, he gave it to his assistant.

A comma follows the subordinate clause when the clause comes before the independent clause.

Examples: That we should reorganize the department was an excellent idea.

We read that the company would be offering stock option plans and that employees would be allowed to participate.

Compound-Complex Sentence

A compound-complex sentence is a combination of two or more

independent clauses and one or more subordinate clauses. In the examples, the italicized subordinate clauses will help you see the sentence structure more clearly.

Examples: We need more computer personnel, but we cannot hire them *until we have decided on our budget.*

The mail clerk, *who is usually efficient*, lost the letter; I don't know what to tell my supervisor.

You should open the mail *as soon as it arrives*, but *if you have a rush job* put the mail off until noon.

I asked her about the figures, and she replied *that she had looked them up, that they were accurate*, and *that I could use them.*

Rearranging Sentence Order

You can rearrange a basic sentence pattern to place the predicate and part of the verb phrase before the subject.

Examples: When the clock struck five, I looked up. (predicate, subject, verb)

Has the tax form arrived at the home office? (auxiliary verb, subject, verb, predicate)

Only when the payroll department complained did she turn in her weekly time sheets. (predicate, auxiliary verb, subject, verb, predicate)

When rearranging your sentence patterns, be sure to join the modifiers clearly to the word or words they modify. When you join descriptive phrases or clauses to the wrong words, you create dangling modifiers. They can create some odd images in your sentences.

Incorrect: Exhausted and bleary-eyed, the report was finished by morning. (An exhausted, bleary-eyed report?)

Correct: Exhausted and bleary-eyed, the staff finished the report by morning.

Incorrect: The engineer left the terminal pleased with the work. (The terminal is pleased?)

Correct: Pleased with the work, the engineer left the terminal.

Incorrect: After standing up well under the stress tests, the company was convinced that the product was sufficiently strong. (The company stood up well?)

Correct: After standing up well under the stress tests, the product was judged to be sufficiently strong.
Incorrect: After considering the report, it was accepted by the committee. (the report considered the report?)
Correct: After considering the report, the committee accepted it.

The phrase at the beginning should modify the first word of the independent clause.

EXERCISES — SENTENCES AND SENTENCE PATTERNS

1. On a separate sheet of paper, identify whether the following groups of words are sentences, fragments, or run-ons. Revise the fragments and run-ons to make proper sentences.

(a) Waiting for the message to arrive by courier.
(b) Use the FAX to forward the material they requested.
(c) They were late for work again and the office manager didn't bother to hear their excuses but simply went ahead and terminated their employment inspite of all their objections.
(d) Because the administrative assistant didn't have the signing authority.
(e) After which the speaker rose slowly to the podium.
(f) The salesperson offered a replacement item but the customer was set on a refund.
(g) Is this the answer to your question or have I misunderstood you?
(h) Because numerous concessions had already been made and the negotiating team had nothing more to offer.
(i) The communications software available.
(j) Connecting all the participants for the conference call.
(k) Despite her numerous objections, her co-workers planned an elaborate retirement dinner.
(l) The final proposal is due on Monday I feel confident it will be completed on time.
(m) The larger issue remains unresolved however it is a good thing some minor issues are no longer important.
(n) Because the answering machine failed to function.
(o) Although his movement was unintentional.

2. Rewrite the following sentences according to the cue given after each one — simple, compound, complex, or compound-complex.

(a) The clients were assembled and they were ready for the marketing presentation. (simple)

(b) She received the spreadsheet and she began to check the inventory. Following her call to the manager. (compound-complex)

(c) The traffic was completely tied up. We delayed leaving for an hour. (compound)

(d) They were pleased to know that their bid was accepted. They also knew that they would have to take a salary cut. (complex)

(e) All the offices will be closed on Friday. Mr. Dan Myers, the President died suddenly. Business inquiries will be handled Monday. (compound-complex)

3. To practise writing varied sentences, rewrite the following, changing the sentence order. Correct any dangling modifiers you find.

(a) To promote the new cat food, the sales manager arranged a contest for all marketing representatives.

(b) She filled out her application as she waited for the interviewer.

(c) Answering the phone, the vase of flowers was knocked over by Jennifer's haste.

(d) Although it was a long time coming, your payment was well received this morning.

(e) The employees greeted their new supervisor with enthusiasm and they were sure he would be easy to work with.

(f) The law of averages would suggest that the current profitable trend can't last.

(g) The conference which was scheduled to be held in Edmonton was cancelled and then it was moved to Montreal.

(h) The letters were full of errors because they had been written at the end of a long day.

(i) He was notorious for monopolizing any discussion involving office procedures.

(j) Don't forget to lock the door and remember to take the mail with you when you leave.

4. A Practical Application

Read the following paragraphs to see how sentence variety can make your writing more interesting and informative. Study the differences in sentence structure between the two paragraphs.

(a) The following is a report on employee productivity. We prepared it for the personnel office. We studied each worker for three months. We studied them for efficiency, ability to work with others, and level of skills. We considered a variety of conditions. Some of the conditions were heat, light, ventilation, noise, equipment, and workload. Employees worked alone or in groups of six or more people. Solitary employees had slightly lower rates of productivity. Workers in groups tended to support one another. Their productivity rates were somewhat higher.

(b) The following is a report on employee productivity which we prepared for the personnel office. Over a period of three months, we rated each worker for efficiency, ability to work with others, and level of skill. The study team considered a variety of conditions including heat, light, ventilation, noise, equipment, and workload. Some employees worked alone while others worked in groups of six or more people. That solitary employees had lower productivity rates should come as no surprise. Employees who work in groups tend to support one another; as a result, their productivity rates are somewhat higher.

PART

C PUNCTUATION AND PUNCTUATION STYLE

Punctuation serves two main purposes in written communications. First, punctuation helps you present your ideas clearly and accurately. It indicates where one thought ends and another begins, how ideas relate to one another, how to separate items in a series, and the like.

Second, you use punctuation in abbreviations and in figures expressing time, quantities, measures, and the like.

In this section, we look at the proper use of end marks, the comma, semicolon, quotation marks, apostrophe, hyphens, dashes, brackets, parentheses, and ellipses.

End Marks — Period, Question Mark, Exclamation Point

End marks usually come at the end of a sentence; however, they also have other uses within a sentence and in individual terms.

Period

The period marks a full stop at the end of a complete sentence. It is a visual marker that one idea has ended and another will follow. Two full spaces follow the period before another sentence begins. Use the period at the end of a statement, command, or request.

Examples: We will ship your order on the third of each month. (statement)
Order your copy today. (command)
Would you please return the enclosed card. (polite request)

You may use periods in many abbreviations. (For a fuller discussion of abbreviations, see pages 336)

Examples: Ave. (Avenue)
Blvd. (Boulevard)
F.O.B. (free on board)
Dec. (December)
M.B.A. (master of business administration)
C.O.D. (cash on delivery)

Question Mark

Use a question mark at the end of a statement that asks a question but not at the end of a statement that contains an indirect question.

Direct question: Do you know who the new consultant is?
Indirect question: She wants to know who the new consultant is.

Although in many business letters a period usually follows a polite request, a question mark is also acceptable.

Examples: Will you please indicate your preference by June 30.
Will you please indicate your preference by June 30?

Use question marks after each question in a series of questions.

Example: What price did you quote for machine parts? for replacement? for maintenance and repair? for field testing?

Place question marks inside quotation marks when the quotation is a question; otherwise, place them outside quotation marks.

Examples: The supervisor asked, "How many parts can be welded in an hour?" (The quoted material is a question.)
Did you say "return the package today"? (The quoted material is not a question. The entire sentence is the question.)

Exclamation Point

Use exclamation points to indicate emotion, surprise, or enthusiasm. In business writing, you will use exclamation points in advertising and sales materials to call attention to a particular message or urge the reader to take some action. Overuse of exclamation points, however, will reduce their effectiveness; therefore, you should avoid using them.

Examples:
You can't allow the competition to get ahead!
This offer represents an unusual opportunity!
Act! Order the ABC Printer today.
Oh!
Wait!

Comma

The comma is the most frequently used — and abused — punctuation mark. Use it to separate items in a series, to join independent clauses, and to set off non-essential expressions.

Series Commas

Use commas to separate items in a series. In most business writing, use a comma before the final conjunction (*and, or, nor*) to avoid confusion.

Examples:
We learned how to use the keyboard, printer, and modem.
Do you want this on the table, on the desk, or near the door? (Series of prepositional phrases)
The sales department ordered men's and women's slacks, sport shirts, boots and shoes and laces. (Is the final category *boots and shoes* or *shoes and laces*? A comma would make the categories clear: boots and shoes, and laces.)

Joining Independent Clauses

Use a comma before *and, but, or, nor, for, yet*, and *so* when they join two independent clauses, unless the clauses are very short.

Examples:
Please have Mr. Tse reply by Thursday, and I will have his cheque ready for him.
We cancelled the meeting, for no one could get to the office.
Have him go ahead, and I'll follow soon.

Do not use a comma when *and, but, for, yet* join two verbs that share the same subject.

Example: Marlene *asked* her co-workers for suggestions and *received* several good ideas from almost everyone.

Non-essential Material

Use commas to set off non-restrictive material or expressions that interrupt the sentence.

Examples: Danielle Glaudini, who was appointed director last year, has been recommended for membership in the local Jaycees. (The material set off in comma is incidental to the meaning of the sentence.)
The arrangements depend, of course, on the number of people coming.
The order, the one we discussed, has been sent.

Set off expressions such as *I am sure, on the contrary, indeed, naturally, in my opinion, for example, that is, incidentally* by commas whether they come at the beginning, middle, or end of the sentence.

Direct Address

Set off words in direct address by commas, no matter where they fall in a sentence.

Examples: Rene, I think you need to trim your expense account.
Please call the field representative, Katarina, and tell him to come this afternoon.
Can you find this address, Dee?

Introductory Expressions, Phrases, Clauses

Use a comma after introductory elements such as *no, yes, well, why* when they begin a sentence. Use a comma after an introductory phrase or subordinate clause, unless the phrase or clause is very short.

Examples: No, we cannot change the schedule at this late date.
By the way, can you work this weekend?
When the final results were compiled, the interviewer was surprised.
Throughout the long meeting, he kept looking at his watch.
At five o'clock we left the office.

Traditional Comma Uses

Use commas in dates (traditional style), addresses, complimentary closings (two-point and closed punctuation), and certain forms of proper names or names followed by a title.

Examples: We would like to set March 5, 19—, as our target date. (When only the day and month are used, no commas are necessary:
The stock offering on May 10 was for 5 000 shares.)
You can write Mr. Garlitz at 355 South LaSalle, Quebec City, Quebec, for a copy of the brochure.

Sincerely yours,
Gabe Van Dusen, Ph.D.

Dear Angelo,
Bill Waters, Jr.

Truly yours,
Amy Nguyen, Director

Comma Faults

Do not use commas to separate subject from verb.

Incorrect: The sales force from Labrador, arrived two hours late. (The subject sales force should not be separated from the verb arrived.)

Correct: The sales force from Labrador arrived two hours late.

Do not separate two subordinate clauses joined by a conjunction.

Incorrect: The supervisor recommended that we work longer hours, and that we divide the work among more operators.

Correct: The supervisor recommended that we work longer hours and that we divide the work among more operators.

Semicolon

Use semicolons to coordinate ideas. A semicolon, like a comma, has one space after it.

Independent Clauses

Use a semicolon to join two independent clauses similar in thought when you do not join them with *and, but, or, nor, for, yet*, and *so*.

Examples: We have repaired your printer; it should run perfectly now.

Check off the items you wish restocked; leave blank those items you have in sufficient supply.

Use a semicolon between two independent clauses joined by linking adverbs such as *accordingly, however, for example, therefore, instead.* Follow the linking adverb with a comma or set it off by commas.

Examples: We need to improve our hiring practices; for example, we are not reaching the junior colleges.

I approved your recommendation; however, I'm not sure Tamara will.

He received a copy of the complaint; he has suggested, accordingly, that his assistant look into the matter.

Use a semicolon to separate two independent clauses if one or both of them contain internal punctuation.

Examples: Carl said we needed a disk drive, a backup system, and a modem; and he recommended we look at the Ottawa Office installation.

Nancy, who talked to the people in the mail room, suggested we mail the letters today; the mail delivery will be slow tomorrow.

Series

Use a semicolon to separate items in a series if the items contain commas within themselves.

Examples: The list of conferees include Carol Hilliard, vice president; Arthur Little, director of research; Gayle Schmidt, director of finance; and Alan Berman, office manager.

Colon

Colons represent a more complete stop than a semicolon but not as full a stop as a period. Insert two spaces after a colon when using it in a sentence.

Before a Series or List

Use a colon to introduce a list, particularly after such expressions as *the following* or *as follows*. When a series immediately follows a verb or preposition, do not use a colon, *unless* you list the items in the series on separate lines.

Correct: The manufacturer gave us five colour choices: blue, orange, yellow, green, and red.
The application form covers the following: schooling, work experience, references, outside interests, and medical history.

Incorrect: The assistant expressed an interest in: telephone surveys, field research, and report writing.
Our best markets are: Lethbridge, Oshawa, and Montreal.
(Omit the colons in both sentences.)

Correct: Our best markets are:
Lethbridge
Oshawa
Montreal

Between Independent Clauses

Use a colon to introduce a question or related statement following an independent clause. In general, a question begins with a capital letter.

Examples: Our biggest problem lies ahead: How do we repay the debt?
There is one reason for our success: we have an excellent staff.

Time

Colons are used in numerical expressions of time. When writing time in figures, do not use the words o'clock.

5:00 p.m. 4:15 a.m.
12:00 noon 10:00 in the morning

Business Letters

Use a colon after the salutation in a business letter (two-point and closed punctuation styles) or a memo.

Dear President Field:	To the Staff:
Dear Customer:	To All Line Managers:
Dear Ms. Johnson:	To All Computer Personnel:

Quotation Marks

Use quotation marks to enclose a direct quotation: someone's exact words.

Examples: The shop supervisor said, "We must deliver the product today."
"We were told," he said, "to deliver this product today."
"I remember distinctly," he said. "We were told today."

When you interrupt quoted material by *he said, she asked*, and the like, the second part of the quote begins with a small letter. If the second part is a new sentence, it begins with a capital.

Punctuation with Quotation Marks

Always place commas and periods inside the closing quotation mark and place semicolons and colons outside the quotation marks.

Examples: She didn't say she was "disappointed in the group's performance." "The group has failed," she said.
Look at the manual under "double-sided copying"; then proceed.
His assistant considered the following as "unnecessary frills": glass mugs and gold-stamped pens.
The manager said, "Please keyboard these letters today."
"Send this order right away," the supervisor spoke hurriedly.

Place question marks and exclamation points if they are part of the quoted material inside the quotation marks; otherwise, place them outside the quotation marks. Use only one end mark or comma at the end of the quotation.

Examples: Did the article say "all employees share in the plan"? (The question mark refers to the entire sentence.)

"Why hasn't this letter been delivered?" she asked.

"We set a new record!" Martin shouted.

Don't say, "Keep calm"!

Who was it that asked "what price progress?" (Question mark applies to the sentence and the quoted material.)

The news release stated, "We are pleased to announce the appointment of Tara Jacobson as vice-president of marketing. She will provide strong leadership for our consumer products division."

Brief and Long Quotations

When quoting a few lines, place quotation marks at the beginning and end of the material.

Example: As the report on office productivity revealed: "There is a strong relationship between employees' feelings of self-worth and their motivation on the job."

Set off long quotations from the rest of the text by indenting and single spacing. Do not use quotation marks. Use a colon after the lead-in sentence.

As the report on office productivity revealed:

> There is a strong relationship between employees' feelings of self-worth and their motivation on the job. Employees in one plant were given responsibility for setting their own productivity goals and reporting on their progress each week. In every case the employees not only met those goals but exceeded them, often by as much as 35 percent!

Single Quotation Marks

Use single quotation marks to enclose a quotation within a quotation.

Examples: He said, "The letter stated that 'every effort should be made.'"
"We are instituting 'quality of work life' here at the plant."

Titles

Use quotation marks to enclose titles of articles, chapters of books, and titles of many reports and government publications. Set off these titles from the sentence by commas.

Examples: He used the article, "Labour's Blue-Collar Blues," for his speech.
The chapter, "Corporate Values and Decision Making," is excellent.
Please get me a copy of the Labour Department's report, "Women's Job Opportunities in the 20th Century."
I'd like to see Martha's report, "Small Business Equipment."

Apostrophe

Use the apostrophe to show possession and to form the plural of numbers, symbols, letters, and signs.

Possessive of Singular Nouns

To form the possessive of a singular noun, add an apostrophe and an *s*. In words or names that end in a *z* sound, you can add the apostrophe without the *s* to avoid too many *s* sounds.

Examples:

the president's opinions
the manager's desk
Gus's record books
Georgia Burns' report

Possessive of Plural Nouns

To form the possessive of a plural noun ending in *s*, add the apostrophe. All other types of plural nouns take *'s*.

Examples:

the managers' staff
the Jones' family business
women's ready to wear
children's sports clothes

Indefinite Pronouns

To form the possessive of indefinite pronouns (*everyone, no one, someone*) use *'s*; however, do not use an apostrophe with personal possessive pronouns.

Examples:	Someone's ID card is here.	That call was hers.
	It was no one's fault.	Is this his book?
	The cat licked its paws.	

Individual and Joint Possession

In hyphenated words, names of organizations and companies, and words showing joint possession, only the last takes *'s* to show possession. In cases of individual possession, both nouns or pronouns take *'s* or apostrophe only.

Examples:	vice president's orders	Harris & May's products
	vice presidents' orders	Donovan Peers' main store
	Margo and Andrew's office (the office belongs to both)	Margo's and Andrew's offices (each one has an office)

When one of the nouns is in the possessive case, the other noun is also possessive whether it is a case of joint or individual ownership.

Example:	Kristijan's and my assignment (they have the same assignment)	Kristijan's and my assignments (they each have a separate assignment)

Units of Measure as Possessive Adjectives

Words such as *minute, hour, day, week, year, cents*, and *dollars* require an apostrophe when used as possessive adjectives.

Examples:	a minute's work	five minutes' work
	a day's pay	two weeks' pay
	one cent's worth	two cents' worth

Plural Forms of Symbols

You may use *'s* to form the plural of letters, number, signs, symbols, and words where confusion might otherwise occur.

Examples: The higher priced items are marked with blue *X's*.
Don't use *&'s* in this letter; use and's.
Instead of writing 5 and 8, he wrote two *8's*.

Hyphens

Use a hyphen with compound numbers from twenty-one to ninety-nine and with fractions used as adjectives. There are no spaces before or after the hyphen.

Examples:

forty-five slides	a three-fifths majority
sixty-two tallies	But: three fifths of the stockholders (*three fifths* is a noun)

Prefixes and Suffixes

Always use hyphens with prefixes *ex-*, *self-*, *all-*, and with the suffix *-elect*. Use hyphens also with all prefixes before proper nouns and adjectives.

Examples:

self-image	president-elect	Pan-American games
ex-manager	all-important	pro-British

Compound Adjectives

Hyphenate compound adjectives when they precede the noun; however, do not use a hyphen if one of the modifiers is an adverb ending in *-ly*.

Examples:

well-planned program	a program well planned
government-owned site	a site that is government owned
a problem-solving sequence	a sequence used in problem solving
a perfectly keyboarded letter	

To Avoid Confusion

Use hyphens to prevent confusion or awkwardness in words.

Examples: re - creation (prevents confusion with *recreation*)
re - educate (avoids awkwardness of *reeducation*)
sub - subsidiary (avoids awkwardness of *subsubsidiary*)

Dashes

Use a dash to indicate an abrupt break in thought within a sentence. Form a dash by using two hyphens with no space before or after them or using one hyphen with one space before and after it.

Examples: Communication—two-way communication—is vital to business.
Call John — he'll be back on Thursday — and have him look at this.

Use a dash to mean *namely, that is, in other words*, and *so on* before an explanation.

Examples: Many explained the method to us — we had to record each number.
Many employees share this value — they desire meaningful work.

Parentheses

Use parentheses ( ) to enclose material that is not essential to the meaning of the sentence but adds additional information.

Examples: Many people feel that etiquette (good manners) is important.
Our survey indicates a declining loss rate (see Figure 3).

If material enclosed in parentheses is at the end of a sentence, the end mark falls outside the closing parentheses. If the material enclosed is a complete sentence in itself, the end mark falls within the parentheses.

Examples: We make three forecasts. (For complete data, see Appendix A.)

We make three forecasts (for complete data, see Appendix A).

Brackets

Use brackets to enclose information within parentheses or within quoted material when the words inserted are not part of the quotation.

Examples: "Our analysis shows it [the new fabric] to be flame retardant."

Health benefits are explained in the manual (see page 42, Health Benefits [Table 3.3] for a detailed breakdown of coverage.)

Ellipses

Use ellipsis points (...) to indicate material that has been omitted from a quotation or quoted material.

Example: "There are recent indications that the market will remain unstable for some time. I suggest we re-evaluate our present marketing strategy."

"...the market will remain unstable for some time... Research and development should be given more funds."

When you omit words at the end of a sentence, use an end mark plus three dots.

Underscore

Underscore any item that would be italicized in print. Underscore the title of books, magazines, movies, plays, newspapers, and other types of periodicals. Underscore the first word *a, an, the* only if it is part of the actual name.

Examples: La Presse (newspaper)

Star Wars (movie)

the Times-Herald (newspaper)

The Empire Strikes Back (movie)

The Whitehorse Star (newspaper)

A Man for All Seasons (movie)
Les Affaires (magazine)
Canadian Almanac & Directory (book)
Canadian Aviation (magazine)
World Book Encyclopedia (book)
A Midsummer Night's Dream (play)
My Fair Lady (play)
The Insider (corporate magazine)

Foreign Words and Expressions

Underscore foreign words and expressions that have not become part of common usage.

Examples: He submitted his brief to the court, acting as amicus curiae.
"The early corporation believe in caveat emptor — buyer beware!"

Vehicles

Underscore the names of ships, spacecraft, airplanes, and other well-known vehicles.

Examples: company yacht: The Atlantic Clipper.
space shuttle: Columbia.
luxury liner: Star of the North.

Words or Expressions

Underscore words used as themselves or expressions you want to emphasize. Such use of the underscore should not be frequent, however.

Examples: Please define the word partner in your memo.
Use a comma after introductory elements such as no, yes, and well.

EXERCISES — PUNCTUATION AND PUNCTUATION STYLE

1. Punctuate the following paragraphs:

(a) Dear Camilla:

I'm writing to ask you about the new Cirrus photocopying machine we're thinking of buying the promotional material indicates that the machine can copy both colour and black and white materials quickly clearly and with top quality the price is not stated would you look over the material I attach and let me know what you think thanks. Anthony.

(b) Sasha I'm calling you attention to some concerns voiced by the information centre analysts at their meeting last Wednesday. The main problems seem to be related to computer security computer viruses and the fact that there aren't enough people to do all the required tasks for example the information analysts specifically need someone full time to handle the routine information inquiries. Shawn De Windt and Laura Kos are preparing a list of all concerns to be presented to you on Monday. I feel we should attempt to solve these problems before they become more serious. Sincerely Gwen

(c) Dear Mr. Santos

I thought you might be interested to know the results of the preliminary home shopping research I recently conducted for you. Specifically I spoke with Charles Yin vice president of Canadian Shopping Network and Carlene Ashcroft sales manager of HS Network. There are four major computer shopping services however a fifth is about to come onto the market. For a membership fee of approximately $30 and an online charge of $10.50 per hour at 1,200 and 2400-baud modem speeds you can shop at home from 600 am to 1200 midnight for anything from fresh lobster to a Cartier 18K gold watch you can even browse through an electronic mall without the crowds. All you need is a personal computer a modem some special software and a credit card. Two of the networks offer nonshopping services movie reviews, news and stock market prices. Please let me know if you would like me to conduct indepth research on your behalf. Lucinda Ruzzo, Research Assistant

2. Insert hyphens, dashes, parentheses, brackets, underscores, or ellipses where needed in the following paragraph:

The management group is pleased to announce a five week seminar on "Improving Communication Techniques in Business." For further details see attached brochures. The seminar open to thirty participants will be led by Ryan O'Connell, a writer and experienced group leader. Meeting times will be 7:00 p.m., Thursdays, in the conference room. Those interested should apply directly to the Personnel Office. NOTE: Should enough interest be generated to warrant a second seminar, participants will receive a one quarter discount on tuition costs. The seminar has been reviewed in The Globe and Mail, Fortune, Working Woman, and other publications. Charles Olson of The Globe and Mail stated, "A must for everyone in business. Do it attend this seminar." The topic as I'm sure you are all aware is of continuing interest in a business such as ours where public relations are especially important.

3. Insert quotation marks and other punctuation where needed in the following sentences:

(a) He asked her what FAX meant.
(b) The President said that complete report on the topic of Employee Morale is on my desk.
(c) Her exact words were the contract has been ratified.
(d) The final memo contained extensive sections on the purpose of the meeting, the issues discussed, and something called significant outcomes.
(e) An employee's worth, Edward Aitken always said is in his or her loyalty and dedication.
(f) She actually asked the interviewer, Is it all right if I'm late?
(g) He asked his co-workers Have you read the article called Effective Customer Relations?
(h) She said she intended to meet with the directors next week.
(i) While you're out he said would you pick me up some doughnuts?
(j) He asked the other executives to support the idea of Equal Pay for Equal Work.
(k) Try our new air conditioner, the ad stated. It will bring comfort to your home or office.
(l) She spoke with authority saying you may be certain that we adhere strictly to the rules of ethical advertising.
(m) He asked the question how can we justify our expense account when others in the company are losing their jobs?

(n) To err is human, to forgive divine.
(o) Of all the assistants I've had, she said, none can compare to you.

4. Re-write the following sentences using the appropriate possessive form.

(a) Sheena and his report is better than the others.
(b) If I'm not in when you call, leave a message with the president assistant.
(c) I found Milos and Gena report in an unmarked file.
(d) Could you please bring last month purchase orders?
(e) List all the software in the university computer lab.
(f) He was asked to return the department van and the warehouse forklift.
(g) They renovated Harry and Betty offices.
(h) He has someone gloves—are they yours?
(i) A company success depends on an employee effort.
(j) The firm sent its representative to the international conference.
(k) Cassidy was unaware of this corporation entry into the electronic field.
(l) The directors homes are all within driving distance of the head office.
(m) A letter was sent to Lam attorney but not to Nemchek.
(n) The Eaton white sale attracted people from all parts of the city.
(o) It is an executive duty to be concerned with employees problems.

PART

D CAPITALIZATION, ABBREVIATIONS, NUMBERS

Style guidelines for capitalization, abbreviations, and numbers are important to good written communications. Study the guidelines in this unit until you are familiar with them. Keep in mind that each company may have its own style rules that may differ slightly from the guidelines given here. In general, however, most organizations and firms accept the style in this section.

Capitalization

Capitalize the personal pronoun *I*, the first word in any sentence, and the first word of a direct quotation.

Examples: When the phone is free, I will make the call.
First impressions are important.
I heard her say, "We have seven vacation days this year."

Proper Nouns and Adjectives

Capitalize all proper nouns and adjectives and the names of persons, organizations, business firms, business products, institutions, and government bodies and agencies.

Examples:

Proper nouns		**Proper Adjectives:**	
	Flin Flon		Canadian
	B.C. Place		English
			French

Allison O'Reilly, Umang Gupta, Brenda Yu
The Canadian Council, Voice of Women, United Way
Tandem Computers, Canadian Airlines, Levy & Son
Coca-Cola, Kodak Instamatic, IBM Personal Computer

Canadian Wheat Board, Office of the Prime Minister
Royal Alexandra Hospital, Dalhousie University, The National Gallery of Canada, Hotel Chateau Laurier

Geographical Names and Regions

Capitalize geographical names and regions; however, do not capitalize points of the compass when used simply as directions (north, south, east, west). Capitalize *earth* only when using it with other planets (Mercury, Mars, Earth); otherwise, it is lowercase.

Examples: Montreal, South America, Western Hemisphere, Canada, Europe, Maine (all cities, townships, countries, states, continents)

Cape Breton Island, Saanich Peninsula, Cavendish Beach, Dease Strait (all islands, peninsulas, straits, beaches)

Lake Winnipeg, St. Lawrence Seaway, Smallwood Reservoir, Rideau Canal, Red Sea, Lac St. Jean (all bodies of water)

Rocky Mountains, Three Sisters, Mount Robson, Torngat Mountains (all mountains and mountain chains)

Coquihalla Highway, Regent Street, Eglinton Avenue, Gardner Expressway, Sussex Drive, Trans-Canada Highway, rue St. Hubert (all streets and major thoroughfares)

Jasper National Park, Sherwood Forest, Fraser Canyon, Revelstoke Dam, Rideau Canal (all parks, forests, canyons, waterways and dams)

the Maritimes, Eastern Canada, the Prairies, the West Coast, National Capital (all recognized regions of the country)

Capitalize the names of historical events and periods, special events, and calendar items.

Examples:

World War II
Confederation
Riel Rebellion

Grey Cup
Manitoba Festival of the Arts
Canada Day

Tuesday	National Book Week
Mothers' Day	New Year's Day
Labour Day	January
Yom Kippur	

Do not capitalize seasons of the year unless personified. *The fall fashions include fur capes. Last night, Fall paid us an early visit.*

Nationalities and Religions

Capitalize the names of nationalities and religions. If you capitalize the name of one racial group, capitalize them all. If you use the lowercase for one racial group, use it for the others.

Examples:	Roman Catholic	Indian	Black or black
	Baptist	Australian	White or white
	Hindu	Belgian	
	Buddhism	Vietnamese	

Languages and School Subjects

Capitalize languages and those school subjects followed by a number. Do not capitalize general school subjects.

Examples:	Chemistry 101	chemistry	French, French II
	History 402	history	German

Academic Degrees and Titles

Capitalize academic degrees of people. Capitalize titles used as part of people's names. In general, however, do not capitalize titles used after a person's name or without a name (exception: when the title refers to the highest national, provincial, or church office, such as the Governor General).

Examples:	President Newmann of Dunn Company	president of the company
	Barbara Harvey, Ph.D.	Lou Childers, director
	Dr. Edward Levi	

Titles of Persons

Capitalize titles of officers in an organization in legal and other documents. Capitalize titles and academic degrees when they appear on envelopes, inside addresses, salutations, and closings in correspondence.

Document: According to the terms of this agreement, the Director of Research and the Vice President of Finance shall report weekly.

Correspondence: Helena LeBrun
President
Consolidated Bathurst
Bathurst, New Brunswick

Dear President Brown:

Sincerely yours,
Louis DeSpain
Vice President

Documents

Capitalize the first word and all important words (and prepositions five letters and over) in charters, treaties, declarations, laws, and other official documents; however, when you use the words *charter, act, treaty*, or *law* alone, do not capitalize them.

Examples: Constitution Act; Criminal Code; Articles of Incorporation; International Treaty of the Sea

Titles of Publications

Capitalize the first word and all important words in the titles of books, chapters, magazines, articles, newspapers, musical composition, and movies.

Examples: *The Manager in the Modern Organization* (book)
"Why GE Won't Get Turned Off" (article)
Beethoven's *Eroica Symphony*

Religious Terms

Capitalize words referring to the Deity and to sacred texts.

Examples: the Creator; God; The Koran; the Holy Bible; the Lord's Prayer; Genesis; the Talmud; the Holy Spirit; the Diamond Sutra

Capitals with Numbers

Capitalize a noun or abbreviation before a number when it designates a formal part of a written work.

Examples:

Paragraph 4 or para. 4	Unit 3
Section 19 or Sec. 19	Act V, Scene 2
Chapter 22 or Chapt. 2	Book IV

Abbreviations

The following abbreviations are acceptable in all writing.

Examples:

A.D. (A.D. 19—)	etc. (and so forth)
B.C. (482 B.C.)	e.g. (for example)
a.m. (before noon)	i.e. (that is)
p.m. (after noon)	

While it is general practice to use periods with these abbreviations, you may also use them without periods: am or pm.

Company Names

Abbreviations of company names may or may not use periods. Below are some of the more common abbreviations.

Examples:

IBM
Wm. H. Brown Printers
Gore-Tex, Inc. (incorporated)
Ford Motor Co. (company)
General Motors Corp. (corporation)
Hollingshed Ltd. (limited partnership)

Be sure to copy a company's name exactly as it is spelled on the firm's letterhead.

Government Agencies

Government agencies also may or may not use periods in their abbreviations. Again, be sure to copy the abbreviations accurately.

Examples: DND (Department of National Defence)
W.H.O. (World Health Organization)
NATO (North Atlantic Treaty Organization)
CRTC (Canadian Radio-Television and Telecommunications Commission)

Unnecessary Abbreviations

Avoid using unnecessary abbreviations in your business communication.

Avoid: We would like to set a time on Mon. to meet with you. We suggest the Heritage Ctr. on Water St. if it's convenient.

Better: We would like to set a time on Monday to meet with you. We suggest the Heritage Centre on Water Street as a convenient location.

Names and Titles

The following abbreviations are customary before or after a name:

Before a name:	Messrs. (two or more men)	Ms.
	Mesdames (two or more women)	Dr.
	Mrs.	Rev.
	Mr.	
After a name:	Jr. (junior)	B.A.
	Sr. (senior)	M.B.A.
	Esq. (esquire)	Ph.D.

A comma should precede Jr. and Sr. (Jones, Jr.); however, no comma precedes a Roman numeral (Jones III) .

Units of Measure

Use abbreviations of weights, measurements, and distance in statistical or tabular material. Do not use them in formal writing. An exception would be some metric measures.

Examples:	1 L (litre)	150 g (grams)	5 ha (hectares)
	4 lbs. 7 oz.	45 mi. (miles)	16 mm (millimetres)
	16 ft. 4 in.	17 km (kilometres)	20 cm (centimetres)

Provincial, Foreign, and Address Abbreviations

In general, use the postal code abbreviations for the provinces, territories, and states.

Province Abbreviations:

Alberta AB or Alta
British Columbia BC or B.C.
Labrador (Part of Newfoundland) LB or Lab.
Manitoba MB or Man
New Brunswick NB or N.B.
Newfoundland NF or Nfld.
Northwest Territories NT or N.W.T.
Nova Scotia NS or N.S.
Ontario ON or Ont.
Prince Edward Island PE or P.E.I.
Quebec PQ or P.Q. or Que.
Saskatchewan SK or Sask.
Yukon Territory YT or Yuk.

State Abbreviations:

Alabama AL
Alaska AK
Arizona AZ
Arkansas AR
California CA
Colorado CO
Connecticut CT
Delaware DE
District of Columbia DC
Florida FL
Georgia GA
Hawaii HI
Idaho ID
Illinois IL
Indiana IN
Iowa IA
Kansas KS
Kentucky KY
Louisiana LA
Maine ME
Maryland MD
Massachusetts MA
Michigan MI
Minnesota MN
Mississippi MS
Missouri MO
Montana MT
Nebraska NE
Nevada NV
New Hampshire NH
New Jersey NJ
New Mexico NM
New York NY
North Carolina NC
North Dakota ND
Ohio OH
Oklahoma OK
Oregon OR
Pennsylavania PA
Rhode Island RI
South Carolina SC
South Dakota SD
Tennessee TN
Texas TX
Utah UT
Vermont VT
Virginia VA
Washington WA

West Virginia WV
Wisconsin WI
Wyoming WY

Foreign Abbreviations:

Canal Zone CZ
Guam GU
Puerto Rico PR
New Zealand NZ
United Kingdom UK
United States of America USA
Virgin Islands VI

Common Address Abbreviations:

Avenue AVE
Boulevard BLVD
Court CRT.
Crescent CRES.
East E
Heights HTS
Hospital HOSP
Institute INST
Junction JCT
Lake LK
Lane LN
North N
Park PK
Parkway PKY
Ridge RDG
River RV
Road RD
Rural R
Shore SH
South S
Square SQ
Station STA
Street ST
Terrace TER
Union UN
View VW
Village VLG
West W

Numbers

You will use numbers frequently in your business letters, memos, and reports. The following guidelines should help you express them in a clear and consistent style.

Figures or Words

In general, spell out numbers ten and under; use figures for numbers over ten. Spell or write out large round numbers (10 000) or write them in a combination of words and figures.

Examples: The letter was *eight* pages long.
The company laid off almost *two thousand* workers.

The insurance covers *352* married workers and *198* single workers.
The tanker held over *25 million* gallons of oil.

Spell out numbers that begin a sentence. If the sentence contains more than one figure, try to rephrase the sentence so the number does not come first.

Avoid: 43 people attended the conference.
Better: Forty-three people attended the conference.
Avoid: Twelve out of 15 employees preferred the shorter work week.
Better: The shorter work week was preferred by 12 out of 15 employees.

Series

Express consistently numbers in a series. Use figures if any number in the series is over ten.

Examples: We bought *24* sheets of music, *7* music stands, and *36* batons.
We need *one* terminal, *two* desks, and *five* chairs.

Words and Figures Together

If two numbers are part of the same construction, express the small number in words. If you use numbers in a sentence in different ways, use words for numbers ten and under and figures for larger numbers.

Examples: Please get me *250 twenty-cent* stamps.
Make sure we get *fourteen 65-cent* labels.
Within *six* years, *three* of the companies had earned *$520 000.*

Place a comma between two unrelated figures. It is better, however, to revise the sentence to separate them.

Examples: In *19—, 420* companies developed high-tech products.
In *19—*, a total of *420* companies developed high-tech products.

Addresses

Express house numbers in figures, except for the number one. Use words for numbered street names one through ten.

Examples: *One* South LaSalle Street
1476 Lynn Avenue
15 Second Avenue

Separate the house number and street name with a hyphen preceded and followed by a space.

Examples: 17 - 20th Avenue 414 - 110th Street

Dates

When writing dates, use the current style (either month/day/year, day/month/year or year/month/day). Use words or figures (with *d, nd, rd, st*, or *th*) for the day when it occurs alone or when the month is part of a prepositional phrase in a sentence.

Examples: We received a number of phone calls on *January 22, 19—.*
We received a number of phone calls on *22 January 19—.*
The director discussed the plan on the *fifteenth of March.*
The director discussed the plan on the *15th of March.*
We send bills on the *second* of every month.
We send bills on the *2nd* of every month.
The office manager said that the new policies would take effect on 19— 06 01. (Numeric date).

Centuries and Decades

Use words for centuries and for decades when you omit the century. Do not capitalize the words. Use figures when you give both decade and century.

Examples: the *nineteenth* century *1990s* or *1990's*
during the *thirties* *1930s* or *1930's*

Money

Use figures to express sums of money whether foreign or Canadian currency, but use words for small sums of money serving as adjectives.

Examples: The order cost *$4 235.98* It cost *£315* and sells for *£760.*
This *ten-dollar* pen leaks. They charge a *ten-cent* fee.

Write amounts in even dollars without the decimal and zeros; however, if other figures in the sentence use decimals, make sure all amounts of money are consistent.

Examples: We can get lumber for *$6* a metre.
We received two invoices: one for *$15.45* and one for *$15.00.*

Use figures and the word *cents* for amounts under a dollar; however, if you use the amount with figures over a dollar, use a zero and decimal point before the cents figure.

Examples: The cassettes cost only *35 cents* to produce.
One item cost *$1.45*, another cost *$0.65*, and the third cost *$2.50.*

Percentages

In general, express percentages in figures plus the word *percent.* (Use the symbol % in statistical or tabular material.)

Examples: The company borrowed $44 million at *10 percent* interest.
Sales have decline *2.5 percent* over the past quarter.

Fractions and Decimals

Express mixed fractions and decimals in figures. Use a zero with decimal fractions not preceded by a whole number; however, express simple fractions in words. If you use the fraction as an adjective, hyphenate it. If it serves as a noun, do not hyphenate it.

Mixed fractions and decimals

10 1/4 feet by *12 1/2* feet
up to *2.25* cm
the rate fell *0.15* percent
the rate rose *1.045* percent

Simple fractions

one-sixth share of the market
three-fifths majority
one tenth of their income
one half of the workers

Ages

Express exact ages in figures. Express approximate ages in words or figures, but be consistent in your usage.

Examples: At *41*, Edgar Thorton is our youngest vice president.
Our computer is only *2* years and *7* months old.
She is *33*, and he is about *40*.
He is almost *eighty*.

Measures

Express measurements, weights, and distances in figures.

Examples: For this wall, use studs that are *5* by *10* cm.
Each box weights *100* kg.
Using air freight, we can cut *900* km out of the route.
(Express fractions of a kilometre in words: The warehouse is *three quarters* of a kilometre from here.)

Temperature and Time

Express temperature in figures with the degree sign, plus the scale being used. Express time in figures when using a.m., p.m., or other modifiers. With o'clock, express time in words.

Examples: The bank sign recorded *5° Celsius* at noon.
We will arrive at either *5:20* in the evening or *2:15* in the morning.
You have a choice between an *11:35* a.m. or a *2:50* p.m. flight.
You are invited to attend a cocktail hour at *five o' clock*. (Time expressed in words is used in more formal correspondence.)

Titles

Express official titles and designations in numbers, but you will need to follow the particular organization's style.

Examples: *First* Ministers' Conference — *1st* Atlantic Savings & Loan

Forty-second District — *3rd* Annual Sports Jamboree

Book Divisions

You generally express major book divisions in Roman numerals and minor divisions in Arabic figures; however, follow the style used in each book. Always express page numbers of books in figures.

Examples: Read from *Part I, Chapters 2* through *6*, to *Part III*.
Check these names against those on pages *144* and *145*.

Express consecutive pages either with *and* or *to*, or with a hyphen:

Examples: pages *344 and 345*
pages *344 to 345*
pages *344-345*.

EXERCISES — CAPITALIZATION, ABBREVIATIONS, NUMBERS

1. In the following sentences, identify those words which begin with a capital letter.

(a) The latest edition of statistics canada documented the increased importance of women in the labour force.
(b) You will find provincial government buildings in edmonton, regina, and victoria.
(c) To reach Medicine Hat from Toronto, travel straight west on highway one.
(d) Jack P. Schussel, vice president of coombes construction, has predicted an upsurge in residential building in greater Yellowknife.
(e) The golden rule, "do unto others as you would have them do unto you," should be the first rule of business.
(f) Professor Carter teaches biology at algonquin community college.

(g) Roberta Evanson, the mayor of Gander, plans to seek election as a member of the legislative assembly for the liberal party.
(h) The rocky mountains form the southern portion of Alberta's western boundary with British Columbia.
(i) The strike was averted by a last minute compromise reached by the negotiations for labour and management.
(j) The conference board of Canada is a nonprofit institution funded by business, government, unions, and universities.
(k) Christmas day, boxing day, labour day, and good Friday are statutory holidays.
(l) The vice president of our firm met with the superintendent of schools.
(m) The plant was located on the prairies about three miles west of Esterhazy, saskatchewan.
(n) In the course of the three hour meeting, the chairman of the board drank coffee from a thermos and ate two bowls of shredded wheat.
(o) The cedar lake reservoir is located in the west central region of Manitoba, north of lake Winnipegosis.

2. Read the following paragraph. Identify every lower-case letter that you should capitalize.

"Labour day, honoring organized labour, is a legal holiday observed throughout Canada on the first monday in september. The contribution of organized labour to canadian society has been recognized since 1872, when parades and rallies were held in ottawa and Toronto. The earliest american labour day has been celebrated since 1889 on May 1, thereby merging traditional may day festivities with labour celebrations... This spring date was briefly observed in Canada, but the north american need for a long weekend at the end of summer brought about the fall observation, recognized by parliament in 1894."

(adapted from John Robert Colombo in *The Canadian Encyclopedia*, p. 956)

3. Write the correct abbreviation for each of the following items.

(a) incorporated
(b) Quebec
(c) for example
(d) 546 before the birth of Christ
(e) 3:34 in the morning
(f) reverend
(g) 4324 kilometres
(h) company
(i) that is
(j) doctor of philosophy

- **(k)** World Health Organization
- **(l)** 8½ by 11 inches
- **(m)** 16 millimetres
- **(n)** 24 cubic centimetres
- **(o)** 50 kilometres
- **(p)** 10 hectares
- **(q)** United Kingdom
- **(r)** crescent
- **(s)** Labrador
- **(t)** Hawaii

4. Revise each sentence to express the numbers correctly.

- **(a)** The present coverage through 3 carriers provides inadequate compensation for seven of every 10 disabled workers.
- **(b)** After the budget was introduced, the comptroller said each department with more than 20 employees would have to save fifty-seven hundred dollars and fifty cents every 6 months.
- **(c)** The dental insurance cost 3000 employees an average one hundred and thirteen dollars yearly.
- **(d)** At a shareholders' meeting of 40 people, the president revealed 3 plans to clear the $2 million deficit.
- **(e)** 4 out of five employers favoured the $2,000,000 policies.
- **(f)** In 19—, 127 of our competitors switched from purchase vehicles to lease vehicles.
- **(g)** On the 15th of June, I recommended that we look at Yorkton Life and Casualty, 44 Bloor Street, Toronto, Ontario and CNA, 7 rue St. Denis, Montreal, Quebec.
- **(h)** Trends which were dominant in the Sixties and Seventies changed in the Eighties.
- **(i)** The vice president was amazed when he was told the leasing rates varied by sixteen percent; the difference in payments was $92.37 per month.
- **(j)** The rate of inflation is predicted to be ten percent.
- **(k)** The average age of retirement in their company is fifty-five and ours is sixty-one.
- **(l)** I would like to move our meeting from eleven thirty tomorrow to 12 on Friday.
- **(m)** The showcase contains ten billfolds, twelve watches, and 22 rings for a total value in excess of two hundred thousand dollars.
- **(n)** During his 7 day trip to the Maritimes, the sales rep hoped to visit twenty-seven customers in 13 locations.
- **(o)** As the top real estate agent in 15 companies for nineteen eighty-eight, Marcia Godfrey sold 32 single-family residences, five commercial buildings, and six apartment houses.

PART E SPELLING

To many writers, the English language seems riddled with exceptions to spelling rules. Most words, however, conform to specific guidelines, and you can categorize even the exceptions for ready reference. The guidelines in this section will help you in spelling most regular and troublesome words. The section also covers word division and provides a list of frequently misspelled words. Always remember that your best guide to correct spelling is an updated dictionary.

Spelling Guidelines

Prefixes

When you add a prefix to a word, the spelling of that word does not change.

Examples: mis + statement = misstatement
im + material = immaterial
un + needed = unneeded
over + run = overrun
pre + existing = pre-existing
in + flammable = inflammable

Suffixes

When you add the suffixes *ness* and *ly*, the spelling of the word does not change unless the final *y* of a word represents a long *e* sound; then, the *y* changes to *i* before the suffix is added.

No spelling change

Examples: wry + ly = wryly
indebted + ness = indebtedness

sincere + ly = sincerely

Final y changed to i + suffix

Examples: happy + ness = happiness
steady + ly = steadily
handy + ly = handily
Exception: *busyness* to avoid confusion with *business*

Drop the final *e* if the suffix begins with a vowel. Retain the final *e* (1) after *c* or *g* if the suffix begins with *a* or *o*; and (2) before adding a suffix that begins with a consonant.

Drop the final e

Examples: cope + ing = coping
use + able = usable
(*Exceptions: saleable or salable*)

Retain the final *e*

Examples: courage + ous = courageous
change + able = changeable
manage + ment + management

Words ending in *y* preceded by a consonant, change the *y* to *i* before adding a suffix. Words ending in *y* preceded by a vowel, do not change.

Change *y* to *i*

Examples: sunny + est = sunniest
accompany + ment = accompaniment
(*Exceptions: trying, studying*)

Retain the *y*

Examples: cloy + ing = cloying
say + ing = saying
boy + ish = boyish

Double the final consonant before a suffix that begins with a vowel if (1) the word has only one syllable or the accent is on the final syllable; and (2) if the word ends in a consonant preceded by a vowel.

Examples: control + able = controllable
omit + ing = omitting
plan + ing = planning
prefer + ing = preferring
(*Exception: preferable*)
occur + ence = occurrence

For words ending in hard *c* sound, add *k* before suffixes *ing, ed, y.*

Examples: panic + ed = panicked
picnic + ing = picnicking
traffic + ed = trafficked
mimic + ing = mimicking

Plurals

Form the plural of most nouns by adding *s*.

Examples:				
	figure	figures	manager	managers
	record	records	file	files

For nouns ending in *s, ss, z, sh, ch*, and *x*, add *es* to form the plural.

Examples:				
	tax	taxes	kiss	kisses
	wish	wishes	buzz	buzzes
	watch	watches	gas	gases
	address	addresses	fez	fezes

For nouns ending in *y* preceded by a consonant, change the *y* to *i* and add *es*. For nouns ending in *y* preceded by a vowel simply add *s*.

Nouns ending in *y* preceded by a consonant change *y* to *i*, add *es*.		**Nouns ending in *y* preceded by a vowel add *s*.**	
secretary	secretaries	holiday	holidays
currency	currencies	Wednesday	Wednesdays
category	categories	delay	delays

For nouns ending in *o* preceded by a consonant, add *s* or *es*. If the *o* is preceded by a vowel, add *s*.

Nouns ending in *o* preceded by a consonant usually add *s* or *es*		**Nouns ending in *o* preceded by a vowel add *s***	
potato	potatoes, potatos	radio	radios
hero	heroes	studio	studios
tomato	tomatoes, tomatos	stereo	stereos

All musical terms ending in *o* add *s* to form the plural.

Many nouns ending in *f* or *fe* simply add *s* to form the plural; however, some nouns change the *f* to *v* and add *s* or *es*.

Add *s*

Examples:	chief	chiefs
	dwarf	dwarfs

Nouns changing *f* to *v* and adding *s* or *es*

Examples:	life	lives	half	halves
	knife	knives	thief	thieves
	wife	wives	self	selves

Form the plural of compound nouns written as one word and ending in *s, sh, ch*, or *x* by adding *es*. In all other cases, form the plural by simply adding *s*.

Compound nouns adding *es*		**Compound nouns adding *s***	
lockbox	lockboxes	firefighter	firefighters
toothbrush	toothbrushes	mainframe	mainframes
		cupful	cupfuls

Form the plural of compounds written as two or more words by adding *s* to the main word. Make hyphenated compounds plural either by adding *s* to the main word or, if there is no main word, adding *s* to the end of the compound.

Compound nouns of two or more words

Examples:	editor in chief	editors in chief
	notary public	notaries public
	vice president	vice presidents

Hyphenated nouns adding *s* to the main word of compound		**Hyphenated nouns adding *s* to the end of compound**	
president-elect	presidents-elect	trade-in	trade-ins
ex-premier	ex-premiers	write-in	write-ins
son-in-law	sons-in-law	grown-up	grown-ups
passer-by	passers-by		

Form the plural of numbers, letters, words, and symbols by adding apostrophe and *s*.

Examples:	three 8's (or 8s)	two 's and three #'s	use x's and o's
	use and's	1990's (or 1990s)	yes's and no's

The I and E Rules

Use *i* before *e*, except after *c* for the long *e* sound in a word. Use *e* before *i* when the sound in the word is not long *e*.

***i* before *e* (long e sound)**		***e* before *i* after *c* (long *e* sound)**	
believe	relieve	ceiling	receipt
grievance	retrieve	deceive	receive
piece	thief		

(*Exceptions: neither, leisure, seized*)

e* before *i	**(no long *e* sound)**
freight	weight
neighbour	height
weigh	eight

Frequently Misspelled Words

The following list contains frequently misspelled words used in business communications. Use this list as a reference, but be sure you also have a good dictionary on hand.

A
abbreviate
absence
accessible
accommodate
accompanies
accompaniment
accrued
accuracy
acknowledgment
advantageous
advisable
analysis
analyze/analyse
apparatus

appreciate
appropriate
argument
arrangement
arrears
ascertain
association
authorize
auxiliary

B
bankruptcy
beneficial
bibliography
bookkeeper
brochure
budget
bulletin

C
calendar
cancelled
cancellation
category
changeable
choose
chose
clientele
column
commission
commitment
committed
committee
competent
competitor
comptroller
concede
concise
conscience
conscientious
consensus
contingency
convenience
correspondents
courteous
criticize

D
debtor
deferred
definite
dependent
depreciation
description
desirable
dilemma
discrepancy
dissatisfied

E
economical
effect
efficiency
eligible
embarrassment
emphasize
enforceable
exaggerate
exceed
excel
exceptionally
exhibitor
existence
exorbitant
experience
extension

F
facilitate
facsimile
familiar
feasible
February
fiscal
forecast
foreclose
foreign
foreseeable
forfeit
forewarn
forty
franchise
fraud
fraudulent
freight
fulfill

G
gauge
grateful
grievance
guarantee
guaranty

H
harassment
hindrance
hypothesis

I
illegible
immediately
imperative
implement
inconvenience
indebtedness
indemnity
indispensable
inflationary
initial
installation
initiative
interfere
interpretation
interrupt
invoice
itemize
itinerary

J
jeopardize
jeopardy
judgment/judgement

K
knowledge
knowledgeable

L
labelled/labeled
legitimate
liable
liaison
likelihood
livelihood
livable
loose
lose
lucrative

M
maintenance
manageable
mandatory
marketable
measurable
mediator
miscellaneous
misspell
misstatement
mortgage
municipal

N
necessity
negligible
negotiate
neutral
ninety
ninth
notarize
noticeable

O
objectionable
observant
obsolete
occasion
occupant
omission
omitted
opinionated
option
overrated

P
pamphlet
parallel
paralysis
parity
parliament
particularly
permanent
permitted
personnel
pertinent
phenomenon
plausible
possession
practically
precede
precise
preference
preferred
prejudice
procedure
promissory

Q
quality
quantity
qualitative
quantitative
questionnaire

R
receive
recommend
recommendation
reconciliation
recurrence
reducible
reference
referred
reimburse
relevant
remittance
remitted
repetition
rescind
respectfully
responsibility
returnable
revenue
routine

S
saleable
schedule
scientific
scrutinize
separate
serviceable
similar
sincerely
software
specifically
subpoena
substantial
supervisor
supersede
superficial
superfluous
susceptible
synonymous

T
tariff
technician
tendency
totalling/totaling
transferring
transmit
transmittal
truly

U
unanimous
undoubtedly
unmistakable
unnecessarily

V
vacuum
vendor
ventilation
versatile
volumn

W
waive
warranty
wholly
withhold

Y
yield

Z
zealous

Word Division

Whether you use a typewriter or a word processor, you will need to know how to divide words properly. The guidelines listed below can help you learn the basic rules of word division. As a basic rule, avoid dividing words at the end of more than two or three successive lines. You should also avoid dividing a word at the end of a page or a paragraph.

Basic Rules

Divide words only between syllables. As a result, never divide one-syllable words such as *missed, rough, through*, and *while*.

When you divide a word, there must be more than one letter on the first line and more than two letters with the last part of the word.

Right: sin-cerely
Wrong: sincere-ly
Right: ap-a-thy
Wrong: a-pathy
Right: jew-ellery
Wrong: jewelle-ry
Right: era-sure
Wrong: e-rasure

Each syllable in word division must contain a vowel; therefore, you cannot divide most contractions.

Right: con-trol
Wrong: con-tr-ol

Right: hy-drau-lic
Wrong: hy-dr-au-lic
Right: couldn't
Wrong: could-n't
Right: isn't
Wrong: is-n't

Final and Double Consonants

If you double a final consonant preceded by a vowel before adding a suffix, divide the word between the two consonants.

Examples: win + ing = win-ning
plan + ing = plan-ning

If the root word ends in a double consonant before you add the suffix, divide the word between the root word and the suffix.

Examples: tell + ing = tell-ing
assess + ing = assess-ing

Single-letter Syllables

Generally, you should leave with the first part of the word a single-letter syllable within a word and not carry it over to the second line.

Examples: bus-i-ness = busi-ness
sep-a-rate = sepa-rate
oxygen = oxy-gen

When two single-letter syllables occur together in a word, divide the word between the single letter syllables.

Examples: grad-u-a-tion = gradu-ation
in-sin-u-a-tion = insinu-ation

When the final syllable *ble, bly*, or *cal* follows the single-letter syllable *a, i*, or *u*, join the two end syllables and carry them to the next line.

Examples: de-pend-a-ble = depend-able
cler-i-cal = cler-ical
in-vinc-i-ble = invinc-ible

Hyphenated Words

Divide hyphenated words and compound hyphenated words only at the hyphen that connects them.

Right:	clearing-house
Wrong:	clear-ing-house
Right:	self-assessment
Wrong:	self-asses-ment
Right:	client-oriented approach
Wrong:	client-or-iented approach

Proper Names

Avoid dividing a person's name or any proper name. Separate titles, initials, or degrees from names only when it is unavoidable.

Avoid:	Mrs. Joan Cunning- ham	**Preferred:**	Mrs. Joan Cunningham
	Mr. Emmett Mei		Mr. Emmett Mei
	Georgia Watson, Ph.D.		Georgia Watson, Ph.D.

Figures and Abbreviations

In general, avoid dividing figures and abbreviations. If you must separate the parts of an address or a date, however, use the following guidelines.

Dividing addresses

Avoid:	15 Water Street	**Preferred:**	15 Water Street
	557 West Boule- vard		557 West Boulevard
	1903 — 71st Avenue		1903 — 71st Avenue
	Halifax, Nova Scotia		Halifax, Nova Scotia

Dividing dates

Avoid:	August 20, 19—	**Preferred:**	August 20, 19—

EXERCISES — SPELLING

1. Recopy the following passage, correcting misspelled words and selecting the appropriate words to fill in the blanks.

Dear Ms. Connolly:

I am pleased you are (excepting, accepting) our new Blue Chip service contract. Our (companies, company's) (principle, principal) concern is to provide you firm with outstanding (personnel, personal) computor products and service. In this regard, I will call you in early Febuary to set a time for our first service call. Our company pride's itself on keeping our customers up to date on the latest developments in computor tecknologys. To often we've heard of managers embarassed by the fact that there new employees no more about the latest hardwear and softwear than they do. We will offer you qualitie products throughly tested by our deadicated analysts and technicians. All our products and servises come with a full (guarantee, guaranty).

2. Identify and correct the misspelled words in each line:

(a)	parallel	faxsimile	ocassion	budget
(b)	fullfill	immediately	bookkeeper	cancelled
(c)	morgage	jeopardy	relevent	livable
(d)	supoena	tendancy	eligible	existence
(e)	embarassment	superviser	consensus	dependent
(f)	measurable	consience	effect	concede
(g)	discrepency	mispell	emphasize	vacuum
(h)	initial	calender	quandary	knowledgable
(i)	changeable	hindrance	municiple	auxiliary
(j)	omited	withhold	columm	preferred
(k)	necisity	itemize	parity	revenue
(l)	competent	livelihood	seperate	objectionable
(m)	serviceable	repitition	overrated	refered
(n)	exaggerat	vendor	argument	dilema
(o)	supersede	catagory	excel	unmistakable

3. Write the plurals of each noun:

(a) church
(b) theory
(c) audio
(d) shelf

(e) motto
(f) chief executive officer
(g) sandwich
(h) passer-by
(i) radio
(j) cupful
(k) fuss
(l) currency
(m) half
(n) looker-on
(o) handful

4. Write the words formed when you join each prefix or suffix to the main word.

(a) happy + ly =
(b) insure + able =
(c) study + ous =
(d) ugly + ness =
(e) impel + ing =
(f) use + able =
(g) ready + ness =
(h) courage + ous =
(i) sale + able =
(j) sincere + ly =

INDEX

2 3 4 5 4917-7 93 92 91 90